Words of Praise for THE GOD CODE

"Brilliant and insightful—I urge all of you to embrace the message of THE GOD CODE. I see Gregg Braden as one of our great visionaries."

— **Dr. Wayne W. Dyer,** bestselling author of
10 Secrets for Success and Inner Peace and
The Power of Intention

"Gregg Braden is a rare blend of scientist, visionary, and scholar, with the ability to speak to our minds while touching the wisdom of our hearts."

— **Deepak Chopra,** author of *How to Know God*

"THE GOD CODE explores a fascinating premise— that there is a tangible, verifiable, and universal message planted firmly within the foundation of life— a message that may provide evidence for a higher intelligence operating behind the scenes of the phenomenal world that we all take so much for granted. Scholar Gregg Braden is to be commended, as he has opened an unprecedented window into our understanding of the great mystery of existence."

— **Hank Wesselman, Ph.D.,** anthropologist, and author of
The Journey to the Sacred Garden and the Spiritwalker trilogy
(*Spiritwalker, Medicinemaker,* and *Visionseeker*)

The
GOD
CODE

Also by Gregg Braden

The Isaiah Effect

Walking Between the Worlds

Awakening to Zero Point

Hay House Titles of Related Interest

Getting in the Gap, by Dr. Wayne W. Dyer (book and CD)

God, Creation, and Tools for Life, by Sylvia Browne

The Indigo Children, by Lee Carroll and Jan Tober

The Jesus Code, by John Randolph Price

The Journey to the Sacred Garden,
by Hank Wesselman, Ph.D. (book and CD)

Mirrors of Time, by Brian L. Weiss, M.D. (book and CD)

The Power of Intention, by Dr. Wayne W. Dyer

Power vs. Force, by David R. Hawkins, M.D., Ph.D.

Visionseeker, by Hank Wesselman, Ph.D.

Sacred Ceremony, by Steven D. Farmer, Ph.D.

All of the above are available at your local bookstore,
or may be ordered by visiting:
Hay House USA: www.hayhouse.com
Hay House Australia: www.hayhouse.com.au
Hay House UK: www.hayhouse.co.uk
Hay House South Africa: orders@psdprom.co.za

The GOD CODE

The Secret of Our Past, the Promise of Our Future

GREGG BRADEN

HAY HOUSE, INC.
Carlsbad, California
London • Sydney • Johannesburg
Vancouver • Hong Kong

Published and distributed in the United States by: Hay House, Inc., P.O. Box 5100, Carlsbad, CA 92018-5100 • *Phone:* (760) 431-7695 or (800) 654-5126 • *Fax:* (760) 431-6948 or (800) 650-5115 • www.hayhouse.com • *Published and distributed in Australia by:* Hay House Australia, Ltd., 18/36 Ralph St., Alexandria NSW 2015 • *Phone:* 612-9669-4299 • *Fax:* 612-9669-4144 • www.hayhouse.com.au • *Published and distributed in the United Kingdom by:* Hay House UK, Ltd. • Unit 202, Canalot Studios • 222 Kensal Rd., London W10 5BN • *Phone:* 44-20-8962-1230 • *Fax:* 44-20-8962-1239 • www.hayhouse.co.uk • *Published and distributed in the Republic of South Africa by:* Hay House SA (Pty), Ltd., P.O. Box 990, Witkoppen 2068 • *Phone/Fax:* 2711-7012233 • orders@psdprom.co.za• orders@psdprom.co.za • *Distributed in Canada by:* Raincoast • 9050 Shaughnessy St., Vancouver, B.C. V6P 6E5 • *Phone:* (604) 323-7100 • *Fax:* (604) 323-2600

Editorial supervision: Jill Kramer   •   *Gregg Braden's editor:* Stephanie Gunning
Design: Tricia Breidenthal   •   *Indexer:* Debra Graf (sagewords1@aol.com)

Photo on page 125 used by permission of Israel Antiquities Authority

Library of Congress Cataloging-in-Publication Data

Braden, Gregg.
 The God code : the secret of our past, the promise of our future / Gregg Braden.
  p. cm.
Includes bibliographical references and index.
 ISBN 1-4019-0299-5 — ISBN 1-4019-0300-2 (trade paper)
 1. God—Name. 2. Creation. 3. Evolution. 4. Hebrew language—Miscellanea.
5. DNA—Miscellanea. I. Title.
 BT180.N2B73 2004
 299'.93—dc22

                                        2003015712

Hardcover ISBN 1-4019-0299-5
Tradepaper ISBN 1-4019-0300-2

07 06 05 04   4 3 2 1
1st printing, January 2004

Printed in the United States of America

This book is dedicated to the first generation in recorded history with the power to destroy, or preserve, all that we love and hold dear.

May our legacy be one of peace to those who will call us their ancestors.

CONTENTS

"As my ancestors planted for me
before I was born, so do I plant
for those who will come after me."

— ANCIENT HEBREW SCRIPTURE[1]

AUTHOR'S NOTE

Regarding the gender of God: While the principle of "God" ultimately implies both male and female, and is thus without gender, historic references suggest that it is the *active* male principle of God in Heaven that merges with the *receptive* female principle of "Mother Earth" to produce the duality of life that is married into our bodies. For this reason, it is understood that references throughout this book to "He" are references to the male principle of God, in the act of creation, only.

Dating convention: The debate continues among archaeologists and historians regarding the notation indicating historic dates as *Before Common Era* (B.C.E.), dates prior to the year "1"; and *Common Era* (C.E.), dates from the year "1" to the present; and the previously used *Before Christ* (B.C.) and *Anno Domini* (A.D.). The now-conventional, and widely accepted, terms B.C.E. and C.E. are used throughout this text for purposes of consistency and clarity.

The term *man:* In many of the ancient texts, modern translations, and traditions referenced throughout this book, humankind is referred to in this way. Clearly, this term is intended within the ancient context to be inclusive of both male and female, as well as of children, and represents the whole of human existence. In an effort to remain consistent with the language of the texts, this convention has been honored throughout *The God Code* as well.

INTRODUCTION

Sometimes the solutions to life's deepest mysteries are found in the most unlikely places. In hindsight, once the discoveries are made and the mysteries are solved, it is not uncommon to find that the most elusive answers were, in fact, present all along and simply not recognized. In these instances, the obvious appears to conceal itself, as suggested in the proverb that the "forest is hidden by the trees." The search for evidence of the Big Bang, for instance—the cosmic explosion believed to have set our universe into motion—is an example of just such a discovery.

In 1960, the Bell Telephone Laboratories facility in Holmdel, New Jersey, constructed a large dishlike antenna as part of a satellite communications project named *Echo*. By 1962, however, new technology had made the antenna obsolete, so it became available as a radio telescope for research. Two employees of the Labs, Arno Penzias and Robert Wilson, were interested in using the antenna to measure faint radio signals between distant galaxies.

When the researchers began using the antenna, they found that it produced a staticlike noise that made it difficult to detect the subtle signals they were looking for. Although the annoying sound had been noticed by the previous researchers, it was believed to be a by-product of the antenna itself, and ignored. After careful inspections eliminated the equipment as the source of the noise, Penzias and Wilson methodically investigated other possibilities, including an above-ground nuclear test in 1962, and even families of pigeons living inside the antenna! All failed to reveal the source of the noise.

At nearby Princeton University, another scientist, Robert Dicke, was exploring theories suggesting that the universe began in the distant past as a primal explosion of unimaginable proportion. If, in fact, such a massive release of energy had occurred, he theorized that there should be echoes of the event in the form of microwave radiation—a constant background noise that would continue to bathe the universe today. Only after the three scientists shared their findings with one another did they realize the source of the static and what they had discovered.

While Penzias and Wilson had intended to learn more about our universe by studying signals *between* galaxies, the "static" that they detected everywhere was actually the lingering echo of an ancient explosion! Surviving from the early moments of the "beginning," they had unknowingly found proof of the Big Bang theory of creation. By the 1970s, the theory was so widely accepted that it was called the *standard model* of creation. John Bahcall, a noted astrophysicist at Princeton University, commented on the significance of the finding, stating, "The discovery of the cosmic microwave background radiation changed forever the nature of cosmology. . . ."[1] Penzias and Wilson received the Nobel Prize for their work in 1978.

The irony of the discovery at Bell Labs is that the evidence holding the key to one of creation's greatest mysteries was so abundant, and appeared in a form that was so unexpected, that it was overlooked, and discounted for at least two years. Perhaps the search for clues to our origins—evidence that could serve as an unprecedented principle of human unity—may reveal a similar irony. Is it possible that the answer to the deepest mysteries of our existence is so abundant in our own world that it has been overlooked as well?

A REMARKABLE DISCOVERY LINKING the biblical alphabets of Hebrew and Arabic to modern chemistry reveals that a lost code—*a translatable alphabet*—and a clue to the mystery of our origins, has lived within us all along. Applying this discovery to the language of life, the familiar elements of hydrogen, nitrogen, oxygen, and carbon that form our DNA may now be replaced with key letters of the ancient languages. In doing so, the code of all life is transformed into the words of a timeless message. *Translated, the message reveals that the precise letters of God's ancient name are encoded as the genetic information in every cell, of every life.*

The message reads: *"God/Eternal within the body."*

The meaning: *Humankind is one family, united through a common heritage, and the result of an intentional act of creation!*

Preserved within each cell of the estimated six billion inhabitants of our world, the message is repeated, again and again, to form the building blocks of our existence. This ancient message from the day of our origins—*the same message*—remains within each of us today, regardless of race, religion, heritage, lifestyle, or belief. As we'll see in Chapter 9, the code is so universal that it produces the identical message when translated into either the Hebrew or the Arabic language!

The discovery of God's name within the essence of all life demonstrates that we are related not only to one another, but also to life itself, in the most intimate way imaginable. From a single blade of grass, to vast expanses of uncharted rain forests; from a fruit fly peering at us through the many facets of a compound eye, to the piercing stare from our nearest primate relatives—any logic that preys upon our differences ultimately dissolves with the evidence that all life is made from the chemical equivalent of a single name. With such tangible proof of a common bond, we're given a reason to look beyond the issues that may have separated us in the past, and a place to begin when our differences seem insurmountable.

To the degree that any work is a product of its time in history, this book is influenced by the extraordinary circumstances that face our world in the infancy of the 21st century. Perhaps the uniqueness of our time was best clarified by Dr. Michio Kaku, cofounder of the revolutionary string field theory and professor of theoretical physics at the City College of New York. "For most of human history," Dr. Kaku observed, "we could only watch, like bystanders, the beautiful dance of Nature." Following the close of the 20th century, however, our relationship to nature has taken on a new meaning. Describing that change, Dr. Kaku continued, stating, "The Age of Discovery in science is coming to a close, opening up an Age of Mastery . . . today, we are on the cusp of an epoch-making transition, from being *passive observers of Nature* to *being active choreographers of Nature.*"[2]

In the last 100 years, we have, in fact, coaxed from creation the timeless secrets of matter, conception, life, and death. Our new-found understandings afford us a rare ability, unknown at any time in our past. With nature's forces at our command, we find ourselves capable of redesigning our genetic code, customizing our weather patterns, and creating new forms of life—powers historically left to God and nature. At the same time, our future now hinges upon our ability to use our newfound abilities wisely.

Today, new discoveries in science and technology have placed at our fingertips the power to preserve or destroy all that we love and hold dear. *For the first time in recorded history, the survival of our entire species rests upon the choices of a single generation.* Perhaps it is precisely the presence of such power that now compels us to recognize that we are a part of all we see, and the expression of something even greater.

Faced with the unique challenges of our time, the key to peace in our world—and perhaps our very survival—appears to exist within each of us, perfectly replicated within each cell of our bodies. Perhaps as a testament to our success as a species, every member of our global family carries the same message as a silent reminder of our heritage, recorded on the first day of our existence. Decoded, the message discloses the following undeniable facts:

- The basic elements of DNA—hydrogen, nitrogen, oxygen, and carbon—translate directly to key letters of the Hebrew and Arabic alphabets.

- In these languages, our genetic code spells the ancient name of God. The same name lives within all humans, regardless of their beliefs, actions, lifestyle, religion, or heritage.

- This relationship was described in sacred texts, such as the Hebrew *Sepher Yetzirah,* at least 1,000 years before modern science verified such connections.

- The odds that this relationship has occurred by "chance" are approximately 1 in 200,000.

The God Code is the result of 12 years of research and the personal quest for a principle of human unity that is so deep, and so tangible, that it cannot be denied. Since 1986, my search has led me into temples, villages, and monasteries hidden in some of the most pristine, isolated, and remote locations remaining on Earth today. In these places, I've met dedicated individuals who consider it their duty in life, as well as an honor, to preserve the memories of our species and the history of our world.

Held in ancient myth, traditional dance, secret language, and hidden records, our most cherished traditions carry a theme that is strikingly similar across cultural, geographic, and religious divisions. As different as the traditions appear on the surface, an underlying theme reminds us that, as the family of humankind, we are greater than any differences that have ever divided us.

It may be no accident that such a powerful message of unity is revealed now, in the first years of the new millennium. Statistics show that the 20th century was the bloodiest 100 years in human history, with more people killed as the result of violence, ethnic cleansing, war, and genocide than from all of the major natural disasters *combined* during the same period of time (see Chapter 1, Figure 1.2). In the first years of the 21st century, that violence continues, with nearly one-third of the world's nations engaged in armed conflict.[3] In addition to battling for profit and resources, many of the hostilities are based upon differences of religion, bloodlines, and borders.

Today, scientists, researchers, and religious leaders suggest that humankind stands alone as the single greatest threat to our future. The human-made realities of drug-resistant disease and the projected midcentury collapse of Earth's ecosystems present us with the greatest challenges of our time. In the presence of such global hazards, the largest buildup of weapons and military forces since World War II now risk engulfing the earth in a conflict of unprecedented magnitude. It is upon such a stage that we live each day, raise our children, and search for peace in our lives.

Perhaps our situation is much like that of a family accustomed to spending so much time together that they forget how deep their life-bond really is. It's not until the unexpected loss of those they love that they're reminded of just how precious their family, and their time together, really is. For the survivors, "loss" becomes the catalyst that awakens them from one way of looking at life and jolts them into a new perspective.

Similar to the way in which loss may transform a family, the unprecedented suffering, deterioration of our world, and attempts to eliminate entire cultures may become the catalyst that awakens us, on a grand scale, to the reality of how precious our global family —and our time together—really is.

> *Unlike the family in our example, however,*
> *all of humankind does not have to suffer such*
> *extremes and tragedy before the awakening occurs.*

To create a world where families and nations celebrate diversity and live in peace, however, requires something that appears to be absent from many of our societies today—a reason to honor life, one another, and believe that we are part of something even greater. Such qualities can be realized only through their direct experience. We may find that the living evidence of God's name within the body of every woman, child, and man—past and present—offers precisely such an experience!

THE GOD CODE IS ULTIMATELY a work of peace. Crossing the traditional boundaries of science, religion, and history, it merges what we know of our past with what we believe of the present into a single unifying principle. While many people suspect that a higher power plays a role in our world, *knowing* that God's name exists within our bodies offers a realization so deep, so personal, and yet so universal, that *it becomes the experience* of greater meaning in our lives. Through that experience, we are given a reason to find peace, and an unprecedented common ground from which we may begin to resolve our differences.

About This Book

In the spring of 1990, I left a successful career as a senior computer systems designer in the aerospace and defense industry to dedicate myself, full time, to developing and presenting such principles of unity. While the research continues, the discoveries described in these pages stand on their own as a complete and meaningful body of information.

I have divided the book into three clearly distinct, yet related, sections: Part I offers a history and context for why the message in our bodies is important in our lives; Part II describes the discovery and translation of the code; and Part III discusses how the message offers a rare opportunity to heal the differences that divide our families and our world.

Everyone reads books a little differently. For some people, it is important to know the essence of the book that they're about to invest their time and energy into before they read it—the bottom line. Others prefer to allow the author's ideas to unfold as a journey, trusting that it will lead them to something useful in its completion. The following guidelines are intended to help you navigate your way through this book depending upon your individual preferences.

For all readers, Part I sets the stage by describing how our longing to know who we are has shaped the history of our world. From persecutions and inquisitions, to holy wars and genocide, we have defined ourselves through our *differences*. At the same time, the most advanced science in history has extended our collective eyes and ears to the edge of our solar system, and now beyond, in our quest to understand how, *together*, we fit into the scheme of creation. Even with the miraculous advances of last century's technology, the irony of our time is that we have yet to discover precisely who we are.

Chapter 3 details how some of the most ancient records of our past have attempted to answer the oldest questions of our existence. From the mysterious "lost" *Book of Adam* to the Gnostic Nag Hammadi Library, it is clear that those who penned these ancient

manuscripts longed to share their discoveries with the generations of their future. The chapter ends by introducing what is
often referred to as the oldest, as well as the most mysterious, book
of the Hebrew traditions, the *Sepher Yetzirah*, or Book of Creation.

For readers who are interested in understanding precisely how
the molecule of DNA may be read as a translatable language, Part
II details the background, history, and specifics of the discovery.
Chapter 4 applies the clues found in the *Sepher Yetzirah* to reveal
the hidden link between the ancient elements of Fire, Air, and
Water, and their direct equivalents in today's language of chemistry—a correlation that has surprising results! While Chapter 4
uncovers the hidden relationship that bridges ancient and modern
beliefs, Chapter 5, "The Discovery," applies this powerful link and
continues our journey into the mystery of alphabets and hidden letter codes. The remarkable finding that reduces letters and elements
to a common denominator of numbers allows us to compare
"apples to apples," and to correlate the oldest accounts of Genesis
with the science of today. In doing so, Chapter 6 reveals how the
ancient and personal name of God—the name recorded more
than 3,500 years before our time—forms the very foundation of
our DNA!

For others who ask how a single message can possibly make
a difference in our world today, I invite you to proceed directly to
the portion of this book that addresses that question: Part III. Following Part II's discussion of the history, science, and translation
of the message in our cells, Chapters 7, 8, and 9 address what the
message means in our lives. While Chapter 7 helps us come to terms
with the implications of God's name in our bodies, Chapters 8 and
9 describe the role that such a message may play in bridging the
differences that threaten our survival.

Chapter 9, for example, describes an indigenous method of conflict resolution based upon the shared vision of a common future.
In such traditions, the vision becomes a common ground—the place
to begin from, or return to, when the differences between people
seem overwhelming. *The key is that the shared vision is a unifying experience that cannot be denied by the vision's participants.*

The section suggests that the experience of recognizing God's name in our bodies may serve a purpose similar to resolving conflict of a larger scale. This approach may be especially useful for conflict based in religious and ethnic differences.

A Well-Researched Book or a Technical Paper: Why This Approach?

This book admittedly touches upon many deeply held and very personal beliefs. To do justice to each and every implication of the code in our cells is beyond its immediate scope. For this reason, I have chosen to focus upon the power of the message to bridge the differences in our lives and bring peace to our world. From the complex issues surrounding terrorism and the 4,000-year-old battle for land in the Middle East, to the predicted collapse of the world's ecosystems and increasing stockpiles of mass-effect weapons, the issues that divide us as individuals, families, religions, and nations have reached overwhelming proportions—and the choices are more difficult than ever.

There is an old adage suggesting that when answers are vague and situations difficult to resolve, it's generally because we don't have all of the information we need—something is missing. A growing body of evidence suggests that this is precisely the case for the most controversial issues of our day. When all of the information is present, the choices become clear and the courses of action apparent. Ultimately, we may discover that our present-day crises are symptoms of a deeper, more fundamental concern. Each asks precisely the same question:

> *What is the "yardstick" by which we measure*
> *the human cost of our scientific and political*
> *choices as we build the world of our future?*

The tangible, verifiable, and universal sign of a message at the very foundation of life offers undeniable evidence of a greater

intelligence underlying our existence. The fact that the message *is* the "stuff" that we are made of tells us that we are part of a much grander scheme. Our relationship to that intelligence is a factor that must now be considered in the policies of science, war, and peace—policies that pave the way for tomorrow.

By its very nature, the subject of this book transcends the traditional bounds of science and spirituality. From the most ancient descriptions of our origins, to our most advanced scientific understandings, it has become clear that to solve the challenges of our time, we must search beyond the thinking that has defined them. By marrying the wisdom of our past with the science of our future, we create powerful new tools to resolve the issues of our day. At the same time, we open an unprecedented window into the mystery of our own creation.

As with any discovery that is technical in nature, the challenge has been to convey the information in a way that is accurate and meaningful to a broad, general audience. When I began this project in 1990, I was counseled by some experts to offer the material from a scholarly perspective. To do so, however, would mean revealing the findings in increments that could ultimately delay the final publication, and the power of the message, by months or even years. (The landmark study of the numeric codes in the Hebrew Bible, for example, was delayed for *six years* while being evaluated by peers and referees.[4])

During the same time, others encouraged me to take a less academic approach. They believed that to leave out many of the charts, graphs, footnotes, and references in exchange for the opportunity to share the message quickly with a larger audience was a worthwhile tradeoff. In consideration of such honest and heartfelt recommendations, I've chosen to take the best of both approaches and offer a book that is "middle-of-the-road."

In representing the many branches of study that form this work, my sense is that I can best honor my audience by offering the discovery as a flowing narrative, rather than a structured report. Within the narrative format, I have included references to the research that has made this book possible. This approach allows me to share the discovery responsibly, while making it

available in a timely fashion. At the same time, I have done my very best to scale down the technical jargon and lengthy explanations in order to allow for the rhythm and flow that appeal to a broad cross-section of readers. Hopefully, in doing so, I have created a book that is meaningful, as well as enjoyable to read!

Even with such considerations in mind, there are undoubtedly portions of this book that will come across as "wordy" and more technical than others. Chapters 4 and 5, for example, delve into the details of how the chemistry of our bodies and the language of ancient Hebrew are related. For those readers who may choose to gloss over these sections due to their depth, a summary of the key points has been included at the end of each chapter.

The Power of the God Code

While we will continue to refine our understanding of matter and life for generations to come, the question that we now face is one of balance between wisdom and power. Will we gain the wisdom to balance our knowledge of science with the forces of nature before we suffer the irreparable consequences of misusing our power? Will we survive our learning process? In his pioneering book *Hyperspace,* Dr. Michio Kaku shares a perspective of our time in history from the late physicist Heinz Pagels. Commenting in the early 20th century on the discoveries of light, energy, and life, Pagels stated that we must find a "moral and political order which will accommodate these forces or we shall be destroyed. It will try our deepest resources of reason and compassion."[5]

There appear to be no clear models to show us the way as we engineer the forces of nature and God. Although we have stepped into uncharted territory with regard to precisely *how* our newfound powers are applied, of one thing we may be certain: From the many lessons that the wars, sickness, environmental disasters, hate, and suffering of the last century taught us, all may be reduced to a single underlying theme. Each reminds us of the sacred and interconnected nature of life—all life—everywhere. To the degree that we remain true to what we've learned, and honor the principle of life in each choice that we make, we cannot go wrong.

The implications of viewing our DNA as a message from a higher power are vast, controversial, empowering, and perhaps, to some, overwhelming. The fruit of our willingness to do so reveals nothing less than a key to lasting peace and an invitation to assume our role as stewards in the miracle of our own existence. In light of the many possibilities that this material may suggest, *The God Code* has been written with one express purpose in mind: to clearly and simply reveal a single principle of unity that transcends any separation of the family of humankind based upon our differences.

In a single sentence, visionary, futurist, and social architect Barbara Marx Hubbard summarized our situation, stating, "We must now decide between conscious evolution, or extinction through misuse of our powers."[6] This book is the story of a reason to believe that we have a choice, and the power of a single name to unify our global family in the presence of differences that, at times, seem insurmountable. *The God Code* is not intended to be *the* solution as we enter into the greatest challenges of science, technology, and peace in the history of our species. In a time when so much emphasis is placed upon our differences, it is simply intended as a place to begin.

— **Gregg Braden**
Taos, New Mexico
December 2003

PART I

Who Are We?
Clues from the Mystery Itself

"Human misery is more often caused
not so much by stupidity as by ignorance,
particularly our own ignorance about ourselves."

— CARL SAGAN, author of
THE DEMON-HAUNTED WORLD:
SCIENCE AS A CANDLE IN THE DARK

Chapter One

HISTORY:
The Story of Our Differences

We are a mysterious species of extremes and contradictions. It has been said that we are capable of dreaming the most beautiful dreams and harboring the darkest nightmares, while having the power to bring each of our visions to life. Perhaps at no other time in our history have we shared our world with so many of our kind while feeling so separate and alone. At the same time, the possibilities of our future have never held such promise, yet so much fear. It is within this context of extremes that we search for unity in our world and deeper meaning in our lives.

What would it mean to discover undeniable evidence—*verifiable proof*—that our species exists as an intentional act of creation? How different would our lives and our world be, knowing that within each cell of every woman, man, and child, evidence revealed the ancient name of God, hidden as the chemical code of life itself? The moment that such a message was shared, the world that we have known could never be the same.

Imagine the implications of discovering that the God of our prayers—the Allah of Islam, the Lord of Judeo-Christian beliefs, the Supreme God of Hindu traditions, and the Great Spirit of the Native Americans—is precisely the same God. Consider the ancient wounds that could be healed knowing that the persecutions, ethnic cleansings, religious wars, and inquisitions in the name of God over the last 2,000 years have arisen from a misunderstanding of the same timeless message!

With the revelation of such a discovery, the reasons that have justified the horrors of our past would become obsolete. From that time forward, ignorance could no longer be used to condone atrocities based on our differences. Through the undeniable evidence of humankind's common heritage, conflict in the name of God could only arise from the choice to create conflict. In such a moment, we would begin anew.

Looking for the Right Answers in the Wrong Places

Does such powerful evidence exist? Could a record of the most sacred trust of humankind have survived time and the ravages of civilization, awaiting discovery since the dawn of our creation? For more than 4,000 years, scholars have asked precisely such questions while seeking clues within the aging records of those who have come before us: the written scrolls, chiseled walls, and fragmented texts of antiquity. Searching the libraries of remote monasteries and crumbling manuscripts that were tediously transcribed one letter at a time, the discoveries thus far, while interesting, have failed to live up to the expectations of researchers. What does exist, however, are clues to the solution of our mystery, suggesting that the written records of our past are incomplete and reveal only a portion of something much greater in scope.

From mysterious passages recorded in the *Sepher Yetzirah,* the Kabbalah's ancient Book of Creation, to the original inscription above the entrance to Apollo's Temple at Delphi, there are references to a universal key—*a time capsule of knowledge*—holding the long-forgotten answer to nothing less than the identity of our Creator and the origin of our species. Through that key, we are given the means to bridge any differences of belief, heritage, or history that could ever divide us. The theme of such passages is deceptively simple. With an eloquence that is typical of many time-honored traditions, we are invited to "Know thyself" and "Seek within" for the answers to our deepest mysteries.

Scholars have traditionally viewed such passages as metaphors, suggesting that through the experience of our lives, we gain the wisdom of the ages. There are few who would argue that the tribulations and challenges of life in the modern world have, in fact, become great teachers in and of themselves. Is it possible, however, that our invitation to "look within" is something more? Could such passages be taken literally and read as directions—*actual instructions*—describing where we may find the clues to our creation?

A new interpretation of the ancient invitations suggests that the key to our mysteries may be found within what our most cherished traditions refer to as the crowning achievement of God's creation: our biology! Rather than sifting through the remains of weathered temples and crumbling manuscripts, the answer to our deepest mysteries may lie hidden within the expression of life itself.

Conceptually, the idea of looking within a creation for evidence of its creator is not so very different from a practice that is common today. From the construction of complex electronics, to the simplicity of an artist's canvas, the desire to let others know of our accomplishments appears to be part of human nature. In automobiles, within household appliances, from the music that moves our souls, to the sculptures that inspire us without making a sound, we need only look to the work itself to find the signature of its maker. If a "signature" from our Creator has, in fact, survived the elements of time and nature, then it makes perfect sense that the sign would remain within our bodies.

The secret to revealing such a signature is that we must first recognize the universal principles that unite us with our world, and, perhaps most important, with one another. In doing so, we may find that our search of the past has been the catalyst, patiently leading us to the most ancient source of knowledge in existence, the library of life.

It has been said that the key to our future lies in our past. Noted anthropologist Louis Leakey, acclaimed for his discoveries of early hominids in Africa's Olduvai Gorge, once remarked, "Without an understanding of who we are, and from where we came, I do not think we can truly advance." Later in the 20th century, anthropologist Richard Leakey, Louis Leakey's son, reiterated the significance of his father's sentiments, stating, "To give meaning to where we are today, we need to look at where we've come from."[1]

History is the story of our journey. Across the pages of time, we have inscribed a living record of our search for identity, our quest to know who we are, and precisely how we fit into the scheme of creation. Our legacy is preserved as the nations, families, wars, and achievements of those who have come before us— the building blocks of our past. Collectively, we have left few stones unturned as we've tested the very limits of our senses and beliefs in an effort to define ourselves.

Much of our history mirrors our attempt to find grace in the presence of a higher power. The massive temples in the deserts of Egypt, observatories hidden in the jungles of the Yucatán, shrines perched upon the mountains of Peru, and great cathedrals of Europe remind us of our efforts throughout history to please and become closer to our ever-changing idea of God. History also reminds us of the consequences experienced by individuals and entire populations who failed to share the accepted beliefs of their day.

A Species Defined by Our Differences

In our world of diversity, it has often been easier to focus on the differences that divide us rather than the principles that unite us. Ours is the story of a species defined by religion, the color of our skin, the wealth of our societies, and the advancement of our technology. Within the 4.5 billion years that scientists estimate our world has been in existence, our nearest human ancestors emerged only about 250,000 years ago. During that relatively brief span of time, we've managed to seek out our differences and parlay them into the invisible boundaries of class and society that fuel our sense of separateness. Based upon those boundaries, countless members of our global family have suffered in ways that seem unthinkable, even unimaginable, to the minds of rational and loving people. Together, we share the darkness of a history punctuated by persecutions, inquisitions, enslavement, and attempts to eliminate entire races from the face of the earth.

Today, we're in awe of the seemingly miraculous technology that allows us to combat disease and extend our lives to advanced ages. At the same time, we find ourselves in a world where the very life that so many people fight to preserve is routinely extinguished through the atrocity and violence of what has been called "man's inhumanity to man." While the development of high-tech weapons in the last century made it possible to destroy huge numbers of lives in a single day, history shows that something much deeper is responsible for creating what historian Eric Hobsbawm called "the most murderous century in recorded history."[2]

In his assessment of the toll taken by what he calls "politically motivated carnage," Zbigniew Brzezinski, former national security advisor under the Carter Administration, estimated that, by 1993, the violence stemming from our differences in the 20th century had cost between 167 and 175 million lives—roughly the equivalent of the populations of Great Britain, France, and Italy combined![3]

Along with the battles to settle disputes over borders and resources, the last century saw a rise in horrors of a different kind—the seemingly relentless efforts to "cleanse" societies based upon principles beyond those of land and the ownership of natural resources. In 1948, the United Nations General Assembly chose the term *genocide* to describe this kind of violence, defining it as "a denial of the right of existence of entire human groups." Article II of the 1948 *UN Convention on Genocide* further defined and described five categories of genocide with regard to human populations:

1. Killing members of the group.

2. Causing serious bodily or mental harm to members of the group.

3. Deliberately inflicting upon the group conditions of
   life designed to bring about its physical destruction,
   in whole or in part.

4. Imposing measures intended to prevent births within
   the group.

5. Forcibly transferring children of the group to
   another group.

Deaths Attributed to Specific Acts of Genocide	
Event	Estimated Deaths
Crusades (1095–1291)	1.5 million[4]
Atlantic slave trade (1700–1850)	18 million[5]
Native American decimation (16th–19th centuries)	20 million[6]
Jewish holocaust (World War II)	5.8 million[7]
Polish holocaust (World War II)	5.0 million[8]
Tibetan genocide (1959–2000)	1.2 million[9]
Balkan genocide (World War II to 1997)	1.5 million[10]
Post-war Vietnam, Cambodia, and Laos (1974–1986)	2.2 million[11]

Figure 1.1: Estimated death tolls from inquisitions and episodes of genocide. Although the Crusades occurred before the time period discussed in the text, they are included for comparison. Statistics for the Balkans are conservative due to unreported civilian deaths, and may run as high as 4.8 million.[12] Estimates are derived from averages of historic record.

The form of genocide based upon differences of race, religion, and heritage that is largely responsible for the magnitude of deaths reported by Brzezinski and others is called *ethnic cleansing*.

Although the history of such persecutions began long before the modern era, it was the 300-year effort to drive the Native North Americans from their land and to eliminate their way of life that began the current trends, and the magnitude, of the genocide that has continued until today (see Figure 1.1). Between the Atlantic slave trade of the Africans and the holocausts of Native Americans in the 17th through 19th centuries, nearly 40 million humans had already perished due to differences of religion, race, and heritage before the horrors of the last century. With the addition of 20th-century atrocities throughout Europe, including the Jewish holocaust of World War II; the Polish holocaust of Christians and Catholics during World War II; and the ethnic cleansings that have occurred in the Balkan regions, Vietnam, Cambodia, Laos, Africa, and Tibet, that number easily exceeds 53 million.

Comparison of 20th-Century Deaths Attributed to Genocide, AIDS, and Natural Disasters	
Cause of Deaths:	Estimated Number
Genocide (all known occurrences)	80.0 million[13]
AIDS	11.7 million[14]
Natural Disasters	3.5 million[15]
Total	15.2 million

Figure 1.2: Estimated death tolls from differences of religion and beliefs, AIDS, and natural disasters in the 20th century. Natural disasters exclude events such as droughts and famines.

To put such staggering numbers into perspective, while the last century is noted for its bloody wars, more than five times as many lives—*80 million children, women, and men of all ages*—were lost to violence based in ethnic, religious, and philosophical conflicts than were lost to all of the major natural disasters and the AIDS epidemic *combined* during the same period of time (see Figure 1.2). While historians generally agree upon these numbers, the numbers themselves are less significant than the magnitude of the story they tell. Perhaps it is for this reason that the last century is also known as the century that "murdered peace."[16]

Peace: More Than the Absence of War

Future generations will study the 20th century as the single most violent century in recorded history. In the first years of the 21st century, much of the thinking responsible for such a grim characterization appears to remain. With the renewed escalation of nuclear weapons programs in countries such as India, Pakistan, Iran, and North Korea, the stage is set in the new millennium for arms races similar to last century's Cold War between the U.S. and the Soviet Union. The threat from terrorism, civil war, and religious differences leaves little doubt that the violence and suffering that marred the last century will be the legacy of the new millennium's early years.

While political attempts to remedy conflict are always the most desirable, when such attempts have failed, the fallback approach has been largely a military one: overcoming the forces of tyranny with a greater force of power dedicated to preventing additional tyranny. It is precisely these forces that have proven themselves in locations ranging from Bosnia and Herzegovina to Sierra Leone and East Timor.

Country of Conflict	Year Mission Began	Country of Conflict	Year Mission Began
Middle East	1948	Georgia	1993
India and Pakistan	1949	Bosnia/Herzegovina	1995
Cyprus	1964	Prevlaka	1996
Golan Heights	1974	Kosovo	1999
Lebanon	1978	Sierra Leone	1999
Iraq-Kuwait	1991	Republic of Congo	1999
West Sahara	1991	Ethiopia and Eritrea	2000

Figure 1.3: Active United Nations Peacekeeping Missions in 2002.[17]

In the second year of the 21st century, the United Nations engaged in 15 such peacekeeping missions, bringing the total number of missions deployed since the commission was created in 1945 to 54 (see Figure 1.3). Today, the majority of UN peacekeeping missions remain focused in Eastern Europe, Africa, and the Middle East.

While the purpose of the UN forces is to provide peace and stability in a particular geographic region, the peace that they provide can be an *imposed peace* only, one where conflict is discouraged by a show of force. Additionally, the international nature of UN forces serves as a reminder that from an "official" position, the majority of the world stands behind the peacekeepers, with the promise of bringing an even greater military presence to bear upon the situation, if required. History has shown, as well, that in the long term, an imposed peace is generally ineffective. Clearly, the number and duration of such missions is teaching us a powerful lesson.

Bringing to mind the image of poking a finger into one part of a water-filled balloon and seeing the balloon bulge in another place, the repression of violence stemming from hurt and anger in one part of the world does not make the conflict go away. While troops and sanctions can do a very good job of making it difficult to carry out violence in a particular location, the underlying tension at the root of that violence remains. It should not surprise us to see the tension of entire regions becoming even greater immediately following the use of force to quell localized outbreaks of violence.

From this perspective, military intervention may be viewed as a Band-Aid of sorts, a quick response to a much deeper crisis at hand. Within the context of present world conditions, such responses may make sense by saving lives in the near-term. For example, it was only with the intervention of peacekeeping forces during the Kosovo crisis in 1999 that the extermination of entire villages and communities was prevented in the former Yugoslavia. The continuing conflict between Israel and the Palestinian people, however, escalated to new proportions in the early years of the new millennium. This renewed wave of violence occurred even with a military presence in place, illustrating the fact that force cannot bring a lasting peace.

Whether we are speaking of a family during their evening meal or the entire world, true peace is more than simply the absence of conflict. Lasting peace happens in the hearts and minds of people before it ever occurs between governments and nations. While the peacekeeping efforts throughout the world may be key in the short-term prevention of violence, and provide a vital step toward a peaceful solution of any conflict, in the end they can do little more than buy precious time. The question becomes one of whether or not, within that time, we have the wisdom to find another way to resolve the issues that divide us.

While the answer to this question will only be revealed in our future, of one thing we may be certain: We can learn from our past. Each conflict, every war and attempt at ethnic cleansing, may be viewed as a mirror of our relationship to our Creator, one another, and to creation itself. When we value life and see ourselves as members of a global family and stewards of Earth, our actions reflect those beliefs. History has shown that it is when we choose to dishonor one another and the principle of life that we experience the downward spiral of violent competition and aggression. From the fall of Rome to the collapse of the former Soviet Union, forgetting this simple truth has destroyed some of the most powerful nations in history.

How do we see ourselves at the birth of a new century? The intensity of late-century wars, ethnic cleansings, and struggles for power may offer a telling clue. So may our global response to such crises.

Today, the search to know ourselves continues. The way that we live each day echoes our longing for greater meaning in our lives. Like a tribe that has wandered for so long that it has forgotten the purpose of its journey, we go through the motions of life looking for a sign, something that will give significance to what we've created and what we have become.

Searching for Our Place in Creation

On April 28, 2001, a milestone in the search to understand our place in the cosmos came and went with little fanfare. Except for a brief mention in the evening news, the event that occurred earlier that day went largely unnoticed. At 10:27 A.M., Pacific Daylight Time, scientists operating a sensitive radio telescope in Madrid, Spain, received a signal from the first man-made object in history to leave our solar system. Having failed to receive any communication from the craft since August of 2000, National Aeronautics and Space Administration (NASA) scientists had transmitted a signal into the vastness of deep space the previous day in an effort to initiate contact with the object from Earth. Traveling at the speed of light, that signal was returned and picked up by the Madrid telescope. With the signal came a renewed faith in the legacy of *Pioneer 10,* a space probe launched from Earth nearly three decades before.

On March 2, 1972, Pioneer 10 began an unprecedented voyage that would eventually lead it to the edges of our solar system and beyond. Pioneer's job was to send back information along the course of its journey, giving scientists new insights into the magnetic fields, gravity, and weather patterns of our distant planetary neighbors—clues that would help us in our search to know who we are. Suspecting that the craft could possibly encounter intelligent life at some point on its one-way voyage, Pioneer was also fitted with our first interstellar "calling card."

Designed by the late Dr. Carl Sagan and Dr. Frank Drake, a six-by-nine-inch gold plaque with key information describing its makers and the source of its origins was fastened onto the tiny craft. Carefully engraved into the surface of the plaque was a diagram indicating that Pioneer had originated on the third planet from the Sun, showing its relationship to the center of the galaxy. Additional information included the likeness of a human man and woman, the silhouette of the Pioneer spacecraft, and chemical symbols demonstrating that we understand the breakdown of hydrogen, which is the most abundant element in the universe (see Figure 1.4).

The signal that was returned to Earth on that day in 2001 was the same signal that we had broadcast approximately 22 hours earlier (Pioneer 10 was almost 11 light years away, so it took 11 hours to send the signal and another 11 for it to be returned). After 29 years of dodging space debris, radiation storms, and enduring the frigid sub-zero temperatures of deep space, Pioneer was still "alive," and its instruments were still working. Although the probe's mission may continue for hundreds of years into the future, the sheer distances it has traveled will eventually make such communication impractical.

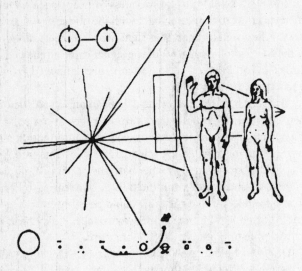

Figure 1.4: Schematic illustration of the gold plaque carried by the Pioneer 10 spacecraft.

At some point along its sojourn, Pioneer may very well encounter intelligent life forms searching, as *we* are, for clues to their origins and others of their kind. On that day, after having traveled so far from our home with evidence of our existence, the 570-pound probe that left our world in the spring of 1972 will become our first deep-space ambassador. Even if those making the discovery don't understand the symbols, Pioneer's very existence speaks for itself. The fact that its sole mission is one of exploration should be a sign to its discoverers that we value life to such a degree that we are willing to apply our technology—reaching into the uncharted realms of our solar system and beyond—to know if anyone else is "out there."

Are We the Only Ones?

Following his lunar landing in 1969, Neil Armstrong, the first human in recorded history to have set foot on another world, admitted that, while we have no proof to date, the odds favor intelligence elsewhere. "If we extrapolate, based upon the best information we have available to us, we have to come to the conclusion that . . . other life probably exists out there—and perhaps in many places."[18]

Armstrong's sentiment is echoed by other scientists and researchers well respected in their fields. "We know that there are planets going around other stars, and we know that it's likely that some of those planets have the right conditions for life. So it would be really bizarre if we were the only ones. It's much more likely that the universe is teeming with life," suggests Dan Werthimer, a physicist at the University of California at Berkeley.[19]

In 1961, astronomer Frank Drake went so far as to propose an equation that could estimate the number of intelligent civilizations that may exist elsewhere in our universe. Known as *Drake's equation,* the formula was based upon seven factors that scientists believe necessary for intelligent life. Using educated guesses, such as the rate of star formation per year and the number of those stars that produce planets suitable for life, Drake's equation suggested that as many as 10,000 intelligent civilizations could be present in the universe as we know it (see Figure 1.5).[20]

(the rate of star formation per year) x

(the fraction of those stars that have planets) x

(the number of those planets suitable for life) x

(the number of those planets where life actually develops) x

(the fraction of those planets where intelligent life emerges) x

(the fraction of intelligent civilizations that develop advanced communications) x

(the number of years an intelligent civilization can survive without destroying itself or succumbing to natural causes) = (number of intelligent civilizations possible in the universe)

Figure 1.5: Radio astronomer Frank Drake's equation for estimating the number of intelligent civilizations that may exist in our universe. *Note:* In this illustration, the letter x is the symbol for multiplication.

For the moment, however, we appear to be unique in the vast expanse of the cosmos. Scientists now believe that the universe we inhabit is nearly 17 billion light years (1 light year = the 9.46 trillion miles that light travels in one year) from one side to another, while our Milky Way galaxy alone is 100,000 light years across. Within the entire universe, estimates for the number of galaxies are a staggering 200 billion, each galaxy holding somewhere in the same neighborhood of the 200 to 500 billion stars that are believed to be in our own.

With such mind-boggling statistics, the odds favor the existence of intelligence somewhere "out there." Some researchers even suspect that we have already made contact in one form or another. In the absence of hard data, many people simply have a deep intuitive feeling, described as a "knowing," that we are not alone. In that knowing is the sense of a greater universal presence associated with God. Even if we find that such a presence is not "the" God, the hope is that by finding other life we will be closer to solving the mystery of our own beginnings.

Commenting on the value of our quest for other life, Carl Sagan observed, "In the deepest sense the search for extraterrestrial intelligence is a search for ourselves."[21] Perhaps the basis of Sagan's sentiment stems from the probability that the search for our origins will ultimately lead us to the most abundant evidence of life's mystery: the mystery of humankind.

Although the odds favor intelligence elsewhere in the universe, for the time being the family of human beings appears to be unique in creation. Even if and when a living presence beyond our world is discovered and openly acknowledged, the chances are that it will not be identical to us. In all probability, our status as a one-of-a-kind life form will not change. In light of our uniqueness, we may find that it is precisely the qualities that make us so distinct that also hold the key to surviving the greatest threats of our future. To find such a key, however, we must first reckon with what is, perhaps, the oldest and most difficult enigma of all . . . we must discover who we are by looking within.

CHAPTER 1 SUMMARY

- In the first years of the 21st century, humankind is faced with the greatest challenges of recorded history. The prospect of a third global war, drug-resistant disease, and the uncertain results of biological technologies such as human cloning now threaten the future of our entire species.

- In the presence of the most advanced science in recorded history, we have yet to answer what is perhaps the most fundamental question of our existence: Who are we?

- History is the story of our search to know ourselves. Our journey is punctuated with examples of how differences of race, belief, heritage, and lifestyle have been used as the basis for the atrocities recognized as "man's inhumanity to man."

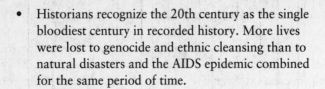

- Historians recognize the 20th century as the single bloodiest century in recorded history. More lives were lost to genocide and ethnic cleansing than to natural disasters and the AIDS epidemic combined for the same period of time.

- Many of the issues at the root of last century's violence remain today. Unresolved, these issues have escalated to regional levels and now threaten the peace of our world.

- The technology of the last 50 years has extended our search for identity to the farthest regions of our solar system, and now beyond. Pioneer 10 continues on its record-setting journey into deep space with the six-by-nine-inch plaque designed as our first interstellar "calling card."

- Ultimately, the search for our origins appears to be leading us to the most abundant source of clues: life itself. Through the understanding of life in general, and who we are specifically, we may discover the key to overcoming the differences that threaten our existence.

"Without an understanding of who
we are, and from where we came,
I do not think we can truly advance."

— LOUIS B. LEAKEY

Chapter Two

BONES, BOOKS, AND CELLS:
When Evidence and Theories Collide

In the first years of the 21st century, we are faced with a single and humbling reality. In what may be the greatest of ironies, while we find ourselves with the most advanced science in the history of our species, we have yet to answer the most basic question of our lives: *Precisely who are we?* Do we owe our existence to a chance combination of elements and evolution, or is there something more to our lives?

In Search of Our Origins

Until recently, scientific discussions of human origins have been largely based upon the discovery of fossilized remains believed to be those of our ancestors. In the footsteps of Charles Darwin's theory of evolution, first published as *The Origin of Species by Means of Natural Selection* in 1859, the general idea is that species develop over long periods of time, with each new generation selecting from its parents the characteristics that ensure its survival. In this way, the traits that bring strength and diversity to individuals are preserved and encouraged. Much of Darwin's theory was based upon observations that he made while studying wildlife in the Galapagos Islands, as well as his findings of fossilized creatures unknown to the world at the time of his journey.

Prior to the release of Darwin's work, the prevailing view of how our world has come to "be" as it is was the result of a literal interpretation of the biblical story of Genesis. This view remains popular today and is best recognized as the theory of *creationism,* which is rooted in religious doctrine proposed by Anglican bishop James Ussher in 1701. Combining Mediterranean and Middle Eastern history with the historical births and deaths recorded in the Bible of his day, Bishop Ussher created what he believed to be an accurate timeline for biblical events from the first day of creation.

Based upon his calculations, Ussher declared that Sunday, October 23, 4004 B.C.E., was the day of the "Beginning," thus setting Earth's age at 6,000 years.[1] From this chronology, Ussher then calculated dates for key biblical events, such as Adam and Eve's expulsion from Eden, which he placed on Monday, November 4, 4004 B.C.E. James Ussher's correlations were printed into authorized versions of the Bible and came to be accepted by many without question.

At odds with the scientific interpretation of Earth's age and the geologic record accepted today, creationism states that life was created all at once by the force of God during the time of the Beginning. Additionally, the theory states that there are essentially no new species to be found. All life existing at present or in the past—including human life—is the result of the original creation, and it has remained fixed and unchanging.

To explain the physical features that form our Earth today, creationists look to past events of catastrophic proportions. This concept, known as *catastrophism,* is believed responsible for creating the mountains, oceans, and continents that we see in modern times. The worldview based in the theories of creationism and catastrophism remained largely unchallenged until a paradigm-shattering work was published in 1785 by a Scottish scientist named James Hutton.

Known as the father of modern geology, Hutton's book *The Theory of the Earth* suggested that our world is continuously

changing and evolving as the result of natural processes that have always existed, rather than a single, divine act of intervention occurring at the time of the Beginning. Hutton's theories also stated that the forces at work earlier in our planet's history were still active, and that the processes continued in the present. It was the continuous form of these changes that could offer modern researchers a window into the past. Through this simple concept, the present became the key to the past.[2] Although these principles appear obvious to us today, theories such as Hutton's were radical for their time.

Darwin was familiar with the work of Hutton and other scientists,[3] and their ideas contributed to his theory of evolution by providing an explanation for what he saw during his famous voyage of the HMS Beagle from 1831 to 1836. Throughout his journey, Darwin observed a greater variety of plants and animals than any other scientist of his day. A journal entry recalling his voyage, dated 1859, offers a clue as to the impression that his journey left on him personally:

"When on board HMS Beagle as a naturalist, I was much struck with certain facts in the distribution of the inhabitants of South America, and in the geological relations of the present to the past inhabitants of that continent. These facts seemed to me to throw some light on the origin of species—that mystery of mysteries, as it has been called by one of our greatest philosophers."[4]

Central to Darwin's findings were his observations of various species of birds in the Galapagos Islands. It wasn't until his return to London that he realized that what he originally thought to be specimens collected of *different* families of finches were actually variations of the *same* family. The question Darwin faced was how to explain variations, such as beak size and shape, among finches that had developed isolated from one another on separate islands. The additional discovery of fossilized remains of creatures resembling modern-day animals, though much larger in size, added to the mystery that Darwin was faced with.

Using sound scientific methods, Darwin applied the best theories of his time to explain what he discovered during his historic journey. Today, we know the result of his work as the theories of *natural selection* and *evolution*. In essence, these theories simply state that there are differences in any population. Members and their offspring having characteristics that support their lives, such as large beaks for consuming large nuts or camouflage-like coloring for protection, have an advantage over other members of the same species without such characteristics.

Over time and changing conditions, individuals with traits that ensure their survival will win out over members without such features. The reason is that they will survive longer and produce more offspring that will also have the desirable traits. Eventually, once-unique changes in individuals become the traits of an entirely new species. In his later book *The Descent of Man,* Darwin stated his belief that humankind, like other forms of life, is the result of precisely such processes, with evolutionary selection occurring over very long periods of time.

Evolution or Adaptation?

Although Charles Darwin returned from his historic journey in 1836, it wasn't until 20 years later that he shared his findings publicly. In a joint paper, *The Theory of Evolution and Natural Selection,* presented to the Linnean Society of London, Darwin offered his findings with Alfred Wallace, a scientist who had arrived at similar conclusions, though without the evidence to support them. A full account of Darwin's theory was then published as *The Origin of Species* and widely acclaimed by scientists the world over.

While Darwin's work was well thought out, meticulously documented, and performed within the guidelines of the scientific method, *a growing body of evidence now suggests that it may not fully describe the story of human origins or prove that we are the result of evolution.* This is not to say that a form of evolution hasn't

occurred, as characteristics that allow groups of people to adjust to their environment are known and well documented. Perhaps the ability to *adapt* better describes what has been observed in such groups, rather than a process of evolution.

The indigenous tribes of the polar regions in the Arctic and Siberia, for example, are shown to have developed extra flesh around their eyes, allowing them protection from the perpetual glare of sunlight that is reflected from the snow and ice that greets them outside of their homes each day. While this characteristic *is* believed to be a direct response to their environment, *it is a change in their appearance only.*

The members of such tribes have lived and adapted to the harsh environment of the polar regions for at least 10,000 years. During that time, however, they have not evolved into a new species of human, and there appears to be no evidence that they will. Genetically these people still belong to the species *Homo sapiens sapiens.* Their bodies have simply adjusted to the conditions of the environment that their world presents.

In a similar fashion, the bodies of people living in the most extreme elevations of the earth are documented as having developed characteristics that skew the chances of survival in their favor. The highest mountain chains of the world include the Andes mountains of Southern Peru and the Himalayan range that juts skyward between the countries of Nepal and Tibet. Studies show that the number of red blood cells in people living full-time at higher altitudes is likely to be as much as 30 percent greater than someone living at sea level.[5]

In general, people who live in these extremes *shift* their body functions to survive the conditions of cold temperature, low moisture, and oxygen levels in the atmosphere. An increase in red blood cells enhances the blood's ability to carry oxygen and, in turn, the amount of oxygen sent to the tissues. While these and similar studies certainly document the ability of human populations to adapt to their environments, they may fall short of actually describing an evolutionary process with regard to our origins and history.

Does the Evidence Support Evolution?

With Darwin's theories in mind, the search for our origins has focused upon the search for physical evidence to link modern humans with our earliest ancestors. A growing body of evidence compiled over the last 150 years appears to suggest that our ancestors did, in fact, change over long periods of time from less advanced to progressively more sophisticated forms of life. Invariably, such discussions of the fossil record lead to the deeply inspiring work of the Leakey family in Kenya.

For more than half a century, the Leakeys and their scientific colleagues, such as Tim White and Donald Johanson, have labored in the remote regions of the East African Rift Valley attempting to fill in the missing links of our family tree. From the time that the excavations began in the 1950s, a number of international teams have diligently sifted through loose soil and grains of dust to recover bone fragments, teeth, stone tools, and sometimes entire skeletal sections of ancient beings that appear to have human characteristics. Numerous issues of *National Geographic* magazine beautifully document the search throughout the past half century that has now pushed the accepted date of human origins back to nearly six million years ago (*Nature*, July 12, 2001).

The search continues today and has produced numerous examples of fossilized remains believed to represent the various stages of human development along the ladder of evolution. Taught in classrooms throughout the world, these ancient examples of hominid ancestors have been commonly referenced through names such as "Cro-Magnon man" and "Neanderthal man."* In addition to pushing the accepted date of our ancestors' origins back four million years earlier than previously believed, recent discoveries in East Africa have added significantly to our understanding of how we got from "there" to "here." A version of the accepted sequence for human development is shown in Figure 2.1.

---

*Also spelled as "Neandertal man." This find is named after the valley in which the discovery was made, Neanderthal, West Germany. Both variations are correct, and a matter of preference.

Traditional Time Line of Human Development[7]

Scientific Name	Common Name	Approximate Age
Australopithecus	Lucy	3.2 million years ago[8]
Homo habilis	Handy Man	2.0 million years ago
Homo erectus	Upright Man	1.5 million years ago
Homo heidelbergensis	Pre-Neanderthal	300–400,000 years ago
Homo neaderthalensis	Classic-Neanderthal	30–150,000 years ago
Homo sapiens sapiens	Cro-Magnon/ Modern Man	10–30,000 years ago

Figure 2.1: One widely accepted chronology of our ancestors interpreted from fossilized evidence. This summary is approximate, as new discoveries continue to shift the dates describing the ages of our earliest ancestors.

As impressive as these and similar findings are, and as much as they contribute to the knowledge of our origins, late 20th-century discoveries have created new questions, and in some cases deepened the mystery, of our past. For example, if the process of change is ongoing, then why has the form and brain capacity of modern man remained virtually unchanged for the last 160,000 to 200,000 years? If we developed from less evolved forms of primates, then how do we account for fossil records that show us living with those forms during the same periods of time? Assuming that humankind evolved gradually over eons, what happened that prompted us to begin walking upright? Two late-20th-century discoveries may begin to shed light on why these questions exist, and what the answers may be saying about our history.

The Genetic Mystery

The first map describing the building block of life was established by James Watson and Francis Crick in 1953. Through their now-famous model of the double helix and the patterns of information held in the DNA molecule, the door was opened for an entire science of identifying individuals on the basis of their unique genetic characteristics. From eye and hair color, to gender and tendencies toward certain conditions of health and disease, the codes that determine how our bodies appear and function are held in the blueprint of our genetic code. Since the time of Watson and Crick's discovery, the science of matching segments of DNA to determine paternity, identify missing persons, and link individuals to a specific crime has become a keystone in crime-scene analysis and forensics.

In 2000, the same techniques used in such investigations—the results of which are recognized in the highest courts of law today— were applied to the study of human origins for only the second time in history. In a report published in the prestigious journal *Nature*,[10] researchers at the University of Glasgow's Human Identification Centre described their investigation comparing the genetic material from our possible ancestors to that of modern humans. Along with co-workers in Russia and Sweden, in 1987 the scientists tested ancient DNA from the body of an unusually well-preserved Neanderthal infant, discovered in a limestone cave of the northern Caucasus.

The exceptional state of the child's body is a story, and a mystery, unto itself. Normally such a high degree of preservation occurs only in remains where the tissues are frozen, such as those found in the icy polar regions. It was this unusual state of preservation that allowed for 30,000-year-old DNA from the infant to be compared to that of humans today. It was also the first time that such tests could be performed on a body that had already been carbon dated.

While scientists are still reeling from the implications of the report, the study found that the possibility of a genetic link between *Neanderthal* and modern humans was remote. The results suggest that "modern man was not, in fact, descended from Neanderthals."[11] While in theory the science of genetic comparison should solve the mystery of our ancestry, the results are actually raising more questions and opening the door to "forbidden" territory regarding our evolutionary lineage and origins.

There is an additional mystery revealed since the discovery of the genetic code regarding the number of chromosomes that distinguish one species from another. Biological instructions are contained within the chromosomes of each species member that determine their bone structure, brain size, metabolic processes, and so on. Higher primates such as apes and monkeys have 24 pairs of chromosomes, or a total of 48 that give them their uniqueness. Humans have 23 pairs, giving us a total of only 46! Although it appears as though we're "missing" an entire set of chromosomes when compared to our nearest relatives, a comparative study of our genetic maps reveals an interesting curiosity.

A closer look at the chromosomes that appear to be absent from our gene pool shows that human chromosome 2 is remarkably similar and actually "corresponds" to chromosomes 12 and 13 of the chimpanzee, as *if they were to be combined* (fused) into a single larger piece of DNA.[12, 13, 14] Further investigation into primate gene maps indicates that this "split human chromosome 2" is common to the gorilla and orangutan as well. Because of these chromosomal differences, it is unlikely that natural processes or an ancient interbreeding have created such a genetic mix. In addition to such mysteries in chromosome 2, a number of other characteristics between human and chimp genes appear to be nearly identical, *but reversed,* between the species.[15] These discoveries now raise the question: What could have happened in our distant past to produce such changes in the fundamental code of our lives?

Based upon a comparison of human physiology with other primates, there is a growing body of evidence suggesting that, as *Homo sapiens*, we are a unique species unto ourselves. Rather than being part of a tidy linear progression descending directly from earlier forms of primates, this theory takes the approach that we developed along with earlier primates in a sort of parallel evolution. A comparison of primate and human characteristics, such as bone density and our ability to shed tears, perspire, and grow hair versus fur for body covering lends credibility to this theory, while fueling controversy for proponents of *both* creationism and evolution theory.

In the British journal *Nature* (June 12, 2003), a paper was published revealing the discovery of fossilized skulls of the earliest known *Homo sapiens*. Found in the Middle Awash region of Ethopia, Africa, the remains are dated at 160,000 years before present, and while not identical, they are very similar to those of the modern human! If the evolution process is ongoing, then why have we apparently changed so little during such a large expanse of time?

While such findings may ultimately raise more questions than they answer today, each stage of investigation adds to what we know about ourselves, further defining our place in the universe and our role in creation. Additional evidence in the fossil record lends credibility to the genetic studies, suggesting that, while we may share DNA with less evolved forms of life, we may have developed in a unique and unexpected way, along our own genetic time line.

Anomalies in the Fossil Record

In addition to the DNA studies, a number of scientific journals have reported discoveries of anomalous human remains—fully modern human skeletons—*within the same layers of earth where the earliest fossils of ancient hominids* from farther down the evolutionary ladder were discovered. In a report published in 1913, Dr. Hans Reck, a contemporary of Louis Leakey, described a find that he made in the same area of Africa that would later produce the oldest examples of humanlike remains.[16] Working in the Olduvai Gorge, Dr. Reck discovered what appeared to be a fully developed, fully modern human skeleton, *excavated from the same geologic formations* that produced the ancient remains of the now famous "Peking man" and "Java man."

The physical location of a modern skeleton within the same layers of earth as the more ancient remains poses a problem for conventional evolution theory: If one form of life descends from another, they cannot co-exist in the same period of time. As the

deeper layers were deposited first, whatever is found within them can reasonably be assumed to be older than anything found in the shallower layers, which formed at a later time.

Generally accepted as a method of dating buried objects relative to one another, from such procedures we can conclude that the modern-looking skeletons would have had to have lived and died during the same period of time as the more primitive humans. If this is the case, they could not have evolved at a later time.

When the stories of Reck's find were first published, skeptics of the day suggested that the modern skeletons were washed, or in some other way deposited, into the strata at a later time. While such conditions, if they were to occur, could certainly explain the mystery, the discovery of similar cases[17] suggests that the finds may be showing us something much more significant. They add to a growing body of evidence suggesting that we may not be the product of a clear evolutionary ladder, such as that seen with Darwin's finches. If modern humans were, in fact, walking the earth simultaneously with what have been considered our primitive ancestors, then we must ask the next question: Where did they/we come from?

Combining the Theories of Our Origins

The word *theory* is defined as an "assumption devised to analyze or explain the nature of specified phenomena." The theories of creation and how evolution may account for life's origin proposed to date are precisely that: *theories*. Each is designed to account for the observed evidence from a very different perspective. During the time in history in which creationism and evolution were introduced, both appeared as reasonable explanations based upon the information then available. While both theories stem from sound observations, a theory can only be as good as the information upon which it is based. Clearly, for both creationism and evolution, the sources of information still developing, leaving interpretations open to revision as new information comes to light.

The primary questions regarding evolution with regard to human origins stem from two assumptions that are key to the theory. These are the ideas that:

- life may arise spontaneously from nonliving material, and

- the characteristics that make us unique are the result of evolutionary forces acting alone.

While there is strong evidence that certain precursors of life, such as ammonia clouds and the building blocks for chlorophyll in plants and hemoglobins in animals (porphyrins) exist in deep space, to the best of my knowledge, life has never been observed to originate from nonliving materials, under natural or laboratory conditions. Evolutionists address this irony by suggesting that, although we do not see the spontaneous creation of life *today,* the conditions for such processes may have been present at some time in the past and then been destroyed by the development of life itself.[18]

Even when the conditions of temperature, moisture, and chemistry are favorable for spontaneous life, however, there appears to be *some force beyond the properties of chemistry* that breathes life into the elements of creation. This force does not appear to be accounted for in the theories of Darwin's time or in the conventional wisdom of today.

As noted previously, if species do, in fact, truly *evolve* with new genetic characteristics, rather than adapt over time, then one possiblity we would expect to see in the fossil record is a linear progression from one life form to the next. Instead, the developing fossil record suggests that species previously believed to have evolved from one another over time appear to have lived with one another during the same period of time, making their emergence as a linear progression less likely.

Similarly, creation theory has been plagued with concerns that include the accuracy of Bishop Ussher's calculations, his

sources, and the rigidity of his claims. As is the case with evolution theory, these concerns come from assumptions upon which the theories are based, including the ideas that:

- biblical records of creation are accurate, and

- biblical records of creation are complete in terms of the accounts themselves.

The best scholars of our day are in agreement that as good as our biblical texts are as documents of traditional and historic events, they are physically incomplete. Following the fourth-century deletion of at least 45 Old and New Testament books under the direction of the Emperor Constantine in 325 A.D.,[19] the canonized version of the biblical text from which Bishop Ussher made his calculations was also incomplete.

While both creationism and evolutionary theory offer useful insights into the nature of our origins, *we may discover that the merging of key concepts from both theories* offers the best explanation of the evidence observed so far. Such a *hybrid theory of creation* takes into account the observations of evolution theory, stating that our world is ancient and that geologic processes do, in fact, occur over long periods of time. Additionally, it incorporates the creationist's view that a special force, beyond that which is acknowledged in conventional science today, is responsible for the spark that we see as "life," and for setting into motion the conditions from which life has arisen.

In the absence of direct observation, a theory is the best answer available to explain a given phenomenon. The fact is, no one living today directly observed the moment that creation began. For now, a combined theory incorporating elements from both creationism and evolution theory appears to be our best explanation for the mystery, and miracle, of life. While acknowledging the physical evidence discovered to date, it also allows for the intuitive sense, held by the vast majority of people in our world, that we are part of something greater.

Life: By Design

In the college text *Chemistry, Matter, and the Universe,* the definition of life is offered from a chemical point of view: "Life is a behavior pattern that chemical systems exhibit when they reach a certain kind and level of complexity."[20] Although this definition may, in fact, describe one aspect of life, it leaves us with an empty feeling, the sense that something is missing. Are we merely the product of random chemicals combining, evolving, and changing over eons of time? Or are we something more? Is it possible that we are, in fact, the result of a well-thought-out and perfectly timed series of events—an intentional act of creation?

If, as the oldest traditions of humankind suggest, human life is the result of an ancient and purposeful act, then we must ask the next question, as well: Who, *or what,* force is responsible for such an awesome display of power, wisdom, and vision? It is in the answering of this question that we may, perhaps for the first time in a very long time, begin to make sense of our world and find greater meaning in our lives.

In *The Origin of Species,* Darwin himself remarked on how unlikely it is that natural selection was solely responsible for the degree of specialization that we see in organs and tissues. Singling out the complexity of an eye as such an example, he stated, "To suppose the eye, with all its inimitable contrivances for adjusting the focus to different distances . . . could have been formed by natural selection, seems, I freely confess, absurd in the highest degree."[21] From such observations, Darwin has left us to our own conclusion with regard to precisely what additional force or forces the complexity of life may be attributed.

In a similar vein, when asked about the possibility that life has arisen from a chance series of events, Francis Crick once remarked that "an honest man, armed with all the knowledge available to us now, could only state that in some sense, the origin of life appears at the moment to be almost a miracle, so many are the conditions that would have had to have been satisfied to get it going."[22] Charles Darwin first made his observations in the 1830s. More than 100 years later, with the benefit of tremendous advances of science and experimental methods, Crick was arriving at very similar conclusions.

Some of the best minds of our time now suspect that in addition to vast amounts of time and the recognized process of nature, life appears to be as it is by design. This chapter began by asking the question: Who are we? As a species, our search to answer this single question has led us upon a centuries-long journey of mystery, bloodshed, and exploration. Regardless of what words we use to describe ourselves today, ours is an unfolding mystery that continues.

For now, we can say with reasonable certainty that we are more than we have ever dared to imagine, and perhaps capable of all that we have ever dreamed. To even the most skeptical scientist, a growing body of evidence suggests that the force of a greater intelligence underlies our existence. In addition to the now-obvious degree of order at the basis of life, the focus of this book will further describe an order of even greater magnitude—an alphabetic language coded as the elements of life itself. It is this higher degree of order that suggests the presence of an even greater intelligence underlying our existence.

What Would It Mean to Discover a Message from "God"?

With the largest populations in our history, we build nations, raise families, assemble armies, and race forward with the most advanced science believed to have ever existed. In light of the difficulties that we face by living in such a world, what would it mean to find a principle that touched the life of each human in the world today with a single, unifying message so deep, so powerful, and so personal that it could not be denied? Slicing through the outward differences that divide us as families, nations, and religions, we may only imagine how differently we would live our lives and build our world, confident in the knowledge that our existence stems from a Creator whose name is literally encoded into each cell of our bodies.

At the very least, such a discovery would become the benchmark of a new era clarifying our relationship to one another and our world. While such a message would fall short of identifying precisely *who* the God of creation is, the universal nature of God's ancient name within the code of life—a name now confirmed through 20th-century science—would add to a growing body of evidence suggesting that something more than a chance combination of chemicals and evolution is responsible for our being here.

At its best, revealing the name of God within all life would provide powerful new evidence that we are here on purpose, sharing our world as one family. Such a principle could offer a much-needed touchstone of hope in a time when our differences are often viewed as reasons to separate us, rather than the diversity that strengthens us. A message discovered within the chemistry of each body, regardless of religion, lifestyle, race, or belief, would be a sign so universal in nature that it could transcend any differences in our past.

Recent studies suggest that the impact of such a discovery may be similar to the shock we experience when we receive news that changes our lives in dramatic and unexpected ways. Perhaps we would integrate such news in stages, similar to reconciling the loss of a loved one. In a very real sense, the knowledge that we are the product of intentional creation would invite us to replace our present belief system with one that incorporates our newfound knowledge. We may, in effect, find that we mourn the loss of our old beliefs as we redefine our role in creation. In such a scenario, the well-accepted stages of loss—shock, denial, rejection, anger, and, ultimately, acceptance—offer a clue as to how deeply such a realization might touch our lives.

The remarkable discovery that follows describes precisely such a principle of unity: the ancient name of God, coded into the very fabric of our existence. Hidden deep within us from the day of our origins, the code has awaited the moment that our search would lead our journey inward, to the essence of all life. Perhaps we should not be surprised to discover that the secret we share with God and life gives new meaning to our time in the presence of one another as well.

CHAPTER 2 SUMMARY

- The theories of evolution and creationism, in and of themselves, are inadequate to explain the evidence that we see as our past. Something appears to be missing in each theory.

- Hybrid theories of creation, combining elements of evolution and creationism, suggest that an added factor—a force that has yet to be accounted for—may have played a key role in the origins of life.

- Ancient traditions suggest that the clues to humankind's deepest mysteries, and the key to our peace and survival, may be found in the crowning achievement of God's creation—life itself.

- The co-discoverer of the DNA structure suggests that for all of the factors to be in the right place, at the perfect time, and for life to arise by chance, borders upon the miraculous.

- The discovery that the chemistry of life—our DNA—is the ancient code of a universal language offers an unprecedented principle of human unity. In the presence of such a message, we must rethink our relationship to a higher power in the social, technological, and scientific choices of our future.

- The discovery of "who" we are may ultimately hold the key to the peace of our world and our survival.

"Everyone who is seriously involved in the
pursuit of science becomes convinced that
a spirit is manifest in the laws of the universe—
a spirit vastly superior to that of man."

— ALBERT EINSTEIN,
TO STUDENT PHYLLIS WRIGHT IN 1936,
WHO ASKED IF SCIENTISTS PRAY

Chapter Three

FROM THE LOST BOOKS
OF CREATION:
The Powers of Heaven
in Bodies of Earth

Population statistics from the 2000 census are believed to be the most accurate in history, indicating that we share our world with approximately 6.2 billion of our kind. Of that number, nearly 95 percent, or 5.9 billion people, believe in the existence of a higher power or Supreme Being of some description. More than half of those people refer to this power as "God." These and similar statistics suggest that the question of our day may be less about whether or not we believe that God exists, and more about precisely *what* such a presence means in our lives.

Making Sense of a Higher Power

While spirituality has long played a role in the evolution of families, communities, and nations, our future may now hinge upon our ability to recognize that we are more than a chance combination of random molecules. Since the mid-20th century, the theme of our search for a greater intelligence has played out in art, literature, and films throughout the world. The 1998 motion picture *Contact,* based upon Carl Sagan's book of the same name, presents two very different perspectives of our relationship to a higher power, mirroring the modern-day dilemma between science and religion.

Early in the film, the main character, Dr. Ellie Arroway, finds herself in the perfect location to pursue her life's passion: the scientific search for intelligence beyond Earth. Sitting on a bench at the rim of the world's largest single-dish radio telescope, the Aricebo facility located in the mountains of Puerto Rico, she describes the possibilities of intelligent life elsewhere in the universe to the character of theologian and author Palmer Joss. In just our galaxy alone, there are more than 400 billion stars, she comments. If only a fraction of those had planets, and if only a fraction of those planets had life, and if only a fraction of the planets with life had intelligent life, millions of civilizations would exist!

Gazing into the night sky, then into one another's eyes, from very different viewpoints they each sense that we are not alone. From Palmer's perspective, the widely shared belief in a higher power is our collective experience of God's presence. Later, during a moment of intimate discussion, he confesses that his belief in such a power is something that is beyond his ability to intellectualize. It simply "is."

In response, Ellie wonders aloud if our sense of God results from a "need" to add meaning to our lives. Following a moment of silence, Palmer replies with the same words that Ellie heard from her father as a young girl, years before his death. *It seems like a waste of space, if we are the only ones.*

In many respects, the spiritual tension between *Contact's* Dr. Arroway and Palmer Joss describes the polarity of our views today. Palmer sees his experience of a higher power through the eyes of his religious training, interpreting his feeling as the presence of "God." Ellie's passion for the sciences, encouraged by her father from an early age, shapes her sense of a greater intelligence as the statistical probability of life in other worlds. Both viewpoints acknowledge the feeling of a universal presence, a force that science has yet to define. Both discover that absolute proof of that presence is elusive, at best, and ultimately must be experienced to be understood. Ellie's revelation results from her odyssey of being transported and then returned through space-time, with no form of proof to share her experience with others. Palmer's revelation arises from his faith in a force that he can show to no one else, and which he has never seen.

Although the odds are in favor of a higher intelligence in the universe, for the moment we appear to be alone. It's in our feeling of "aloneness," despite having the largest populations in the history of the world, that the irony of not knowing who we are takes on even greater meaning. While science races boldly into the 21st century, at a gut level we still need to understand precisely how we have come to exist.

Ancient Clues to the "Beginning"

As good as our science appears to be, the greatest minds of today admit that our current understandings are incomplete. Within the clarity of the genetic code, Einstein's equations of energy and matter, and the marvel of Internet communication, there are gaps that remain unfilled in our scientific view of creation. To quote a common observation: The more we discover, the more we really understand how little we know.

At the same time, the answer to our question of "how it all began" may already exist in a form that has survived the tests of man and nature. Sealed in earthen vessels and buried under centuries of desert sand, the written records of our past may also hold the most complete records of our origins. Additionally, we may find that the flecks of inked letters and crumbling parchments that preserve such history hold the secret of our capabilities and destiny as well. In much the same way that the native populations of North America described their first experience of the steam locomotive in the language of their time as the "iron horse," the key is to recognize that the secrets of our past have been recorded as the thoughts and ideas of another time.

In the words of their day, those who have come before us described how they received answers to the same questions that we ask today—questions about our origins, life's meaning, and how to survive the suffering of this world. Before the vocabulary of higher dimensions and quantum holograms came into vogue, the principles explaining creation's mysteries already existed. In the only words that they knew, ancient scholars described the visions and revelations that helped them to make sense of their lives. In such a vocabulary, "dimensions" become "heavens," for example, while the forces of nature become the Angels of the Sun, Wind, Earth, and Air; and consciousness becomes the breath of God.

Throughout history, there have been rumors of knowledge preserving such visionary experiences, whose sources are said to date to the time of our beginnings. Through the investigation of time-honored legends, it's not uncommon to discover a factual basis underlying the stories and myths, some of which have persisted for thousands of years.

Heinrich Schliemann's discovery of the city of Troy in 1870, for example, was based upon his belief that Homer's literary classic *The Iliad* was a factual account of historic events. Using *The Iliad* as a verbal map, Schliemann followed the clues of the text and made one of the great archaeological finds of the 19th century. Additional examples of discoveries resulting directly from the investigation of ancient legends and myths include Hiram Bingham's discovery in 1911 of Machu Picchu, the Lost City of the Incas, and the late 20th-century discovery of Noah's Ark on Mt. Ararat in Turkey.

The Lost Book of Adam: Angels' Wisdom in the World of Man

As in the case of the city of Troy, the persistent rumors of an ancient book of wisdom, presented to Adam and Eve during their time in the Garden of Eden, suggests that this legend may, in fact, be based upon a historic event. The mystery of this legend, however, has never been solved. Only one copy of the book is said to have ever existed, the letters of which were imbued with a mysterious substance that prevented the pages from being copied or reproduced. Through the shape, shading, and qualities of the text, the secrets of creation and the origins of humankind were veiled within the letters themselves. To protect the book's contents from being misused, it could be understood only by those whose spiritual maturity allowed them to make sense of its symbols. For all others, legend states that possession of the book was meaningless, and any attempt to misuse its secrets would lead to unhappiness in their lives.

Although the details of the book, known as the *Book of Adam,* have faded over the course of time, rumors of its existence have continued until as recently as the 18th century. During this time it is said to have come into the possession of Israel ben Eliezer, later known as the father of Chassidut Judaism. Until then, the *Book of Adam* had been in the possession of only six individuals: Adam, Joseph, Moses, Joshua ben Nun, and Solomon.[1]

The legend recounts that in a town some distance from Israel ben Eliezer, there lived a rabbi who, while not in possession of the book, knew of its existence. Sensing that he was near the end of his life, the Rabbi Adam Tzaddik entered a "dream-question" requesting guidance in his final act of goodness before leaving this world. His question, simply stated, was to whom should he hand down the *Book of Adam* before his death to assure that the truth of man continue? Later that night, he was awakened from his sleep and led to a cave in the Holy Land where many of the matriarchs and patriarchs of times past were buried. In this cave, he found the single *Book of Adam.*

Rabbi Adam asked his son to locate the young Israel ben Eliezer and hand the book to him personally. The legend continues, describing how Rabbi Adam's son found Israel living in a barn where he would stay up late at night absorbing the words of the Torah, the Jewish Holy Scriptures.

One evening, upon investigating the source of a glow coming from behind the door, the Rabbi's son witnessed a miracle assuring him that Israel was, indeed, worthy of receiving the book of secrets. As he peeked into the window, concerned that the intense

light came from a candle that had set the straw on fire, he saw only a brilliant glow emanating from the body of Israel himself. Rather than a blaze from burning straw, the source of the light was the inspiration that Israel received as he read the words of the Torah.

The next day, Rabbi Adam's son fulfilled his father's last request and handed Israel the mystical book. Through his teachings based upon the *Book of Adam,* Israel ben Eliezer became known as Baal Shem Tov—meaning *Master of the Holy Name.* This is the last time that the *Book of Adam* is mentioned anywhere in the open literature.

Lost Books of the Bible

The 20th century witnessed the recovery of some of the most significant and intriguing records of human history. From lost biblical texts of the Dead Sea Scrolls and the translation of thousands of Sumerian tablets, to the Gnostic and New Testament finds of Egypt's Nag Hammadi Library, a growing body of evidence suggests that the chain of knowledge linking ancient wisdom with our modern world has, in fact, been broken on more than one occasion. Each time the records of our past have been deleted, hidden, or reworded, the mystery of who we are has only been confused further.

As so much of the way we view our present is based upon an incomplete understanding of our past, it should come as no surprise that many of our scientific principles, medical practices, spiritual understandings, and historic facts—as well as how they serve us—also remain incomplete. Perhaps one of the greatest interruptions in our chain of knowledge resulted from the biblical edits of the early Christian Church in the fourth century.

Scholars openly acknowledge the editing and deletion of material from the early Christian texts by a panel that was convened to establish Church doctrine in 325 C.E.[2] Under the direction of the Roman Emperor Constantine, the bishops, clergy, and historians that formed the Council of Nice were presented with the daunting task of converting centuries of disparate religious works into a single document that would be meaningful to the people of their time. Taking into consideration a loose assemblage of parables, teachings, and historic records, many of the books that came to their attention were redundant and poorly written, with overlapping versions and repeated stories. In some instances, the Council found the texts to be so mystical that they were believed to be beyond any practical value. Such was the case with the *Book of Enoch*. As a result of their efforts, the Council recommended that at least 45 documents be removed. The outcome remains with us today in the form of one of the most powerful and controversial books in the history of our world, the Holy Bible.

It's clear from the letters left behind by the Council's members that the original edits were well intended. When asked why he chose to translate and publish such ancient texts rather than his own contemporary works, for example, the Archbishop of Canterbury Wake replied, "Because I hoped that such writings as these would find a more general and unprejudiced acceptance with all sorts of men than anything that could be written by anyone now living."[3] How could the members of the Nicean Council have known that the book they would produce would eventually become the basis for one of the great religions of the world and be considered the most sacred book for over one-third of the world's population?

In recent years, many of the books that were removed during the fourth-century edits have been recovered, translated, and made available to the general public. To the best of my knowledge, there is no single compilation containing all of the texts in their original order, as the translations are the result of different authors working in different languages over the centuries. There are, however, groups of translations that have been made available from time to time, such as a compilation of lost biblical books published early in the 20th century.[4] Following is a partial listing of books that are now known to have been removed during the edits of the Council of Nice.

Letters of Herod and Pilate	I Infancy
Trallians	II Infancy
Romans	Ephesians
Polycarp	I Hermas-Visions
Philidelphians	II Hermas-Commands
Philippians	III Hermas-Similtudes
Paul and Thecla	The Apostle's Creed
Paul and Seneca	Christ and Abgarus
Nicodemus	I Clement
Magnesians	II Clement
Mary	Barnabas

While many of the books listed above were relegated to obscurity following their removal, a number of others were not. Considered to be secondary, or supporting documents, the following is a partial listing of texts that are typically reserved for scholars.

The First Book of Adam and Eve	Simeon
The Second Book of Adam and Eve	Levi
The Book of Enoch	Judah
The Psalms of Solomon	Issachar
The Odes of Solomon	Zebulum
The Fourth Book of Maccabees	Dan
The Story of Ahikar	Naphtali
The Testament of Reuben	Gad
Asher	Benjamin

Fragments of a Greater Wisdom

Arguably, one of the most significant archaeological finds of the last century was the discovery of an ancient library hidden in caves above the shores of the Dead Sea—the Dead Sea Scrolls. This find is highly controversial, as a number of the documents discovered within the caves are now recognized as books that were "lost" during the fourth-century edits. While there are still more scrolls to be found, according to some scholars, the library of documents that came from the 11 caves above the Dead Sea constitutes the most significant cache of biblical texts discovered to date.

Between 1946 and 1956, more than 22,000 fragments of animal hide, copper, and papyrus manuscripts were pieced together, yielding approximately 900 scrolls and revealing the original version of such Old Testament books as Genesis, Isaiah, and the words of Moses. Hershel Shanks, editor of the pioneering journal *Biblical Archaeological Review,* commented on the significance of the find, stating, "Over 200 biblical manuscripts were hidden in the Qumran caves, some dramatically different from accounts in the Bible."[5]

The recovery, translation, compilation, and publication of the scrolls have remained the subject of tremendous controversy since the time of their discovery. Until the last decade of the 20th century, access to the Dead Sea library was limited to a team consisting of only eight scholars. As a result of political and academic pressure, in the 1990s the contents of the scrolls were released to the public. In 1991, Southern California's Huntington Library received a complete set of photographs of the scrolls and announced that they would be made available to the public. Following suit, Emanual Tov, chief of the official scroll team, proclaimed "free and unconditional access to all the photographs of the Dead Sea Scrolls, including previously unreleased scrolls"[6] in November of that same year.

Two years before the Dead Sea Scrolls were unearthed, another library of ancient wisdom was discovered, one that had already begun to change the way we thought of early Christianity. In December of 1945, two brothers found a collection of scrolls buried within a sealed jar near the Nile River village of Nag Hammadi, Egypt. Before coming to the attention of the authorities in Cairo, the collection—consisting of 12 complete manuscripts and eight pages of a 13th—passed through an amazing number of hands. Now kept in the Coptic Museum in Cairo, no one is certain as to precisely how many additional scrolls were destroyed in their use as kindling and fuel for local ovens before the find was authenticated and entered into the museum register on October 4, 1946. The scrolls that remain, known collectively as the *Nag Hammadi Library,* are amazingly well preserved, however, and offer fresh and, in some cases, surprising insight into ancient Gnostic and early Christian traditions.[7]

Figure 3.1: Two pages from the Gnostic "lost" Gospel of Thomas. The manuscript is written in Greek and was among the texts discovered in Egypt's Nag Hammadi Library. [Photo taken through glass by Melissa E. Sherman]

When considered together, these two libraries offer perhaps the most complete view of the ancient world and early Christian traditions discovered to date. Revelations from such wisdom have been tremendously useful in filling the gaps and inconsistencies of traditional scripture. With the history more complete, we are given new insight into the mystery associated with some of our most cherished beliefs. Although this brief discussion doesn't do justice to these texts in their entirety, they are mentioned to illustrate the fact that, through the loss of these and similar bodies of information, universal principles that give meaning to our modern world have been forgotten.

From Heaven's Angels:
Instruments of Death and the Origin of War

Among the most significant and mysterious documents recovered in the last 200 years is the lost biblical *Book of Enoch*. It is clear that historians of the early Catholic Church held the *Book of Enoch* in high regard, as it is referenced in Christian commentaries by respected scholars such as Irenaeus, Clement of Alexandria, and Celsus. The second century C.E. historian Tertullian, for example, describes Enoch's unique place in sacred literature, acknowledging that while the words of the Old Testament prophet had not been accepted by the Hebrew canon, they were nonetheless divinely inspired and should be given the same credibility as other scriptural documents such as the Books of *Isaiah* and *Psalms*.[8] Specifically, Tertullian states, "As Enoch has spoken in the same scripture as the Lord, and 'every scripture suitable for edification is divinely inspired,' let us reject nothing which belongs to us."[9]

Lost for nearly 1,500 years, the first mention of Enoch's text in modern times is with its discovery by James Bruce in 1773. Bruce, a Scottish explorer, noted, "Amongst the articles that I consigned to the library at Paris was a very beautiful and magnificent copy of the prophecies of Enoch."[10] One copy of this manuscript was presented to the Bodleian Library at Oxford, where it was rediscovered and subsequently translated by Richard Lawrence in 1821.

The *Book of Enoch* begins with an account of the prophet dictating the hidden history of the human race to his son, Methuselah, as it was revealed to him by the Angel of Peace. Methuselah records that his father's words were spoken as Enoch saw a "vision in the heavens . . . with his eyes wide open."[11] While in his awakened, yet altered, state, Enoch describes the reasons for humanity's decline and the source of the suffering that he and Methuselah witnessed in their time. Beyond the vague and general references that often seem to accompany the visions of ancient prophets, Enoch clarifies his experience with an uncanny precision.

Specifically, Enoch describes how certain angels divulged the secrets of creation to humankind before our species had gained the wisdom to use such powers wisely. Without the maturity to apply the knowledge responsibly, he is shown how the secrets of plants and herbs, language, writing, and alchemy were revealed and subsequently misused by humankind for purposes of war and power. In response to his request to be shown "all that was concealed," Enoch is further allowed to know the names of the "angels who have descended from Heaven to Earth, and have revealed secrets to the sons of men, and have seduced the sons of men to the commission of sin."[12]

Singling out specific angels and the secrets that each divulges, Enoch describes how the angel Azazyel has "taught every species of iniquity upon the earth, and has disclosed to the world all the secret things which are done in the heavens."[13] The angel Gadrel, he continues, "discovered to the children of men the instruments of death, the coat of mail, the shield and the sword for slaughter."[14]

In addition to such disturbing revelations, Enoch was also shown the awe-inspiring source and beauty of creation's mysteries. "There too, my eyes beheld the secrets of the lightning and thunder . . . there I perceived the place from which they issued forth, and became saturated with the dust of the earth. . . .There I saw . . . the cloud itself, which continued over the earth before the creation of the world."[15]

Making a distinction between knowledge and the wisdom that comes from applying knowledge in our lives, Enoch describes how the secrets of Heaven were eventually lost in the realm of man. "Wisdom went forth to dwell among the sons of men, but she obtained not habitation." He concludes this portion of his vision, stating, "Wisdom found not a place on earth where she could inhabit; her dwelling therefore is in heaven."[16]

The Powers of Heaven in Bodies of Earth

The discovery and translation of additional texts suggest that even before Heaven's knowledge was shared upon the earth, the angels of the heavens questioned humanity's readiness to receive such information. By combining the qualities of angels and a material body, the human race had already been granted a status unprecedented in the eyes of God's angels. The commentary of the mystical Jewish *Book of Haggadah,* for example, describes how man "unites both Heavenly and Earthly qualities within himself."[17] The text further reveals God's reason for the creation of our species, stating that "I [God] will create man to be the union of the two, so that when he sins, when he behaves like a beast, death shall overtake him; but if he refrains from sin, he shall live forever."[18]

According to Gnostic and noncanonized religious texts, to further empower humankind with the secrets of the heavens was the subject of tremendous controversy among God's counsel in the heavens. The Haggadah text continues: "The angels were not all of one opinion,"[19] describing how the Angels of Truth and Peace opposed man's creation, while the Angels of Love and Justice were in favor of God's plan. Of particular concern were the implications and consequences of empowering a single species with the combined secrets of Heaven and Earth before they had gained the wisdom to apply such knowledge responsibly.

Books such as the Haggadah represent only a sampling of a theme that is present throughout ancient accounts of our creation. Additionally, the oldest insights into our collective past reveal a viewpoint that is abundantly clear in their translations: Those who have come before us viewed our relationship to God, the cosmos, and one another in a very different light from the prevailing worldview of today. Through their writings, we are left with little doubt as to the magnitude of the role they believed that God plays in our world and our lives. While the discovery detailed through this book stops short of defining precisely who or what God is, in a similar fashion it describes the modern evidence of a timeless intelligence underlying our very existence.

Through a legacy of massive temples, mysterious pyramids, extensive libraries, and mystical texts, members of ancient societies dedicated their lives to preserving and communicating such secrets of creation—secrets that were already ancient in times of antiquity. Within their secrets was knowledge so universal, yet so subtle, that

even today the best science of our time has struggled with its meaning and implications.

The Mysterious Sepher Yetzirah: The Book of Creation

Some of the most complete, as well as detailed, records of our origins appear to be preserved in the language and traditions of ancient Hebrew. With a continuous history that may be traced back more than 5,000 years in time, we may read the words penned by Hebrew scholars precisely as they were written more than five millennia ago. Through those words, we're given insight into the creation of the universe, the formation of the earth, and ultimately, the origin of our bodies. Perhaps the best-known source of Hebrew knowledge is a collection of mystical writings known collectively as the Kabbalah.

Although referred to as a single name, the Kabbalah is actually a collection of works—some whose origins have been lost since times of antiquity—that form the bulk of Hebrew esoteric tradition. In general, the most important works of the Kabbalah are believed to be the *Zohar* (the Book of Radiance), the *Midrash* (the Book of Illumination), and the *Sepher Yetzirah* (the Book of Formation). Each of the works contributes to the overall understanding of God, humankind, and creation in very different, yet complementary, ways.

Historians generally acknowledge that the *Sepher Yetzirah* is the oldest and perhaps most mysterious aspect of these works. Although its precise origins are unknown, traditional Jewish scholars believe that the text was originally received directly by the patriarch Abraham. If this is the case, then the first versions of the *Sepher Yetzirah* would date to approximately 3,800 years ago, making it contemporary with some of the earliest mystical texts of other traditions, such as the *Vedas* of ancient India.

While the *principles* contained in the *Sepher Yetzirah* may well have been handed down from such time-worn traditions, without direct evidence to support the claims, the book itself is commonly thought to have originated sometime during the first century C.E. It is during this time that historic records first mention it by name. One of the earliest such statements is attributed to the first-century rabbi Yehoshua, who declared, "I can take squashes and pumpkins, and with the *Sepher Yetzirah,* make them into beautiful trees."[20]

With unparalleled detail, this concise text of only about 1,500 lines offers a vivid description of the events leading up to, and including, the birth of the cosmos and ultimately, our bodies. The entire text is written from the perspective of an ancient observer narrating the miracle of God's works step by step. The first chapter begins by stating that our world is the result of three kinds of information, recorded in three distinct volumes: text (*Sepher*), number (*Sephar*), and communication (*Sippur*). From these three books, the text continues: "He [God] created His Universe."[21]

Through the remainder of the *Sepher Yetzirah,* the narration describes God's act of creation with progressively greater levels of detail in each chapter. From the formation of the first elements of the universe, represented as the Hebrew letters of God's ancient name, to the way the remaining letters of the Hebrew alphabet formed "all that was ever formed,"[22] the universe unfolds before our eyes as precise combinations of these letter-elements. With a level of detail unparalleled in other creation stories, the *Sepher Yetzirah* offers precise instructions as to how the 22 letters interact with one another to create the "stuff" our world is made of.

When all of the combinations of letters are taken into account and arranged graphically as a circle, there are 231 lines that connect the possibilities. The *Sepher Yetzirah* identifies these lines as the 231 "gates." As we'll see in Chapter 6, through one of these gates we are given insight into the message in our cells.

Of the many ways that the wisdom of the Kabbalah may be interpreted, its works are often classified according to the approach that they take in relating their secrets: theoretical, magical, and meditative. The *Sepher Yetzirah* is generally viewed as simultaneously belonging to two of the categories. It is considered first as a meditative text, leading the reader through contemplation into the deepest secrets of the spiritual realms. Additionally, it has strong links to what is sometimes called ancient "magic," revealing to the trained practitioner the instructions and techniques to bring the knowledge of their meditations into the physical world.

In his highly acclaimed translation of the *Sepher Yetzirah*, the late rabbi Aryeh Kaplan clarifies this view, stating, "This position [that *Sepher Yetzirah* is a meditative text with strong magical overtones] is supported by the earliest Talmudic traditions, which indicate that it could be used to create living creatures."[23] The creation and destruction of such a creature, called a *golem*, was said to demonstrate the highest levels of mastery in the Hebrew mysteries. Though fragments of such texts are available today, those who study and practice this aspect of the Kabbalah consider its secrets so powerful that the texts have never been published in their entirety.

In addition to preserving the oldest and most mysterious works of the Kabbalah, the *Sepher Yetzirah* is undoubtedly the most controversial. The popular view of this proselike work is that, while interesting, it is largely a metaphor for creation's mysteries. Perhaps this traditional viewpoint is best summarized by scholar and foremost authority of world religions Karen Armstrong. In her groundbreaking and highly acclaimed book *A History of God,* Armstrong states that through the *Sepher Yetzirah,* "there is no attempt to describe the creative process realistically; the account is unashamedly symbolic and shows God creating the world by means of language as though he were writing a book."[24]

A closer examination of this mystical text suggests, however, that it offers us much more than a tale of symbol and metaphor. The discoveries linking the Hebrew alphabet with modern elements indicate that the *Sepher Yetzirah* is actually a very ancient and very rich account of the intentional act of creation. The step-by-step process closely parallels the discoveries of 20th-century science!

The controversy and mystery regarding the origins, accuracy, and interpretations of the *Sepher Yetzirah* remain a source of heated debate today. There are at least four major versions of the text and an almost uncountable number of minor versions, if all of the variations over the years are taken into account. From the approximately 1,300 words of the *Short Version* to the 2,500 words of the *Long Version,* Rabbi Kaplan suggests that the reason for so many variations is because of the secrecy required to preserve such teachings. Between the 6th and 10th centuries, scholars acknowledge an attempt to confine the power of the *Sepher Yetzirah* to a small circle of students. "The leaders of these schools may have deliberately released spurious versions," suggests the rabbi, "so as to confuse those who would be tempted to penetrate their mysteries."[25]

According to Rabbi Kaplan, it was the Kabbalists themselves who eventually produced a composite of the many versions that matched the earlier teachings. Originally created in the 16th century, this version was then further refined in the 18th century as the Gra Version (after the Gra Rabbi Eliahu), which is the basis for the monumental effort that resulted in his book, *Sepher Yetzirah: The Book of Creation.*[26] It is this version that will be referenced most frequently through the remainder of this text.

The discovery of a direct link between the elements responsible for life and the ancient languages of Hebrew and Arabic (see Chapter 5) gives new meaning to more than half of the world's most deeply held traditions of religion and spirituality. The shared history of the Jewish, Christian, and Islamic traditions, acknowledged by biblical scholars through the patriarch Abraham, suggests that the God of each belief is precisely the same God. Although the actual name may vary from tradition to tradition, each religion describes our universe as the willful and intentional act of that God. From this perspective, the ancient may be viewed as a precise account of God using the letters of his name (our chemical elements) to produce the universe, the world, and our bodies. Through that understanding, we share God's essence in the foundation of our genetic code.

While the *Sephar Yetzirah* is not the only text to describe these relationships, it is one of the most complete. In its completeness, the understandings gleaned from this powerful narrative become a

framework to understand other accounts of creation that may be less complete, including the scientific theories of evolution and creationism that we explored in Chapter 2. Through such insights, we are able to fill in the missing pieces and bridge the many stories of our past, in sometimes unexpected ways.

CHAPTER 3 SUMMARY

- Nearly 95 percent of the world's population believes in the existence of a higher power or Supreme Being, of some description. Of that number, more than half refer to this power as "God."

- As good as science appears to be, the greatest minds of today admit that our present understandings are incomplete. Despite the clarity of the genetic code, Einstein's equations of energy and matter, and the marvel of Internet communication, great gaps remain in our scientific view of creation.

- Acknowledging the monumental efforts of science to explain life, creation, and the universe, the answers to such great mysteries may already exist within our most ancient traditions in a form that we have yet to recognize.

- Scholars acknowledge that through intentional edits as well as natural processes, the chain of knowledge linking our oldest traditions with the modern world has been interrupted on more than one occasion.

- The 20th-century recovery of texts and libraries, such as the Dead Sea Scrolls and the Nag Hammadi Library, revealed information that had been hidden from general readership for nearly two millennia.

- As the oldest, most mystical, and most controversial aspect of the Kabbalah, the ancient *Sepher Yetzirah* is traditionally viewed by scholars as a collection of metaphors describing the processes of creation in abstract terms.

- The discovery of a direct link between the Hebrew letters and the elements of life now suggests that the ancient *Sepher Yetzirah* is the precise account of God using the letters of his name (our chemical elements) to produce the universe, the world, and our bodies.

PART II

The Discovery:
All Life from the Name of God

"The Lord God formed Man from
the dust of the earth . . ."
— THE TORAH

"We created you out of dust . . ."
— THE HOLY QURAN

Chapter Four

THE UNIVERSE MAKER:
In the Words of Another Time

Sealed within mysterious texts such as the *Sepher Yetzirah*, ancient tradition suggests that we're offered the identity of our Creator, and the knowledge to bridge the spiritual and material worlds. Through this knowledge, we are given the power to heal our bodies and bring peace to our lives. As is so often the case, ancient scholars viewed such secrets as a double-edged sword. In addition to offering the "wisdom of the Heavens" and the key to transcending life's suffering, they believed that the ability to bridge Heaven and Earth also held the power to destroy all that humankind had worked so hard to achieve. It was left to those inheriting the knowledge as to whether the power would become a blessing or a curse.

Through our advancement as a civilization from wood-burning fires to microwave ovens, is it possible that we could have left something behind? Could the clues for surviving the greatest threats to our existence be buried within the oldest records from our past? If so, then discoveries of science and technology, in combination with the recovery of such ancient records, have placed the wisdom of the heavens within our reach for the first time in a very long time. Now our job is to understand the messages left by those who have come before us.

Shared Threads of a Common Past

Among the recurring themes of ancient creation stories are the descriptions of human origins. Through common threads woven into such stories, we may glean insights into the oldest memories of how we have come to "be" in this world. The oral traditions of the Midrash and early Kabbalah, for example, describe how the Creator asked His angels to "go and fetch me dust from the four corners of the earth, and I will create man therewith."[1]

In very similar terms, the Holy Quran refers to God's creation of humankind from natural elements: "We created you out of dust."[2] At another point in the Quran, however, the birth of humankind is attributed to God acting through fluid, stating: "It is He [God] who has created man from water."[3] While these two descriptions may appear to conflict, a closer examination of the verses resolves any mystery.

In the first description, the story of Adam originating from "dust" is part of a larger sequence describing the events that led to the first life. The verses reveal that after Adam's origin as "dust," a process of progressively more lifelike forms began to take shape. The description states that from the dust there formed "a small life-germ, then from a clot, then from a lump of flesh, complete in make and incomplete. . . ."[4] In this way, the Quran adds to the traditional descriptions of Adam by filling in details of how "dust" becomes flesh.

Similarly, in Western traditions, when we ask someone what the first human on Earth was made of, the reply is generally that we're made of the same "stuff" that the world is made of—minerals, water, and air. To support such statements, we are often directed to the biblical creation story in Genesis. Shared by nearly two billion people of the Hebrew and Christian traditions, the story of Adam provides the most basic description of human origins. Deceptively simple in its form, Genesis recounts the miracle of human creation through a very few simple words:

"The Lord God formed man from the dust of the earth."[5]

Different Words/Same Meaning

Through the nuances of culture, there are instances where subtle relationships recorded in one tradition are lost when they are translated to another language. While the original version may preserve an idea through a single word, there may not be an exact translation for that word in the new language.

In ancient Sanskrit, for example, the single word *prana* describes the living field of energy that surrounds and permeates all life. In the English language, the concept of *living energy* has been historically overlooked. There is no single English word with the precise meaning of *prana*. To convey such a concept, we must make do by using words that, of themselves, have no direct relationship to the original idea.

Combining the word *life,* for example, to indicate that we're speaking of living systems, and *force,* to imply an energetic field that stems from within the system itself, results in the phrase "life force." Though the definition of the two words independently has no association with the word *prana,* the substitute phrase *life force* allows us to acknowledge the subtle energy of living systems in our own language.

The description of the first human in Genesis is another example of precisely such subtlety being lost in translation. The first portion of the Christian Old Testament is derived from the first five books of the Torah. Hebrew tradition states that Moses received the books that we know as Genesis, Exodus, Leviticus, Numbers, and Deuteronomy nearly 3,500 years ago, in the language of his time: ancient, or "biblical," Hebrew. It is in the translation from ancient Hebrew to modern English that the nuances of key events recounted in the Torah may have become clouded.

As we've noted in English translations, the biblical relationship between humankind and the earth describes us as being made of "dust." While this description is adequate in general terms—it tells us that we are made of natural elements—the precise description of our origins is perhaps best preserved in its original form.

In Hebrew, the word for *man* is "Adam" (ADM), derived from the root word *adamah*. Interestingly, *adamah* is also the Hebrew word for "land" or "ground," indicating a much more direct and personal relationship between Adam and our world. In deriving the word *Adam* from *adamah*, we are actually shown that the first human was formed as the elements of the earth. A very literal translation would state that Adam is the person, or human being, "of the ground." Through such subtleties of the original language, we're shown that man and the earth share a common origin.

From Adam to Hermes: Tales of Forbidden Secrets

Until the birth of molecular biology in the 20th century, the idea that we are made of the simplest elements, "the dust of the earth," has remained a basic tenet of human understanding. Perhaps the earliest traditions describing this relationship are those of ancient *alchemy*. In its simplest form, alchemy may be defined as a philosophy of nature. It may also be defined as the use of that philosophy to change, or transmute, matter from one form into another.

Legend suggests that it was to the first member of our species, Adam, that the alchemical secrets of Heaven and Earth were originally revealed. Describing the very process responsible for his creation, Hebrew tradition states that an angel greeted Adam at the gate of Eden and instructed him in the mysteries of Kabbalah and the elements. Along with this instruction, the angel offered the promise that when humankind had mastered the wisdom of these "inspired arts," the curse of the forbidden fruit would be lifted and man could return to the "Garden of the Lord."[6]

While the source of more traditional forms of alchemy is unclear,[7] the beginnings of the ancient science are commonly thought to be from the legendary Egyptian figure Thoth, also known by the names Tehuti and Djehuti. Portrayed upon temple walls and papyrus texts as the body of a man and the head of the

long-billed ibis, many of the advancements that set Egypt apart from other civilizations of the time are attributed to the wisdom of Thoth. In addition to introducing writing, law, and medicine to the ancient Egyptians, mystical tradition suggests that Thoth also divulged the alchemical secrets of nature.

The wisdom of Thoth's secrets is said to have been recorded as 42 books that were later incorporated into separate texts, known as the *Emerald Tablets*.[8] As the knowledge of Egypt was assimilated by the Greeks, the alchemical traditions continued as well, with Thoth becoming known as the Greek master of hermetic principles, *Hermes Trismegistus* (meaning three-times-born). A number of the hermetic traditions, such as homeopathic medicines based upon principles of "like treats like" and "as above, so below," continue today.

From such legends, it's suggested that the science of alchemy is one of the two oldest sciences known to humankind. The second is the study of the celestial bodies known as *astrology*. Both were believed to be divinely inspired keys to redeeming humankind from the "fall" that we're told happened early in our history.

Ancient Records of the First Sciences

At its most basic level, the philosophy of ancient alchemy sounds very much like our present-day practice of altering and combining Earth's elements into new and useful products—modern chemistry. Clearly, the knowledge of alchemists served as a link between our earliest understandings of nature and our modern sciences. While alchemy itself has been replaced by its descendant, chemistry, recent discoveries suggest that subtle relationships originally described in the alchemical language may have been lost in their modern translations.

From the perspective of both alchemy and astrology, the sciences that have evolved from them today, including chemistry, physics, and astronomy, are incomplete. Until recently, each has focused upon the physical aspects of the study—the things that we can "see"—while largely ignoring the subtle energy fields that are responsible for the birth of stars and the behavior of atoms. Although science has proven effective for changing forms of matter that already exist—the combining of elements to produce stronger, lightweight metals, for example—it is only in the last years of the 20th century that serious consideration has been given to qualities of the elements that cannot be seen. In recognizing the effects of their "invisible" fields, modern sciences, such as quantum physics, are only now beginning to acknowledge the interrelated nature of creation's elements and what such deeply rooted relationships mean in our lives.

The Alchemy of Fire, Air, and Water

For some individuals, the very word *alchemy* brings to mind the image of a bearded magician from a dark time in history, working in a cold, windowless room hidden within the belly of a medieval castle, surrounded by dried animal parts and boiling flasks of mysterious liquids. Such a view is largely the result of the way modern cinema and novels have portrayed alchemists. Today, we find records describing useful ways to combine nature's products among the most ancient and established traditions of history. From clay tablets and temple walls, to meticulously prepared scrolls and oral tradition, we've learned that the fundamentals of alchemy were known to the Phoenicians, Babylonians, and Chaldeans, as well as in the Orient, Rome, and Greece.

In general, the basis of alchemical studies began with a single tenet stating that our world, and everything in it, is made of three simple elements. Those elements, well known to students of sacred traditions, are Fire, Air, and Water. Lacking a scientific vocabulary to describe this knowledge, alchemical scholars did their best to preserve and convey the wisdom they possessed, which was already ancient in their time. If we could "translate" alchemy's simplest ideas about Fire, Air, and Water into their equivalents in modern chemistry, what secrets would the ancient formulas reveal today?

Creation As a Trilogy

In the language of the alchemical era, Fire, Air, and Water were known to represent the extremes of polarity and balance. Using trilogies of elements to describe creation: "Fire" is typically equated with the giving, or "male" aspect; "Water" with the receiving, or "female" aspect; and "Air" with the all-important neutral balance in-between, or the "child." Many traditions share a foundation of these three properties: the "positive," asserting, or projecting; the "Negative" attracting, or receiving; and the center of "neutral" (see Figure 4.1 below).

Creation As a Trilogy					
Natural Elements	Polarity/ Sex	Biblical Tradition	Modern Physics	Electrical Charge	Indigenous Tradition
Fire	Male	Father	Proton	Positive (+)	Eagle/Condor
Water	Female	Son	Electron	Negative (-)	Serpent
Air	Child	Holy Ghost	Neutron	Neutral (0)	Puma/Jaguar

Figure 4.1: Examples representing "positive," "negative," and "balance" from different worldviews.

These include the Christian tradition of the Father/Son/Holy Ghost, the indigenous cultures' animals representing Earth, Sky, and creatures between (the chart depicts native Andean traditions), as well as the foundation of 20th-century physics: the proton, electron, and neutron. While recent discoveries in the field of quantum physics are changing our view of the atom itself, the "clouds of probability" that are rapidly replacing the imagined particles of the past continue to carry the trilogy of attributes (positive, negative, and neutral) associated with protons, electrons, and neutrons.

In the early descriptions, although three elements are identified, those who understood the natural order of our world always implied the existence of a fourth, secret element. The missing element, "Earth," is explicitly mentioned in later alchemical traditions. The pre-Christian scribes of the Dead Sea Scrolls, the ancient Essenes, described all four forces of creation as "angels" and named them accordingly: the Angel of the Wind, the Angel of the Sun, the Angel of the Water, and the Angel of the Earth. Alchemists believed that understanding how the fourth element was derived was the key to understanding creation, life, and immortality.

Although the details of such worldviews are obviously ancient and the vocabulary outdated, the thread of similarity that links the most well-established stories of our origins cannot be denied. If we allow for the possibility that our ancestors were attempting to convey a powerful teaching to their descendants—including us, the people of their future—what could they have been saying? Were our scientific forebearers simply telling us that heat, liquid, air, and minerals make up our bodies and all that we see? Or could they have been sharing something much more precise? The evidence presented in the remainder of this, and the next two chapters, suggests that in the words of their day, ancient alchemists were describing the precise makeup—*the actual chemistry*—of the earth and of our cells.

Viewed through the eyes of today's scientific analysis, early formulas of Water, Fire, and Air have proven surprisingly accurate! If we assume that differences in language are all that stand between modern knowledge and an ancient wisdom, then the keys to our most empowering insights could exist in a form that we have yet to recognize.

The Mystical Science of Kabbalah

For clarity, we will use the term *traditional alchemy* to describe what is often considered the medieval form of the science. Although the mysteries of traditional alchemy are well documented and readily available, the underlying principles are less obvious. To preserve the secrets of the "oldest science" during a time when such knowledge often cost people their lives, the meaning of the symbols that form the core of traditional alchemy was shrouded in secrecy during the Middle Ages. Even today, the details of the "first science" remain hidden to all except those who are directly involved with the tradition, to prevent the misuse of its power.

Predating traditional alchemy by over 2,000 years, however, *an even earlier form of alchemy* offers what is perhaps the most complete record of creation's origins and our relationship to our Creator. This is the portion of the Kabbalah that describes the universe using the precise combinations of Hebrew Letters: the *Sepher Yetzirah*.

Throughout the *Sepher Yetzirah*, phrases appear that are laced with alchemical-like references. The verses describe the earliest interactions of Fire, Air, and Water—in a time before time began—represented as Hebrew letters. Depicting the union between Heaven and Earth, we are included as part of that creation. Here, within these ancient descriptions, we find a direct link to the principles of nature in traditional alchemy—and the first key to decoding the message within our cells.

The Tree of Life: Blueprint for the Universe

The narrative of the *Sepher Yetzirah* begins with a description of the ten worlds, or *Sefirot,* that define the relationship between the forces of creation. Surprisingly, the latest theories of creation also state that our universe is made of at least ten domains of energy—ten dimensions. These subtle worlds are actually required to explain the observations of quantum physics! The Sefirot are typically represented as spheres, and arranged to form the familiar pattern of the Tree of Life (see Figure 4.2). From this tree, the teachings of the Kabbalah offer meaning and relevance within the context of daily life.

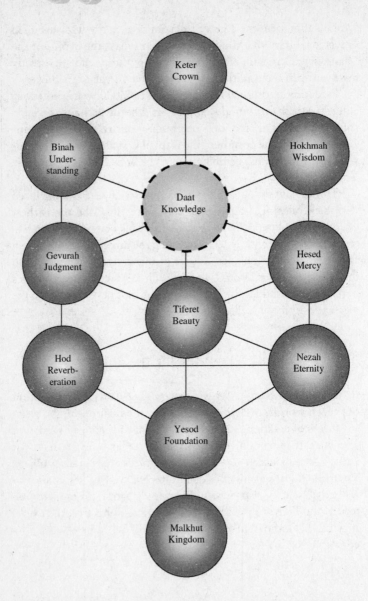

Figure 4.2: The ancient Hebrew Tree of Life showing the attributes of this world as the ten Sefirot (after Halevi).⁹

Each Sefirot represents a particular attribute with which God created the universe, and that we can aspire to in our lives. For example, the second and third Sefirot of *Binah* and *Hokhmah* are exemplified through the principles of Understanding and Wisdom, while the fourth and fifth Sefirot of *Gevurah* and *Hesed* represent the qualities of Judgment and Mercy.

The second chapter of the text makes the first clear connection between the mystical nature of the Tree of Life and something more concrete in our world. The clue is in the first three letters that God used to create the universe, known in the Hebrew alphabet as the *Basics,* the *Mothers,* or the *Mother Letters: Alef (A), Mem (M), and Shin (Sh).* Although each of the remaining 19 letters of the alphabet is imbued with its own power and significance, this book will focus upon these first three, and their very special place in creation.

In no uncertain terms, the text states that it is through these letters, and these alone, that the mystery of creation may be traced to its origins. The Three Mothers are immediately linked to the familiar alchemical elements of creation: Fire, Air, and Water. Within the same sentence that identifies the elements, a single sweeping statement clarifies their relationship to the universe and beyond:

The three Basics, A, M, *and* Sh, *are a great, concealed, mystical exalted secret, from which emanates Fire, Breath and Water, from which everything was created.*[10]

To understand the mystery of *A, M,* and *Sh,* and the implications of the previous statement, it is necessary to highlight the wisdom that's the essence of the Kabbalah itself. In the words of Halevi,[11] "the relationships set forth in the Tree underlie the whole of existence." So broad are the concepts offered through the Tree of Life that they have been applied to a seemingly endless number of topics, from the reasons for marriage, divorce, illness, and health, to the physics of creation. It is through the way the Beginning, *and the time before the Beginning,* are defined using the elements represented by the Hebrew letters that we find meaning in the mystery of the three Mother Letters.

Through a remarkably small number of phrases, the *Sepher Yetzirah* uses the Tree of Life as a metaphor for creation, stating that the first Sefirot represents the "Breath of the Living God." Kabbalists traditionally interpret this as a description of the moment of creation, the first breath or the first light, and also as the primal substance from which all else is formed. Following the Beginning, the reader is led upon an alchemical journey deriving the elements that form the universe. In the following description of the first four Sefirot, each statement details the element that it births.

1. *Ten Sefirot of Nothingness: One is the Breath of the Living God. Blessed and benedicted is the name of the Life of Worlds. The voice of breath and speech. And this is the Holy Breath.*[12]

2. *Two: Breath from Breath. With it He engraved and carved four directions (breaths) of Heaven: east, west, north and south. And there is a breath in each one of them.*[13]

3. *Three: Water from Breath. With it He engraved and carved chaos and void, clay and mire. . . . He poured water on them (the letters) and it became dust, as it is written.*[14]

4. *Four: Fire from Water. With it He engraved and carved the Throne of Glory and all the host on high. It is thus written, He makes His angels of breaths, and his ministers of flaming fire.*[15]

After these initial descriptions, the text continues with a degree of clarity that leaves little doubt as to the relationship between the Mother Letters and the elements:

"Three Mothers, A, M, and Sh, in the Universe are Air, Water, Fire."[16]

Once the attributes of Fire, Air, and Water are established, the text states that the building blocks are in place, and the act of using them for the miracle of our universe may continue. Through the remaining Sefirot, the Tree of Life defines the boundaries of God's universe and the rules of creation. It is here, as well, that we find the clue linking the three Mother Letters to the modern elements of our physical world, and the miracle of life.

Emergence of the Three Mothers

Following the preceding passages, we're led to understand that *A, M,* and *Sh* are more than simply symbols of nature's elements. Described through a form of "verbal alchemy," the verses show us how knowledge of the power in each letter is the key to understanding the forces of the universe.

> *"He made the letter Alef king over Breath*[17]*. . . .*
> *He made Mem king over water*[18]*. . . .*
> *He made Shin king over fire. . . ."*[19]

In terms that have withstood the tests of time and translations, these descriptions testify to the depth of the knowledge possessed by the authors of the text, as well as their remarkable ability to convey what they knew in a language that remains meaningful today. In the absence of scientific language, it appears as though the ancients were conveying wisdom inherited from an even earlier, as yet unidentified, source. Through the only words that they knew, they described nothing less than the building of the universe!

This description of the first acts of creation closely parallels those of traditional alchemy from the Middle Ages, as well as the creation of nature's angels described by the Essenes from a time 500 years before the birth of Jesus. Here the "Breath of God" becomes Air and the Angel of the Wind. In a similar manner, the "Water from Breath" becomes the element Water and the Angel of the Water, while "Fire from Water" becomes Fire and the Angel of the Sun. With these links in mind, the question becomes:

What ties these primal letters of creation to the chemistry of modern science?

From the "Why" to the "How"

Much of our present-day technology is based upon modifying processes that historically have been left to nature. From influencing weather patterns and creating new forms of matter, to the genetic engineering of crops and disease, in order for each of these seemingly miraculous technologies to be designed, it was first necessary to understand *why* natural processes work.

From the perspective of our ancestors, however, there was little need for such information. Ancient healers, alchemists, and miracle makers were less concerned with understanding *why* our world works as it does, and more concerned with *how* to apply the time-honored principles of nature in their lives. Because they weren't attempting to improve nature, there was little need to dissect it in order for their families, villages, and communities to benefit from it.

The power of prayer to enhance healing—a phenomenon that modern science and Western medicine have only begun to explore in earnest—offers a perfect example of this distinction. In a pilot study conducted at Kansas City's Mid America Heart Institute, 990 patients suffering from a range of life-threatening heart conditions were divided into two groups before undergoing their respective medical procedures and surgeries.[21] One group received treatments of prayer from five volunteers on a daily basis, while the second group did not.

To the amazement of the researchers conducting the tests, *the individuals in the group receiving the prayers experienced statistically measurable benefits* in their healing and recovery. The project's lead researcher stated, "The patients who were prayed for just did better."[22] The well-publicized results of this study made national headlines and have led to additional studies at Georgetown University Medical Center and Harvard University in an effort to

understand precisely why the group receiving the prayers fared so much better.

While the research is interesting, many of those who routinely incorporate prayer into their lives each day may feel that it is not necessary. They are already comfortable in their acceptance of prayer's power and in their ability to share that power with others. Because they already know that their prayers work, they do not ask why.

Science Confirms the Ancient Model: Rethinking Air, Water, and Fire

Until late-20th century discoveries gave us the power to engineer nature, the focus of science had largely been one of gathering information that explains our bodies and our world. With the development of computers and data storage, in a single generation we have amassed and stored unprecedented amounts of data. Dr. Michiu Kaku describes the tremendous momentum of our knowledge gathering abilities, stating, "Human knowledge is doubling every 10 years. In the past decade [1987 to 1997] more scientific knowledge has been created than in all of human history."[23] History may reveal that today's unprecedented knowledge of Earth began with the largest cooperative research effort of the last century, the International Geophysical Year (IGY).

During an 18-month period that lasted from July of 1957 to December of 1958, 67 nations participated in a joint project to document the composition and natural process of Earth in a way that had never occurred before or has since.[24] Ironically, it is precisely this modern data that now allows us to bridge the principles of ancient alchemy and the most sophisticated science of our time.

In ancient alchemical texts, the element of Air is never clearly defined. Later interpretations assume that it refers to the air we breathe. Modern science shows that, in fact, our atmosphere nourishes us with the invisible element that gives life to each cell of our bodies: *oxygen*. Correlating ancient alchemy with modern chemistry would therefore lead us to believe that oxygen is the equivalent of alchemical Air. The study of our atmosphere during the IGY, however, *revealed that this is not the case.* Although oxygen is without question the element in air that we most require for life, there is a relatively small amount of this precious substance present in the air that we breathe!

A full 78 percent of our atmosphere is composed of another element that *combines with oxygen* to stabilize the air. While the IGY study revealed that oxygen accounts for about 21 percent of our atmosphere (argon, carbon dioxide, and some trace elements make up the remainder of our air),[25] the bulk of each life-sustaining breath is nitrogen!

When the ancient alchemists identified Air as a primary element of creation, is it possible that they were saying to us, in the language of their day, that nitrogen was the substance they were referencing? For the purpose of this discussion, we will assume this is the case and see where the correlation leads us. A similar line of reasoning may be applied to modern elements for alchemical Fire, Water, and Earth.

The water that makes up more than two-thirds of the surface of our planet is described chemically through the familiar formula H_2O. In the simplest terms, this recipe tells us that there are two hydrogen atoms for each oxygen atom in the oceans, lakes, rivers, and streams of the earth, the rain in our skies, and the water in our bodies. Adopting the same perspective that views Air as a code word for nitrogen, perhaps Water is a code describing another physical element.

From a percentage basis, NASA studies indicate that water is dominated by the invisible element oxygen. The water that covers approximately two-thirds of our world is made of approximately 85.8 percent oxygen (around 88.89 percent for pure water) by percent composition, while the remaining percentage includes hydrogen and various trace minerals.[26] (Although the formula indicates that there are twice as many hydrogen atoms for each oxygen atom, the oxygen atoms are larger, thus accounting for the higher percentage of composition). For the purposes of our discussion, let's

consider the ancient references to water to be a code for the element *oxygen.*

Alchemical references to Fire are generally believed to represent the energy that is the original source of all fire: the sun. Ultimately, the fires that have consumed wood, coal, and other combustible products used throughout history are made possible only because of the sun's energy released from within them. In the last half of the 20th century, improvements in technology have enabled us to make a detailed analysis of the elements that compose the fiery body at the center of our solar system.

The heat that we feel on a warm summer day is largely due to the unimaginable temperatures burning at the sun's core (believed to be as high as 27 million degrees Fahrenheit!). Science views our nearest star as an immense celestial engine, burning a limited supply of gases until the supply runs out. Recent studies confirmed that two primary elements fuel the sun's fire. It is made of approximately 71 percent *hydrogen* and 27.1 percent helium.[27]

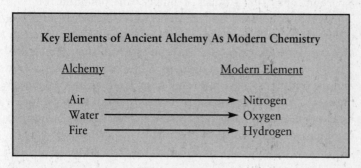

Key Elements of Ancient Alchemy As Modern Chemistry

Alchemy	Modern Element
Air ⟶	Nitrogen
Water ⟶	Oxygen
Fire ⟶	Hydrogen

Figure 4.3: Modern translations of the ancient elements of creation.

Following the logic applied to the elements of alchemy, we may also assume that the ancient references to Fire are, in fact, references to the element that produces the source of all fire: hydrogen. From these discoveries, it now becomes possible to translate the time-honored references of Fire, Air, and Water, into their chemical elements acknowledged by modern science (see Figure 4.3).

Through studies such as the IGY, we now know that relatively few elements compose most of the earth's outer crust, including the layers beneath the oceans. Silicon, oxygen, hydrogen, and aluminum account for more than 90 percent of the composition of this layer. Of even greater significance is the discovery that two of those four elements—hydrogen and oxygen—also account for more than 99 percent of our bodies as well!

From these studies alone, we may conclude that we are truly made "of the earth" (see "Different Words/Same Meaning" on pages 69 to 70). There are differences, of course, between the human body and the crust of the planet. In our bodies, the elements carbon and nitrogen replace the silicon and aluminum found in the earth. Of the remaining elements, while silicon remains an important part of our chemical makeup, it is only found in very small amounts and is therefore identified as a "trace" element. Interestingly, aluminum isn't found in our bodies at all as a naturally occurring element, although we sometimes absorb it from our environment as a by-product of industry and pollution.

Having established a direct link between ancient descriptions of our bodies with equivalents from modern chemistry, we may now cross-reference modern science with the Kabbalah. If these correlations are accurate, then the story preserved as alchemical lore and the traditions of the Kabbalah begins to take on even deeper meaning. A reinterpretation of the oldest and most complete description of our origins reveals new and astonishing answers to the unanswered questions of our past!

CHAPTER 4 SUMMARY

- A common theme in the ancient stories of human origins states that we are created from the "dust" or "clay" of the earth. All life comes from the same dust.

- The secrets of our creation and our ability to transmute life's circumstances (bridge Heaven and Earth)

are preserved through the hidden traditions of ancient alchemy. Within those traditions, the keys state that our world and our bodies are made of the elements: Fire, Water, and Air.

- A detailed account of the alchemy leading to the creation of the universe and the origins of humankind, is also revealed through the mystical Hebrew Book of Creation, the *Sepher Yetzirah*. The book is available today and, in its completeness, offers a detailed account of a higher power forming the universe and our world.

- *New discovery:* Modern science confirms the ancient models, revealing that the alchemical elements of Fire, Air, and Water actually represent three of the most abundant elements of our bodies: hydrogen, nitrogen, and oxygen, respectively.

"Let those who seek, continue seeking until they find. When they find, they will become troubled. When they become troubled they will be astonished . . ."

"Recognize what is in your sight, and that which is hidden from you will become plain to you."

— THE LOST GOSPEL OF THOMAS

Chapter Five

THE DISCOVERY:
When Letters Become Elements

During a time when the rate of human knowledge is doubling every ten years and machines can be reduced to the size of atoms, we still find ourselves relying upon the oldest records of our past to understand who we are—records preserved as the letters of ancient alphabets. At the same time, the origin of the world's alphabets, and subsequent languages, remains one of the great and unsolved mysteries of our time.[1]

In the 40,000-year history of modern man, the use of writing has played an increasingly important role in allowing us to preserve and convey information to others in the present, as well as the future. During this time, we have recorded the events of our lives through one or a combination of only four forms of writing. These forms are grouped into categories described as the following:

- Picture images
- Word signs
- Signs representing individual syllables
- Entire alphabets

Through symbols, each form allows for varying degrees of complexity to be represented and has served the needs of a given people at a specific time in history.

Letters and Alphabets: Symbols of a Deeper Reality

Although the use of complete alphabets is the most recently developed form of communication, this does not suggest that the *thoughts* underlying ancient picture writing are any less sophisticated than those behind today's words. Rather, it is only *the symbols themselves* that have become more sophisticated over time.

The simplest forms of picture images, *pictographs,* for example, generally portray broad and high-level concepts, without providing the kind of details that give greater meaning to the event being recorded. On the opposite end of the spectrum, complete alphabets allow for the specifics of an event to be recorded, conveyed, and preserved for future use.

The single image of a starburst recorded on the underside of a cliff in Chaco Canyon, New Mexico, for example, illustrates this concept. The symbol, which is believed to record the explosion of a supernova in 1,054 C.E., is painted into a sandstone overhang. The brilliant celestial display was seen in broad daylight throughout North America, and its remnants are still visible to astronomers today as the *Crab Nebula.* While the pictograph appears to have recorded the event itself, it offers no specifics, such as the time of day, degree of brightness, or the event's effects upon people, animals, and the living conditions of the time. It simply records that the explosion occurred. Chinese astronomers during the same time, however, documented the event through a more sophisticated language of alphabet, and thus were able to preserve specifics, such as the exact date that it occurred, for future generations.

Preserving a greater level of detail than ancient pictographs, are the languages of word signs (*logograms*) and syllabic signs (*syllabograms*). By using one symbol to represent an entire syllable or word, these forms of writing have the ability to preserve greater amounts of information for the events that they record.[2]

The most precise method of recording written information is through groups of symbols that represent specific sounds: *alphabets.* In an alphabet, the symbols are combined to produce words

that preserve information in a precise and meaningful way. The need to record our experiences is believed to be uniquely human. It is the catalyst that led our ancestors to create our many languages and the alphabets that represent them. Even at very best, however, the words formed by any alphabet are only a symbol of the event or experience that they record. *Implied in the letter symbols are many additional layers, each with deeper levels of meaning.*

Along with the uncertainty of their origins, a deeper mystery has emerged regarding the multiple meanings associated with early languages. Scholars openly acknowledge that from the ancient and obsolete languages of our past to the most modern languages of today, the symbols that we call letters actually serve a dual purpose. Outwardly, the letters form the words and sentences that store and communicate information, such as dates, times, and events. Underlying these outer meanings, less obvious layers of information reveal subtle relationships within the words themselves.

Through the power of its Hebrew letters, the Torah has the distinction of being an outwardly written document of history, as well as an inwardly coded guidebook to creation's secrets. To those who understand the code, the words are pathways into even deeper meanings of the same text. Torah scholars believe that within the very letters that record the acts of God and the patriarchs are the hidden keys to the miracles that the words describe. For example, just as a deeper link was revealed between "Adam" and "Earth," when the Torah states that "God created the Heaven and Earth," the deeper meaning of the words describe precisely *how* Heaven and Earth were formed.

By studying these hidden relationships, we can uncover the power of their author's original message. Any serious study of language must take into account the various levels, or layers, of meaning underlying the symbols of a given language.

When Letters Are More Than Letters:
The Hidden Code of the Hebrew Language

As the taxi rolled to a stop in front of the museum, lines of people were already bulging beyond the entrance, spilling down tiers of concrete steps into the drizzle of a spring storm. Earlier in the afternoon, I had completed an interview with a writer from one of the national news services that included a lengthy discussion of the Dead Sea Scrolls.

"The Scrolls are here in town!" she had exclaimed following the interview. "At the Chicago Field Museum."

"Really?!" I replied. "How far is the museum from where we are right now?"

"With traffic, maybe 15 minutes by taxi," she answered.

"Although I have seen the Coptic manuscripts in Egypt and studied the words of the scrolls extensively, I have never seen the actual Dead Sea Scrolls! I would love to see them," I said. "Maybe we should have a field trip."

That was all it took. In a matter of minutes, we were in a cab and off to the museum.

As we stepped from the taxi into the icy wind, I pointed to the lines of people. "Are they all here to see the scrolls?" I asked.

"Some are," she replied, "but many are probably here to see Sue." It just happened that the time we chose for our visit to the scrolls was also the opening of the exhibit for the most complete remains of a *Tyrannosaurus rex* discovered to date, nicknamed "Sue." Both were in the same museum, only a few hundred feet apart. Approaching the ticket booth, our suspicions were confirmed, with the bulk of the lines heading in Sue's direction. To the side of the main hall, smaller groups were forming that would be allowed access to the scrolls in timed intervals for crowd control. We were there just in time for the last group of the day!

Weaving our way through the specially designed exhibit, I could feel my anticipation building, as well as the excitement of those around me. As we entered the room, I heard gasps of awe from my fellow museum patrons. To minimize the harmful effects

of the heat from the lights, the bulbs illuminating each scroll fragment were on timers that brightened and dimmed every few moments. Each case housing one of the delicate fragments was set on a different timer, creating an eerie effect, as portions of the room alternated from light to dark. Immediately, I was drawn to a small grayish parchment in a freestanding case near the center of the room. As I stood in front of the fragment—part of the ancient *Book of Enoch*—I noticed a wave of warmth that flooded my body as I realized the full magnitude of what I was seeing.

There, on a tattered patch of animal hide, were the letters of a message created by the hand of another human more than two millennia ago! Nearly 200 years before Jesus walked the earth, an unknown scribe had taken the time to record words of wisdom that were already ancient when they were written. The flecks of black ink forming each of the perfectly proportioned letters still clung to the parchment's surface, precisely the way that hand had applied them so long ago.

For a split second, the centuries separating us dissolved. Through the mystery of the letters, now only inches from my face, the forgotten scribe had defied the limits of time. In that brief moment, I understood language in a way that I had not before, and have not since. Beyond a logical knowing, I could actually *feel* the symbols bridging the past and the present, through the power of the Hebrew letters.

For over three millennia, the letters of the Hebrew alphabet have held a unique place in the study of sacred languages. While other ancient forms of writing such as Egyptian hieroglyphics and Sumerian cuneiform are thousands of years older, they are no longer used today. It is entirely possible that in our modern interpretations of such languages, although we generally understand them, we may have missed subtleties that can be known only in their use. This is not the case with the Hebrew alphabet—it has been used continuously for 3,000 years, and perhaps longer.

While changes in the meaning and use of some letters have occurred during that time, we know with certainty that the alphabet has remained the same for at least the last 1,000 years. One of the oldest versions of the complete Old Testament written in Hebrew, the *Leningrad Codex,* was written in 1,008 C.E. When this manuscript is compared to modern versions of the same Bible, the texts match identically—letter for letter! Due to the length of time that the language has been in use and the stability of its alphabet, when we translate the words of an ancient Hebrew document, we may feel confident that we know precisely what the author intended to convey when the words were recorded thousands of years ago.

Even those who do not read Hebrew say that they feel a sense of holiness, awe, and mystery in the presence of its letters. Although many languages have hidden number values associated with each letter of their alphabet, perhaps none of these number systems has been documented as extensively and applied as frequently as ancient Hebrew.

Attributing tremendous power to the forces of the Hebrew alphabet, the *Sepher Yetzirah* states that it is from the letters themselves that God "depicted all that was formed and all that would be formed."[3] Historically, scholars have viewed this state-ment as a metaphor symbolizing the power of God as the source of creation. As we explored in the previous chapter, the correla-tions between the chemical elements and the most ancient, con-tinuously used language known in existence offer a powerful new perspective on this statement, and perhaps on the origins of life itself. In its completeness, the encoded text describes precisely how and by whom (what force) our species came into existence.

The Science of Letters As Numbers

While the original reason for the hidden meaning of a partic-ular letter is a mystery unto itself, from the oldest markings of Sumerian cuneiform to today's languages, *each letter of every alphabet has always been linked with a very specific number value.* The study of these relationships is known historically as *gematria.* Through the one-to-one correspondence between letters and numbers, gematria reveals the hidden relationships and deeper

layers of meaning that would normally be overlooked by simply reading the words themselves. Beyond the scope of this book, it is worthy to note that even the relatively recent English language alphabet, the fusion of ancient Greek and Latin influences, has a deeper level of meaning through the codes associated with its parent alphabets.[4]

Of the many ways that we may define "science" today, *The American Heritage Dictionary* suggests that "any methodological activity, discipline or study"[5] is a science. Through this widely accepted definition, the study of gematria can be considered an ancient science, as it yields precise and repeatable outcomes from specific operations between letters, phrases, and words.[6] As ancient Hebrew texts are the source of key concepts in this book, we will explore the science of gematria from the perspective of Hebrew words. We may ultimately discover that these relationships solve the mystery of the subtle and unseen forces that challenge science today, such as morphogenic fields and quantum effects.[7]

A Brief Introduction to the Hebrew Alphabet

The Hebrew language is one of consonants. It is written differently than it's spoken, with vowels typically left out of the text altogether. Historically, the vowels that make the words pronounceable were only implied through the way the words were used, making the translation of passages written in biblical Hebrew an art, as well as a science. Due to this curiosity, it is useful to know the context of what has been written *before it is translated* in order to assign each word the proper meaning.

In later times, the vowels of the Hebrew language were introduced to its written form through the use of dots and symbols placed beneath certain letters in a word. These symbols, known as *vowel points,* are used today to ensure the correct pronunciation, and thus the meaning, of each letter and word. The *primary* Hebrew alphabet consists of 22 letters, each letter being assigned a unique sound and number. In this way, the language is given the power of both an obvious outer, and a hidden inner, meaning.

The first letter of the alphabet, *Alef* (א), is associated with the number 1; the second letter, *Bet* (ב), with the number 2; and so on, until the letter *Yod* (י) and the number 10 are reached. The sequence then continues as multiples of 10, with the next letter, *Kaf* (כ) having the value of 20; *Lamed* (ל) the value of 30, and so on until *Kuf* (ק) and the number 100 are reached. From this point on, the primary Hebrew alphabet continues as multiples of 100, ending with the letter *Tav* (ת), which has the value of 400.

In the older traditions of the Kabbalah, the alphabet is extended even further, however, by additional increments of 100 until the sequence reaches 1,000, which is indicated by a larger version of the alphabet's first letter, *Alef* (distinguished as the "Big Alef"). This extended letter set is especially important when exploring the deeper meaning of Hebrew texts. Figure 5.1 illustrates the letters of the primary Hebrew alphabet and the hidden number value historically associated with each one.

Numeric Values of the Hebrew Alphabet[7]							
Symbol	Name	Sound	Value	Symbol	Name	Sound	Value
א	Alef	Silent	1	ל	Lamed	L	30
ב	Bet/Vet	B/V	2	מ	Mem	M	40
ג	Gimel	G	3	נ	Num	N	50
ד	Dalet	D	4	ס	Samekh	S	60
ה	Hey	H	5	ע	Ayin	Guttural	70
ו	Vav	V	6	פ	Peh	P/F	80
ז	Zayin	Z	7	צ	Tzadi	Tz	90
ח	Chet	Ch	8	ק	Kuf	K	100
ט	Tet	T	9	ר	Resh	R	200
י	Yod	Y	10	ש	Shin	Sh/S	300
כ	Kaf	K/Kh	20	ת	Tav	T	400

Figure 5.1: Primary letters of the Hebrew letter set, showing the "hidden" number value associated with each letter.

The Hidden Meaning of Soul and Heaven

The depth of hidden word meanings is best illustrated through an example, such as the Hebrew words for *soul* and *Heaven,* and their relationship to life and death.

Almost universally, our most cherished beliefs suggest that the soul within each of us continues to live after death, when it returns to the realms of its origin, the place that we know as Heaven. Traditionally, this relationship is only implied through religious and spiritual writings. Revealing the direct link that exists between the words as numbers, however, shows this relationship specifically and graphically. The following analysis from the work of one of the great Hebrew scholars of our time, Rabbi Benjamin Blech, offers unprecedented insight and, perhaps, much-needed comfort regarding the mystery between Heaven, Earth, and the human soul.[8]

The Hebrew word for *soul* is "NeShaMaH," which is written without the vowels as *N, Sh, M,* and *H.* Assigning the number codes described in the last section, the values of *N, Sh, M,* and *H* are as follows:

N	Sh	M	H
50	300	40	5

The addition of these individual values produces a new, combined value of 395.

$$50 \quad + \quad 300 \quad + \quad 40 \quad + \quad 5 \quad = \quad 395$$

In numeric terms, 395 *is* "soul," and this number allows us to explore a relationship that is not obvious in the alphabetic form of the words. To understand precisely how the realm of Heaven is related to the 395 of soul, we apply the identical process of assigning number values to the letters in the word *Heaven.*

In Hebrew, *Heaven* is spelled as Ha-ShaMaYiM. As consonants only, the word is written as follows:

H	*Sh*	*M*	*Y*	*M*
5	300	40	10	40

Representing each letter as its numeric value, we discover a direct and perhaps surprising relationship between the two words:

$$5 + 300 + 40 + 10 + 40 = 395$$

Adding the number values for *Heaven* yields the number 395—*precisely the same value* as the word *soul!*

One of the rules for the science of gematria is that two words related in number are related in nature as well. Regardless of the meaning that has been assigned by culture or society, the relationship of number speaks directly to the true meaning underlying the letters. Such a relationship is clearly demonstrated by the words *soul* and *Heaven*. Beyond an obvious casual similarity, their numerical values are identical! Therefore, gematria informs us, Heaven and soul are the same.

As implied in many traditional religious descriptions of our origins, "God created the Heaven and Earth" as two distinct, yet related, realms of experience. The texts go on to describe humankind as a bridge between the two realms, a marriage between Heaven (spirit or soul) and Earth.

> *"He [humankind] unites both heavenly and*
> *earthly qualities within himself . . . I [God] will*
> *create man to be the union of the two . . ."[9]*

Throughout our lives, the qualities of the two realms are merged into a single existence. At the end of our lives, the Heaven and Earth that have merged as our bodies return to their respective abodes. Our bodies return to the dust of the earth, while our souls and Heaven are already one. This perspective of life and death offers a tangible sense of why the experience of death does not mean an end to our existence. The hidden number code assures us that it is so.

Number: The Language of Creation

In his historic work *Republic,* the Greek philosopher Plato stated that the reality of our world can truly be known only through our experience—any attempt to describe life through language is an abstraction at best. When we do describe our world through language, however, Plato suggested that numbers are the way to do so: "They [the geometers] make use of the visible forms and talk about them. . . . What they really seek is to get sight of those realities which can be seen only in the mind."[10] Pythagoras, whose earlier work strongly influenced Plato, also described this all-important relationship between numbers and the world simply and concisely: "All is arranged according to number."[11]

The significance of numbers in the Hebrew alphabet is undeniable. With every letter of the language assigned a unique value, the entire Torah may be viewed as a vast array of numbers. Scientists and historians alike now believe that when the Torah was first revealed to humankind, it was given in the traditional form of the language, as a single, continuous string of 304,805 characters, with no punctuation or vowels.[12] The 18th-century scholar known as the *Genius of Vilna* stated, "All that was, is, and will be unto the end of time is included in the Torah, from the first word to the last word."

Within this number code, it is said that we were given the message of our past, as well as the keys to our future. If this original description of the Torah is correct, then our deepest mysteries of healing, peace, and origins were revealed to us as one very long string of numbers! While it may not be clear as to precisely *how* such information is coded into the relatively brief books of the Torah, it is clear that the scholars find a meaning in its pages that goes far beyond the obvious message of the written word.

Acknowledging this direct link between the letters of the Torah and our world, the already arduous task of transcribing the text implied tremendous responsibility as well. It's said that with a mistake in one word, a scribe could irrevocably alter the course of human history forever. Due to the burden of maintaining such accuracy, the error of even a single letter while transcribing the texts was considered intolerable. Such a flaw could warrant the destruction of an entire scroll section, one that may have taken months to create. Thus, only accurate copies of "The Book" (the Torah) were left for future generations.

It is through the reliability of the Hebrew texts, and the secrets encoded in their letters, that we are now given unprecedented insight into our relationship with our world and one another.

The Power of Comparing "Apples to Apples"

Through the science of language and number, we've seen a powerful link between the letters of Hebrew words and the ideas that the words convey. Is it possible that in a similar fashion, there exists a hidden relationship between the origins of life described in the Hebrew texts and the contemporary language of science today? Could the chasm that is believed to exist between religious and scientific explanations of life and the Beginning simply be a matter of different languages from different eras describing precisely the same events?

The key to bridging science and spirituality, or any seemingly dissimilar ways of knowing our world, is that all viewpoints must be converted into the same language before they can be reasonably compared with one another. For example, if we are asked, "Which is greater, one mile or 7,920 feet?" both measurements must be converted to the same units to make a meaningful comparison. In doing so, we create a *common denominator* that allows us to compare "apples to apples" rather than "apples to oranges." Converting the mile measurement into 5,280 feet makes it easy to compare and answer the question. Clearly, 7,920 feet is the longer of the two distances.

Similarly, to find a common denominator between the languages of spirituality and science would infuse new meaning into some of our oldest and most deeply revered traditions. To do so would also offer a much sought-after bridge between what many view as the incompatible worlds of science and spirituality. The key to discovering such a bridge is to find a common link that joins the two worlds. *The hidden number code underlying the Hebrew language offers precisely such a link.*

The Discovery: From Alphabet to Elements

By the close of the 20th century, the composition of everything that we could ever imagine in the physical world had been reduced to approximately 118 elements. Ranging from the invisible gases that form our atmosphere to the dense minerals that form the earth, many of the elements have familiar names, and they have played significant roles in the history of our world. The rush to find gold in California, New Mexico, and Colorado, for instance, contributed to the development of the American West during the early 1800s. Others, such as element 105, *dubnium* (originally *Nielsbohrium*—renamed in 1997), are so rare that they only appear under laboratory conditions and exist for mere seconds before they disintegrate into more stable materials.

Each of the 118 elements is classified according to traits that set it apart from all others—properties that are described by number—and arranged in the form of a chart. This chart is known as the *Periodic Table of the Elements,* or simply the *Periodic Table* (see Appendix B), and it continues to grow as additional elements are discovered. By sorting and organizing these traits, scientists determine where each element "fits" within the chart. *It is these qualities of number that link the elements of our DNA to the letters of the Hebrew alphabet.* This key allows us to read the ancient message coded as the DNA of our cells.

Of the many possible characteristics that describe each element, my 12-year study reveals only one that stands out as a bridge between the four elements of life and the Hebrew alphabet: the quality known as *atomic mass.*[13] Though technical sounding in name, the idea of "mass" is a deceptively simple concept telling us how easily matter allows itself to be moved.[14] For the purposes of this book, let us refer to the term *atomic mass* simply as mass, *and consider it the common denominator that allows us to bridge the Hebrew letters with the chemical elements of creation.*[15]

Something exciting and wonderful begins to unfold as we view the oldest accounts of creation through the lens of such modern terms. Suddenly, the esoteric references to the Beginning take on a powerful new meaning. Earlier, in Chapter 4, we discovered that ancient references to the alchemical elements of creation—Fire, Air, and Water—were actually descriptions of the chemical elements that make Fire, Air, and Water possible: hydrogen, nitrogen, and oxygen. To reveal the secret held by these three elements in ancient literature, we must now determine which letters of the Hebrew alphabet they represent. This is where the common denominator of mass comes into play. By applying the same processes that showed us the hidden meaning between "soul" and "Heaven," we reveal the link between hydrogen, nitrogen, and oxygen and the alphabet.

Following the principles of gematria that allow us to simplify numbers to one digit, we find that the mass of hydrogen, 1.007, needs no simplification, as it is already represented by the number 1. The same process reveals that the *simple mass* for nitrogen, 14.00, and oxygen, 15.99, can be found by adding the whole numbers to the left of the decimal point to their mass numbers taken from the Periodic Table.

Specifically, for nitrogen, the value "14" becomes the *simple mass* of "5" (1 + 4 = 5). For oxygen, the value is calculated to be "6" (1 + 5 = 6). Figure 5.2 summarizes these values. This formula presents us with a new way to think of Fire, Air, and Water. It establishes the common denominators that enable us to search for a match with the hidden number values of the Hebrew letters.

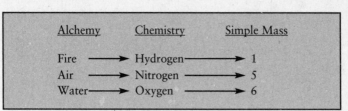

Alchemy	Chemistry	Simple Mass
Fire ⟶	Hydrogen ⟶	1
Air ⟶	Nitrogen ⟶	5
Water ⟶	Oxygen ⟶	6

Figure 5.2: The value of "mass" gives us another way to think of the ancient elements "Fire," "Air," and "Water." It is this value that becomes the common denominator linking the ancient concepts to modern elements.

The Secret of the Three Mothers

As we discussed in Chapter 4, the *Sepher Yetzirah* states that, following the formation of the 22 letters of creation from which all else would be formed, three letters were selected and given a place of honor and respect unlike any other letters of the alphabet. In addition to being the "stuff" that our world is made of, these letters were also to become the foundation for the name of God: the one name by which God would be known on Earth.

> *"He chose three letters from among the Elementals
> [in the mystery of the three mothersAlef Mem Shin]
> And He set them in His great Name . . ."*[16]

By combining the three Mother Letters, God "sealed" and defined the space of his creation. As the letters themselves have already been revealed in the outward text, the answer to our question of hidden meaning now becomes one of correspondences. We may state this question in the familiar form of a proof of logic:

If

the three Mother letters *A, M, Sh* were created first,

and

if these letters are truly the "Mother" of creation,

and

if *Y, H,* and *V* are the letters of God's name (*YHVH*)
and the source of all creation,

then

through a process that is not outwardly apparent,
A, M, Sh must become *Y, H, V!*

The relationship that allows the evolution of *A M Sh* to *Y H V* is held so sacred in the ancient traditions that an entire section of the *Sepher Yetzirah* is devoted to describing the secret of their link.

> *"Three Mothers: Alef Mem Shin, A great,*
> *mystical secret covered and sealed with six rings.*
> *And from them emanated air, water and fire.*
> *And from them are born Fathers,*
> *and from the Fathers, descendents."*[17]

The answer to our mystery may be stated in a single sentence: *Scholars of the Kabbalah state that the three letters of God's name (YHV) are actually derived from, and correspond to, the three Mother Letters (AMSh).*[18] The meaning underlying this answer, however, could fill volumes.

In the Kabbalah, a distinction is made between the creation of our Universe of Order and the universe *before* ours, the Universe of Chaos. While modern physicists struggle with the dilemma of

whether or not anything existed before the time of the Big Bang, for the student of the Kabbalah, the existence of a universe before time is a given, and even required to understand the teachings.

The Kabbalah describes this "time before time and order" as the Universe of Chaos, or *Tohu*. It is in Chaos that the letters of *Alef, Mem,* and *Shin* were born and first described. In this world without order, the elements, or *vessels*, that existed before the ten Sefirot were unable to interact, making it impossible for them to experience the very essence of life—they could not give or receive. Because of this condition, they were incapable of holding the light given by God, and their experience was incomplete.

Due to their condition, they shattered, which is an act known as the *Breaking of the Vessels*. As portions of the shattered vessels fell into lower spiritual realms, they were rebuilt as new containers that *could* give and receive. These containers became the ten Sefirot that form the Tree of Life for our world, the *Universe of Rectification,* or Order.

In the Universe of Order, the Hebrew letters of Chaos were given new meaning, and our mystery begins to make sense. The "great mystical secret" of the *Sepher Yetzirah* is that the letters of God's name in our world *(YHV)* and the Mother Letters from the Universe of Chaos *(AMSh)* are equal. They represent the same force manifested in different realms. In other words, *Yod, Hey,* and *Vav* come from their counterparts of *Alef, Mem,* and *Shin,* respectively. Bearing these relationships in mind, we now have the information necessary to answer the question of how the three Mother Letters of the Hebrew creation stories equate to the elements of modern science.

Mother Letters in the World of Chaos		Mother Letters in the World of Order
A	=	Y
M	=	H
Sh	=	V

Reviewing what we know:

1. Fire, Air, and Water are the ancient equivalent of hydrogen, nitrogen, and oxygen.

2. The bridge between letters and elements is one of number.

3. Hydrogen, nitrogen, and oxygen respectively have number values of 1, 5, and 6.

An examination of the hidden number code for the Hebrew letters reveals that not only does a direct relationship between the letters and the elements exist, the relationship is so precise that it cannot be mistaken!

Alchemical Element	Fire	Air	Water
Elements of Our Body's DNA	Hydrogen ↓	Nitrogen ↓	Oxygen ↓
As Reduced Atomic Mass	1	5	6
As Hebrew Letter Code	1	5	6
Same Elements	↑	↑	↑
As Hebrew Letters	Y	H	V

Figure 5.3: The ancient elements of alchemy, and their equivalents as Hebrew letters, show that there is a direct link between three of the four elements of life (hydrogen, nitrogen, and oxygen) and the three letters Y, H, and V that form God's ancient name (the H is used twice to become YHVH).

In the Hebrew alphabet, there are exactly three letters, and only three, whose hidden number codes precisely match the simple mass for the ancient elements of creation. The hidden value of the Hebrew letters Y, H, and V are found to resolve to the numbers 1, 5, and 6, respectively (see Figure 5.3 above).[19]

Through these simple apple-to-apple relationships in nature, we may now replace the elements of human DNA with their counterparts from the Hebrew alphabet. By simply matching the numbers in the boxed rows, it is possible to directly link the ancient letters of the Hebrew alphabet with the elements of modern science. This concrete and verifiable relationship speaks volumes to us about the knowledge of our ancestors.

From records such as the *Sepher Yetzirah,* we now understand that prebiblical scholars recorded knowledge regarding creation's secrets from an even earlier time of antiquity. In the language of their day, they preserved their wisdom regarding this knowledge just as we do through our books today, for generations they knew would follow their own.

Beyond theory and metaphor, those secrets are now recognized as the details—*the actual combinations of elements recognized and verified by today's science*—that are responsible for the process of creation and life itself! In addition to giving credibility to such accounts, our correlations provide a language that allows us to translate the oldest descriptions of creation with a degree of accuracy never before possible.

The final part of our mystery is to answer the question of where the fourth element of life—carbon—comes from. If, as the texts suggest, all was created from the *A, M,* and *Sh* that became *Y, H,* and *V,* then, through a yet-to-be revealed process, the fourth element of life must also come from these three Mother Letters as well.

Solving the Mystery of the Fourth Element

Throughout the history of alchemy, in addition to the three stated building blocks of Fire, Air, and Water, the fourth, or "hidden," element was always implied. This was the familiar substance of "Earth." In later traditions, while the Earth portion of the code was revealed directly, precisely *where it came from* remained hidden to all but those initiated in the mystery of creation's secrets. For students of the *Sepher Yetzirah,* the key to this mystery is revealed indirectly through the text itself:

> *"From these three (Breath, Fire and Water)*
> *He founded His dwelling."* [20]

With a simplicity that is eloquent as well as profound, we are told that the Creator's home was formed through the use of only these three substances. This leaves little doubt that, either alone or combined, the elements of Fire; Breath (Air); and Water (hydrogen, nitrogen, and oxygen) are responsible for all the creation that becomes the dwelling of the Creator, the world, and our bodies.

The clue to solving the mystery of the fourth element was that it had to come from elements that were already in existence. To create the new element, the three existing elements had to interact in some way. It is this union, often described as the "marriage" of Fire, Air, and Water, that becomes the key to understanding our relationship to the world and, ultimately, to the act of creation itself.

Since the text informs us that only these three elements were available to God at this point in creation, we are left with very clear analytical choices: We must either add, multiply, divide, or subtract the numeric values of those elements from one another to create the fourth element of Earth. When such choices present themselves, an approach to choosing which option is most likely to give us the clearest answers, known as Occam's razor,[21] often narrows the possibilities better than a trial-and-error approach. Briefly, Occam's razor states that in an ideal world, the simplest solution tends to be the best. Such is the case with the possibilities that may lead to identifying the fourth element, as simple addition reveals the value that solves our mystery.

From the three letters that God used to "create His Universe," *Yod, Hey,* and *Vav,* we are left with their number values of 1, 5, and 6. Combining these values through the simplest of the mathematical processes—addition—produces a new number with very different properties from the original three: the number "12."

<u>Yod</u>	<u>Hey</u>	<u>Vav</u>		
1	+ 5	+ 6	=	12

Now "12" represents the value for the fourth element of "Earth." Next, following the now-familiar process of reducing two-digit numbers to a single digit, we add the 1 + 2 of 12 to produce a new value 3. Finally, we use this value to search the Periodic Table for our mystery element.

A brief look at the chemistry of the human body will quickly narrow our search to just a few possibilities. From the 118 elements known to exist, only 4 of those elements account for over 99 percent of the human body: hydrogen, nitrogen, oxygen, and carbon.[22] Carbon is the only element in this group that has not been accounted for. So we can streamline our search by examining the properties of carbon for a "fit" as a bridge between alchemy and chemistry.

The mass value for carbon is 12.00. Applying the standard process of simplifying this value as 1 + 2, the new value (simple mass) for carbon is 3. Perhaps not coincidentally, the 3 of carbon is the only value from the 118 possible elements that precisely matches the 3 produced by combining the letters of God's name: Y, H, and V (1, 5, and 6).

From the perspective of the *Sepher Yetzirah,* this makes even greater sense. As we are told that God had only Fire, Air, and Water to work with, now recognized as colorless and odorless gases, the substance of carbon is the only element of life that makes us solid. In the absence of this fourth physical element, our bodies would not exist!

When the ancients recorded that we are made of Fire, Water, Air, and Earth, in the language of their day they were saying that we are made of hydrogen, nitrogen, oxygen, and carbon—precisely the findings of 20th-century science. In a time before the development of sophisticated test equipment, high-powered microscopes, materials analysis, and the mathematics of chemical equations, our ancestors revealed the composition of our bodies, describing the building blocks of every human cell.

With the revelation of such precise information, we must now ask: What else has been left by those who have come before us that we may have failed to recognize? It is in response to this question

THE GOD CODE

that the last portion of our table becomes significant. What is the equivalent of carbon in the language of Hebrew letters?

Following the procedures that we applied in the last section of this chapter produces an unexpected, yet telling, result. Only one letter of the Hebrew alphabet has the same numeric value as carbon's simple mass: the fourth letter, *Gimel* (ג), represented as the capital letter *G*. *From the perspective of number, Gimel is "carbon" in the Hebrew scriptures, and in ancient alchemy it is "Earth"* (see Figure 5.4 below).

Ancient Element ➝	Fire	Air	Water	Earth
Modern Elements ➝ of DNA	Hydrogen	Nitrogen	Oxygen	Carbon
Same Elements As Hebrew Letters ➝	Y	H	V	G

Figure 5.4: By converting the ancient elements, modern elements, and the Hebrew alphabet to their common denominator of number, the alchemical elements of creation become the modern elements of DNA, and they translate to the Hebrew letters *YHVG* in each cell of our bodies.

This final step in understanding the deeper meaning of ancient Hebrew letters now allows us to create a primer of sorts, a key to solving the mystery of God's name in our bodies. At the same time, however, the link between modern elements and the alphabet poses new questions about the secrets left to us as ancient stories of creation. Why are these correlations so important? What does the discovery of an ancient message tell us in our modern world? We may begin to answer these questions by examining how great the odds are against this message occurring simply by chance.

As mentioned in Chapter 5, there are a total of 22 letters in the standard Hebrew alphabet. These letters represent the field of possibilities from which we may string letters together to create

meaningful words in the language. Just as a sentence depends upon the order of its words, the message in our cells depends upon the order of its letters. This particular portion of the message in our cells, *YHVG*, consists of 4 of the 22 possible letters. From this information, we may calculate the odds of randomly forming a meaningful four-letter sequence from the Hebrew alphabet as 22^4, or only 1 in 234,256!

Stated another way, there is the slim probability of .00042 percent ($1/22^4$ x 100) that the letters *YHVG* would arrange themselves purely by chance. That probability decreases further to a .00016 percent when we take into account the extended Hebrew alphabet of 28 letters! While these aren't necessarily astronomical odds, when combined with the translation of the message they strongly suggest that something more than "chance" or "coincidence" is responsible for the code. These already-slim odds are further amplified when we consider that it is these four letters, *and only these four letters,* that equate to the only four elements in the Periodic Table that create human DNA!

While we now have all of the information necessary to read the chemical code within each cell of our bodies as a text message, a mystery remains. Precisely what does the message mean? To solve this mystery, we must delve into the controversy of God's ancient name, and the way it is revealed in the cells of life.

CHAPTER 5 SUMMARY

- Nearly all forms of written communication fall into one, or a combination, of only four forms of symbols: picture images, word signs, signs representing individual syllables, and collections of symbols as entire alphabets.

- In their original form, the letters of many ancient alphabets were also associated with precise number values. These "hidden" codes represent even deeper

meaning underlying the outer message conveyed by the words themselves.

- Some of the oldest and most complete accounts of human origins are recorded in the ancient language of Hebrew, a language that has changed very little for at least the last 2,000 years.

- The key that links ancient accounts of creation with modern science is a common denominator of numbers that allows us to make an "apples-to-apples" comparison.

- *New discovery:* Of the 17 characteristics that define today's *Periodic Table of Elements,* only one matches precisely with the hidden number values of the Hebrew language—the *atomic mass,* or simply *mass.*

- In solving the mystery of the fourth element from alchemy and the Kabbalah, "Earth" is found to be the fourth element of life as well: carbon.

- *New discovery:* Through determining their *simple mass,* the elements of DNA (hydrogen, nitrogen, oxygen, and carbon) within our bodies may now be replaced with four letters of the Hebrew alphabet: *Yod, Hey, Vav,* and *Gimel,* thus revealing that our DNA may be read literally as a translatable alphabet within each of our cells. The odds of these four letters randomly creating a meaningful message from the Hebrew alphabet are only 1 in 234,256, or the slim probability of .00042 percent.

"He chose three letters. . .
He set them in His great name. . .
a great, concealed, mystical exalted secret
from which emanates Fire, Breath and Water,
from which everything was created."

"All that is formed, and all that is spoken, is one name."

— SEPHER YETZIRAH

Chapter Six

THE CODE WITHIN THE CODE:
In Each Cell of Every Life, the Name of God

In the presence of those who accept the idea of a single Creator, we celebrate our most beautiful dreams and mourn our greatest tragedies, while asking how the same power could possibly be the source of both. As we strive to understand and, at times even please, a God that we identify through time-worn fragments of our most cherished traditions, we're presented with many and varied descriptions of the nature of the Creator. If there is a single God, why are there so many ideas of what that God is like? How can we justify devoting our lives, praying to, giving up our lives, and even killing in the name of a presence so mysterious that we ask for signs just to validate Its very existence?

Ultimately, such questions may be asking us to answer something even more fundamental: Are we simply the product of elements and molecules that combined by "chance" to produce the miracle life, or are we the result of an intentional act of creation?

A God That Defies Description

As a child, I was fascinated by the concept of God. The very idea that there was something so large, so wise, and so present that it could not be explained compelled me to understand what such a presence meant in my life. I remember lying with my stomach pressed against the cool tiles of the living-room floor during the sweltering Missouri summers, studying the children's version of *The Golden Treasury of Bible Stories*[1]—my first window into the biblical mysteries of creation. The book stood out from its place on the shelf as an intimidating source of authority, so thick that it would stand on its own with no support from the other books that surrounded it.

I always started at the very beginning, opening the heavy black cover and carefully scrutinizing each illustration and every word for clues before turning to the next page. I clearly recall the feeling that, surely, such an impressive book must hold the answers to all of my questions regarding God and creation. My job was simply to find them. Somehow, I felt that if I opened the book enough times and read each word the right way, my answers would be revealed and the mysteries solved.

At the beginning of each chapter, a single drawing illustrated the theme of the story that was to follow. The first illustration for the story of Genesis has remained in my memory to this day: the artist's portrayal of God performing the act of creation. Lying horizontally on an invisible plane, the black-and-white lines depicted a very old man with an outstretched hand turning the cosmos and giving life to creation. Locks of wavy white hair cascaded across his shoulders and mingled with his equally wavy beard, as they disappeared into the emptiness of the universe. In this and many other images depicting the mysteries of biblical times, God is often portrayed in very human terms. He is shown as a man performing the miracle of creation in a way that made sense at the time it was written.

While such an image may represent one aspect of God's work, few people suspect that there is actually a physical man lying on his stomach somewhere in space "above" our homes, orchestrating the cosmos. We know that the illustration is a metaphor to describe our sense of the all-knowing, all-seeing, and ever-present source of creation.

In the Judeo-Christian tradition, scientists and scholars have traditionally interpreted such references to God as an attempt to name the un-nameable: a symbol for the source of creation. Even the earliest roots of Western traditions state that it is impossible to know or to represent God directly. The reason is because God exists everywhere in everything and, by His very nature, cannot be known or described.

The Many Names of God

The oldest myths of our past attribute the power to create, sustain, and destroy life itself to the Supreme God of the cosmos, the *Creator*. By the very nature of His/Her omnipresence, *the One* or *the Eternal* is beyond gender, beyond direct name, and is known to the people of Earth only through the miracles that manifest as nature and life.

In the sacred *Bhagavad-Gita* of Hindu cosmology, for example, the power of creation is expressed as three facets of precisely the same force: *Brahma*, the creator; *Vishnu*, the protector; and *Shiva*, the destroyer. Each aspect works in harmony with the others to perpetuate the cycle of life and death and assure the continuation of the cosmos. This theme of a single Creator, whose name is linked with the events manifested in a moment of time, is shared by many native, indigenous, and Eastern traditions. It plays a key role in ancient Hebrew and subsequent Christian traditions as well.

Perhaps the most direct explanation of our inability to know God in His entirety may be found in the words of present-day teacher of the Kabbalah, Z'ev ben Shimon Halevi. In the eloquence of a true teacher, he summarizes God's mystery in three simple words: "God is God."[2] Through his scholarly interpretation of ancient Hebrew texts, Halevi follows this explanation with examples from the Kabbalah that illustrate the unknowable nature of God.

Referring to the ten Sefirot of the mystical Tree of Life, Halevi describes how entire realms of creation may be represented by one of God's many mystical names. The first realm, for example, the Sefirot of *Keter*, or the Crown, is associated with the name EHYEH ASHER EHYEH (I AM THAT I AM), or the beginning and the

end of creation. This is the very precise name that Moses received when he asked God the question: "Who shall I say has sent me?" when asked to deliver a message to the Israelites.[3] Subsequently, each Sefirot of the Tree of Life is associated with a specific name indicating an attribute of God's nature (see Figure 6.1).

Name of Sefirot	Attribute	Ancient Name of God
Keter	Crown	EHYEH
Keter	Wisdom	YHVH
Binah	Understanding	ELOHIM
Daat	Knowledge	No Name
Hesed	Mercy	EL
Gevurah	Judgment	YAH
Tiferet	Beauty	YHVH ELOHIM
Nezah	Eternity	YHVH ZEVAOT
Yesod	Foundation	EL HAI SHADDAI
Malkhut	Kingdom	ADONAI

Figure 6.1: Equivalents between the Sefirot of the Tree of Life and the names of God with which they are associated.[4]

In the earliest versions of the Kabbalah, God is referred to by the name of *Ayin Sof,* meaning the *Infinite* or *Infinite Being.*[5] The *Sepher Yetzirah* further references God through *at least* another six names, each very different and each clarifying one particular way that the Infinite Being is manifest in creation.

Examples of these names are *Yah, the Lord of Hosts, the God of Israel, the Living God, King of the Universe,* and *El Shaddai.*[6] Ultimately, the traditions of the Kabbalah and the *Sepher Yetzirah* describe the many combinations of a single force stemming from a single name, and the effects of a power that cannot be directly known.

I Am That Which I Am

Ancient Hebrew and Christian traditions record at least two instances when God is said to have revealed himself clearly by one very personal name. Both accounts are preserved in the second book of the Torah, as well as the Old Testament Book of Exodus. Although the Quran also describes the general theme of these stories—complete with Moses receiving "The Law" from God upon Mt. Sinai when Hebrew tradition states that God's secret name was revealed—the *personal name* of God does not appear to be revealed outwardly in the Islamic tradition. As we shall see later in Chapter 9, however, *the Islamic, Jewish, and Christian names for God appear to stem from the same source,* and seem to be equivalents of the same power of creation.

The event of God revealing his name to this world is first recorded in the third chapter of Exodus. In the miracle of the burning bush, the account is described as a direct conversation between Moses and God, where God declares himself to be the same God described by Moses' ancestors, the God of Abraham, Isaac, and Jacob, as well as Moses' father. After requesting that Moses deliver a message to Pharaoh of Egypt, Exodus records that Moses, in turn, asked a single question: "When I come to the Israelites and say to them 'The God of your fathers has sent me to you,' and they ask me, 'What is His name?' what shall I say to them?"[7]

According to the oldest versions of the writings, God answered Moses directly. Beginning in Exodus 3:14, God offers the mystical words "EHYEH ASHER EHYEH," and continues, "Thus shall you say to the Israelites, 'Ehyeh sent me to you.'" With these words began the mystery and controversy that has continued from the moment of their utterance more than 3,200 years ago.

The debate revolves around the seemingly incremental way that God revealed himself, and the possible translations of the words that he used. Laying the foundation to share his identity with Moses, God placed the word *Asher* directly between two occurrences of the word *Ehyeh*. In this instance, Asher functions as a specific form of pronoun, a *relative pronoun* referring to the word that immediately precedes it. The word itself is a striking example of the power of the Hebrew language.

Without changing the spelling, Asher can simultaneously mean "who," as well as "which" or "that." Each is an accurate translation, depending upon how the word is used. In the case of God revealing his name to Moses, the most widely accepted translations have historically been as "that," reading as "Ehyeh that Ehyeh."

There is little question that the Hebrew word *Ehyeh* is derived from the root words "to be" in the first person singular.[8] What is not clear, however, is precisely which tense was intended when the name was offered. Some Torah commentaries suggest that this uncertainty could lead to a number of different translations, each correct depending on how the word is used. These translations could result in "Ehyeh" meaning "I am," "I shall be," or "I will be." Additionally, the fact that the word appears twice in the same sentence suggests that the first occurrence could have a different tense than the second occurrence. If so, the first could result in "I am," with the second reading "I will be." Or both occurrences could represent the same tense, reading "I will be who I will be," or "I am who I am."

Thus, the words that God used to preface the revelation of his name, "Ehyeh-Asher Ehyeh," may be read a number of ways, including "I AM (WHO/WHICH/THAT) I AM," "I SHALL BE (WHO/WHICH/THAT) I SHALL BE," and "I WILL BE (WHO/WHICH/THAT) I WILL BE." The most common translation of the sacred scriptures is "I AM THAT WHICH I AM." *It suggests that God identified himself first through his accomplishments* (the source of all that has been, is, and will be) *before offering His precise and personal name to Moses.*

The Personal Name of God

Following the initial revelation of his identity in Exodus, the Torah records that the next statement further clarified the mystery of God's personal name: "Thus shall you speak to the Israelites: *The Lord,* the God of your fathers, the God of Abraham, the God of Isaac, and the God of Jacob has sent me to you: This shall be my name forever, this my appellation for all eternity."[9] For the first time, we are offered direct access to the *personal name* that God revealed to Moses.

Modern translations of both Hebrew and Christian texts show that in this statement, God identified himself as "the LORD." *Older versions of the same texts, however, reveal that another name was originally given to Moses:* the mystical, sacred, and unspeakable name of *YaHWeH.* Following the convention of omitting the vowels from ancient Hebrew, God's name is revealed as the three remaining consonants of His name, written as the four letters ' *(Y)* ה *(H)* ו *(V)* ה *(H): YHVH.*

When reading the Hebrew language, letters are read from right to left, so the word *YHVH* appears as יהוה. Please note that I follow this convention throughout this book wherever I incorporate Hebrew words, although their English translations may be read left to right.

It is with the letters of the name YHVH that we begin to see the confusion regarding precisely which of the names given to Moses is actually the personal name of God. Although God initially identified Himself as "Ehyeh-Asher Ehyeh" (I AM THAT I AM), it's possible that YHVH may be an ancient variation of the name EHYEH.[10] While the name YHVH was clearly known to the patriarchs before Moses, during the time of Genesis they apparently never understood its significance as the actual name of the Creator.

As there were many names attributed to the various aspects of God in Heaven during the time of Genesis, it was originally assumed that the name YHVH was simply another aspect of the living God. During the centuries that passed from the days of the patriarchs to the time of Moses, the name "had hardly been more than a customary appellation."[11]

The Unspeakable Name of God

In the Hebrew language itself, we're given a possible indication that God never intended his name to be spoken commonly among the people of the earth. In reference to His holy name, Torah scholars suggest that a warning regarding its use is inherent within the words themselves. Specifically, they believe it is revealed in the precise way in which God described his name to Moses. When God states that YHVH shall be his name "forever," the Hebrew word *forever* is written **לצלם**, rather than with its traditional spelling of **לצולם**, with the letter *Vav* (ו) in the center. Scholars suggest that the missing Vav indicates that it is to be understood as something hidden.[12] Reflecting upon this clue, the commentary further states: "No man should pronounce the Name according to its letters."[13]

Based upon the two revelations in Exodus, the ancient Hebrew texts referred to God by his preferred name of YHVH approximately 6,800 (by some accounts precisely 6,823) times. This particular name was believed to be so sacred, hold such power, and command such reverence, that to pronounce it improperly or to disrespect it in any way was to dishonor God in the worst manner possible. The Torah itself provides a biblical foundation for this belief, admonishing: "You shall not misuse the name of YaHWeH your God."[14] Traditionally, the Name was spoken only by the high priest during temple services, intoning it on the Day of Atonement.

Sometime between the destruction of the Second Temple in Jerusalem in 70 C.E. and the compilation of the *Talmud,* a collection of Jewish literature compiled sometime between the fourth and fifth centuries, the name by which God identified himself in Exodus was replaced in the texts by a substitute name to prevent its misuse. Afterward, all of the approximately 6,800 occurrences of God's name became the word *Adonai,* meaning *Lord,* or *Ha Shem,* literally meaning "the Name."

Because the name revealed to Moses was originally recorded in biblical Hebrew without the vowels, today we're left with no way of knowing precisely how the name of YHVH was spoken.[15] Although its correct pronunciation was preserved in the oral traditions of the Temple, when the practice of substituting another word for the name of God was adopted, the actual speaking of the original name became something of the past. The majority of scholarly opinion holds that, in the days of Moses, YHVH was pronounced "Yah-Weigh."[16] In the pronunciation, the letter *V* is replaced with the sound of the *W,* although there is no *W* in the Hebrew alphabet.

Portions of the Dead Sea Scrolls, such as first text of Isaiah discovered in 1947, offer tangible evidence that the practice of substituting an alternate word or symbol to replace God's name was already established even at the time of the Scrolls' creation, approximately 2,200 years ago. Figure 6.2 shows a portion of column XXXIII from the first Isaiah Scroll (1Qisa), illustrating the convention of placing four dots between the lines as symbols representing the sacred and unspeakable name of God.

Figure 6.2: Portion of the first Isaiah scroll, showing four dots placed in the middle of the page above the second sentence, as a substitute for the sacred name of God.[17] [Photo by John Trevor]

In Moses' second encounter with what the Hebrew commentaries describe as "the Deity," God identifies Himself again, clarifying any misunderstanding that may have remained following their first meeting. In Exodus 6:2–3, God states to Moses in no uncertain terms: "I am YHVH." He then goes on to confirm that he is the same God that appeared to the Israeli elders and explains why they may not have known his name at that time.

"I appeared to Abraham, Isaac and Jacob as El Shaddai, but I did not make Myself known to them by My name YHVH." In these instances, scholars suggest that God had once again identified himself to Jacob, Isaac, and Abraham through an attribute, rather than his personal name. The expression El Shaddai is generally thought to mean "God Almighty"[18] or "Omnipotent Almighty."[19]

Thus, in His own words, twice in the earliest records that form the foundation of more than half of the world's religions, God offered one very specific name by which the people of this world would know him throughout time.

Ancient Evidence of God's Oldest Name

The recent recovery, translation, and release of some of the oldest known Hebrew texts offers additional support for the argument that the name YHVH is, in fact, the name revealed to Moses nearly 3,500 years ago. In addition to the approximately 22,000 fragments of papyrus, animal hide, and copper originally pieced together as the Dead Sea Scrolls Library, there are an additional 3,000 fragments that have been catalogued, translated, and compiled only recently. These are broken portions of the Scrolls that are so small that they cannot be linked to any one specific document. Nonetheless, they are still part of the extraordinary find of Dead Sea Scrolls. In an effort to create as complete a record as possible, these fragments, identified as "bits and pieces" by the Scroll scholars themselves, now yield what may become one of the most significant finds of the Dead Sea Library.

On one of the tiny fragments, with each letter crisp and clear, a single word remains. Surviving the elements of time and nature, preserved exactly as their author carefully crafted each line and curve over 2,000 years ago, the letters bear the unmistakable form of one word that immediately catches the attention of both the scholar, as well as the casual reader. That single word is the personal name that God used to describe Himself to Moses, the word יהוה: *YHWH* (see Figure 6.3).

Figure 6.3: Enlargement of one of the oldest records of יהוה, the ancient name of God. This portion of text, fragment number 66 from Cave IV, was among 3,000 fragments that, while part of the Dead Sea Scrolls library, cannot be linked with any one particular scroll.[20] [Photo by Israel Antiquities Authority]

In a review concerning the find, Hershel Shanks, editor of the archaeological journal *Biblical Archaeology Review,* commented on the irony of finding this name intact among the thousands of fragments. "Was this simply coincidental? Or is it that the name is used so often in these religious documents that it would be expected to appear (and survive) frequently? Or is there some deeper significance?"[21]

Before writing *The God Code,* it was necessary to establish as accurately as possible by what name the presence on Mt. Sinai identified himself to Moses. Following 12 years of research and the discovery of evidence that will be presented later in this chapter, I am confident beyond any reasonable doubt, and despite the academic controversy on this point, that of the many words and names used to describe the power and presence of God, one survives as the personal and preferred name through which God clearly identified himself. That name is the tetragrammaton: *YHVH.*

The Power of the "Name"

In the absence of a personal revelation regarding the secrets of creation, we're left to ancient accounts of such encounters, and our interpretations of those accounts to add meaning to our lives and make sense of our world. The mystery surrounding the name of

God has endured, preserved through the priesthoods, hidden sects, and secret societies of our past, and it remains today. Additional evidence of the power within the name YHVH may be found within the legends and rites preserved in the traditions of the Masons.

Among such accounts is the story of Hiram Abif, the lead architect of King Solomon, who was murdered and brought back to life through the use of a single word. Legend states, however, that until the true word wielding such power could be recovered and restored, the word *Mah Hah Bone* was used as a substitute "password." The real word of life was the unspeakable name of God: YHVH.[22] As with any legend, without the ability to verify the account, its acceptance becomes a matter of personal belief. Given the powers of life and creation that are attributed to the Name, however, it is not surprising that it would be associated with resurrection as well.

The basis of the mystery regarding God's name is the spelling, pronunciation, and vocalization of what is believed by many to be the single most powerful and sacred name "under Heaven." In addition to the archaeological evidence suggesting that the name YHVH is, in fact, the personal name of the Creator, further evidence may be gleaned through the attention the name is given in the *Sepher Yetzirah*.

As we have seen, in its first chapter, the *Sepher Yetzirah* offers a broad overview of the process used by a supreme force—identified by no less than five names—to set into motion the birth of our universe. In the very first sentence of that chapter, we are told that God created His universe with three ways of knowing and conveying information.

> *"With 32 mystical Paths of Wisdom engraved YH,*
> *YHVH of Hosts, God of Israel, the Living God,*
> *El Shaddai, high and exalted, dwelling in eternity and*
> *Holy is His name. He created His universe with*
> *three books, with script, with number and telling."*[23]

It is generally accepted by scholars of Biblical Hebrew that the first name given to the Creator in this sentence, YH, is an ancient form of the name YHVH.[24] The uncertainty surrounding this name appears to arise from precisely how the name was derived. It may have actually been the original form of the name from which YHVH was expanded. Or it may have been a contracted form of YHVH, shortened to the essence of the name YH,[25] translated as the "Eternal."[26] The use of YH in traditional scriptures may be found today in the restored version of both the Hebrew and Christian Bibles. In the Torah, Exodus 15:2 states: "The Lord (Yah) is my strength and might." While the English versions translate this reference to God as "The Lord," the Hebrew text clearly shows God's name, Yah, as the letters *Yod* and *Hey*.[27]

In the Haggadah, we are given what is perhaps the most direct indication of Yah as God's name. Presented through the story of Adam's marriage to Eve in the Garden, the text is written in a way that leaves little doubt in the mind of the reader as to the name by which God revealed himself on Earth, even before the time of Moses. Following their marriage, both Adam and Eve changed their names to reflect the shift that their union had caused within them. As described in the text, they were the first of our kind incorporate God's name into their own:

> Adam called his wife Ishah, and himself he called Ish, abandoning the name Adam which he had borne before the creation of Eve, *for the reason that God added his own name Yah to the names of the man and the woman*—Yod to Ish and He to Ishah—to indicate that as long as they walked in the ways of God and observed his commandments, his name would shield them against all harm.[28] [Author's italics]

Although there appears to be mixed agreement in the Hebrew commentaries regarding whether or not YH is a divine name, from the perspective of the Haggadah and *Sepher Yetzirah* there is little doubt that it is. In this first, very key statement of the *Sepher Yetzirah*, the text describes how the divine presence, named YH, performed the act of creation through the use of three kinds of information, which are identified as *written, numeric,* and *spoken*.

The Universe from a Single Name

Rabbi Kaplan translates this portion of the *Sepher Yetzirah* as God creating his universe with "text *(sepher)*, with number *(sephar)*, and with communication *(sippur)*" [author's parentheses]. The rabbi further clarifies the subtleties of these three ways of knowing by expanding his translation of text, number, and communication to include quality, quantity, and communication, respectively.[29]

Following its introduction, the text describes how "Ten Sefirot of Nothingness," the ten realms of the mystical Tree of Life, were created. As each Sefirot was formed within the void of the universe, it brought specific qualities into being: qualities that are mirrored throughout all elements of life and creation. Due to the resurgence of interest in the Kabbalah, there are a number of excellent texts dedicated to the understanding and application of its timeless wisdom in the modern world. For the purposes of this book, however, we will focus only on the portions of the *Sepher Yetzirah* that lead directly to the living message hidden within each cell of our bodies.

After the emergence of the ten Sefirot from the void, the *Sepher Yetzirah* details the actual process by which God implemented his creation. Through concise, proselike paragraphs, the verses describe huge concepts ranging from the origin of the universe to its relationship with our bodies. In terms that leave little doubt as to their meaning, the phrases state that it is through these letters alone that God constructed the universe.

The 22 letters; He engraved them, carved them, permuted them, weighed them, transformed them and from them He formed all that was ever formed and all that would ever be formed."[30]

The meaning is so clear that it leaves the mind reeling in its implications. Within our bodies, the letters that allowed for the birth of the universe—and all that God accomplished through His name—are produced, replicated, and stored as the miracle of each human cell.

It is only in the last half of the 20th century that the DNA molecule was characterized as a "language." Although the ancients did not have modern words for cells and molecules, in the idiom of their day they invited us to "look within" to discover the knowledge of our existence. Now, centuries later, their wisdom allows us to carry the modern metaphor of DNA as a language one step further.

By simply following the instructions preserved in ancient records from our past, we're shown the code that allows us to substitute the elements that form our DNA with the letters of the Hebrew alphabet. In doing so, we are able to translate the language of life and read the message. To understand how the genetic code can be translated as a language, however, we must first develop a brief understanding of the way DNA works in our bodies.

DNA: The "Rosetta Stone" of Life

In the overall scheme of the cosmos, we have existed only briefly as a species within our planet's lifespan. In a college text, I remember seeing the age of the universe and the birth of humankind depicted on the face of a typical clock to illustrate the relative times of their appearance. With each hour of the clock representing vast expanses of Earth's existence, it was only in the last two to three minutes before 12 o'clock that the first evidence of human life appears.

Although the controversy continues regarding precisely *what* happened before the moment of creation and the beginnings of human life, there appears to be a growing consensus as to *when* each began. With new evidence supporting the Big Bang theory, the birth of the universe has now been revised to approximately 13 to 14 billion years ago.[31] Within this mind-boggling period of time, Earth is believed to have formed approximately 4.5 billion years ago, with the first evidence of our species arriving only about 160,000 years ago. Assuming that the estimates of such staggering periods of time are even close to correct, a full 99 percent

of our planet's life-to-date had already passed before the appearance of our first ancestors!

Regardless of the controversy over precisely *how* we originated or how long we've been here, from the moment of our appearance on Earth there has remained a single experience that we have always shared with our earliest ancestors. For approximately a quarter of a million years, the process of conceiving and giving birth to a human life has remained the same—that is until the last generation of the 20th century.

We Have Discovered the "Secret of Life"!

In 1978, the bond that we have shared with the earliest members of our species changed forever with the birth of Louise Joy Brown. On July 25 of that year, at 11:47 A.M., Louise was born in a hospital in Great Britain—the first human successfully conceived outside of her mother's womb. Giving rise to the term *test-tube baby*, which is used to describe such conceptions, on that day the requirement of sexual union to create a new life became an option, rather than a necessity.

Since that time, more than 20,000 additional children have been conceived outside of the womb, allowed to develop in an external environment for a period of time, then placed into the womb of a woman prepared to carry and deliver the child full term. In addition to redefining the act of conception and pregnancy, this line of exploration has led to the miraculous abilities that allow us to select the characteristics of children *before* they are conceived, alter their characteristics *after* conception, conceive life for the purpose of harvesting specialized cells, and incubate particular cells to create specialized tissue. The advances of such miraculous-sounding technologies all began with the publication of a single report in the mid-20th century.

In 1953, the British journal *Nature* published a report by James Watson and Francis Crick entitled "Molecular Structure of Nucleic Acids: A Structure for Deoxyribose Nucleic Acid."[32] With the publication of their article, the door was opened to alter, manipulate, and engineer the very essence of life: the *DNA molecule*. While the work of Watson and Crick included the research of two other scientists from King's College in London, Rosalind Franklin and Maurice Wilkins, it was their own stroke of insight into the double helix structure that solved the mystery of genetic behavior and led to their acceptance of the Nobel Prize in 1962.*

As is often the case, it was during the informal moments following an intense period of research that Francis Crick entered the Eagle Pub in Cambridge, England, and boasted the magnitude of their discoveries earlier in the day. As Watson later recalled, Crick declared that through their efforts, they had "found the secret of life"![33] It was that secret that led to the technology making Louise Brown's unconventional birth possible. The ethical repercussions of Watson and Crick's discovery continue today, through heated debate of issues such as human cloning, stem-cell research, and our responsibility to the earliest stages of human life.

The Alphabet of DNA: Translated

Almost from the moment that the code of life was discovered, scientists and nonscientists alike have described the genetic blueprint of life as a "language." In a rare press conference held during the summer of 2000 regarding matters of science, then-President Bill Clinton stood beside the leaders of two companies that had completed one of the largest cooperative research efforts in history: the *Human Genome Project*. Through their combined efforts, they'd produced the first map of our genetic code and opened the door to a new era of medical and life sciences in the 21st century. In describing the significance of the milestone, Clinton declared that the genome was the "language in which God created life."[34]

As frequent as such references are, more often than not they are used only figuratively to describe the building blocks of life—the "language" of life's chemical code. From the relationships described previously in this book, however, it is clear that DNA

---

*In 1962, the Nobel Prize in physiology/medicine was shared by Watson, Crick, and Wilkins for their work in the discovery of DNA structure. Rosalind Franklin died in 1958 and was not named in the award.

may now be regarded as the very real language of an ancient and translatable alphabet. It is that language that preserves the single message transcending any differences that could ever separate us as the family of humankind. To reveal the message in our bodies, we must understand the alphabet of life.

THE GENIUS OF WATSON and Crick's discovery lay in their description of the DNA molecule itself. In very nontechnical terms, the building blocks of life are surprisingly simple, and they're arranged in a way that is both remarkably efficient and, at the same time, pleasing to the eye. The essence of genetic research is based in the understanding that all life is formed as combinations of only four chemical compounds. These basic units of life—*adenine, thymine, guanine,* and *cytosine* (A, T, G, and C respectively)—called *DNA bases,* carry all of the information required to produce every form of life that is known to exist. From the smallest single-celled organisms to the estimated 100 trillion cells that make up a single human body, the code of each life form is made from different arrangements of these four bases.

Through a process that is only partially understood, the bases arrange themselves into precise pairs, known as *base pairs,* with each pair containing the patterns that combine with other pairs to produce the blueprints of life. In other words, each base only works with a specific partner: guanine always pairs with cytosine (G-C), and adenine always pairs with thymine (A-T). The pairs are arranged opposite one another, forming the rungs of a twisted, ladderlike structure, the familiar *double helix*[35] (see Figure 6.4). These base pairs make up the gene-code notation that has become so familiar over the last few years.

Figure 6.4: Illustration of the double-helix structure of DNA, showing how specific bases always pair with one another: C with G, and A with T.

On June 26, 2000, the world watched in awe as the announcement was made that two competing companies, one private and one federal, had pooled their resources to produce the first map of how the bases that form human DNA are arranged. In illustrating this map, seemingly endless streams of alphabetic letters were flashed upon our television screens and across the pages of popular magazines. The sequences, some of which were hundreds of letters long, represented the bases that had been identified at different places on the human DNA molecule. These combinations are known as *genes*. It is groups of genes that form the 23 pairs of living information *(chromosomes)* that make us unique as a species.[36] Following is a portion of human chromosome 1 to illustrate the appearance of this code:

GATCAATGAGGTGGACACCAGAGGCGGGGACTTGTAAATAACACTGGGCTGTAGGAGTGA
TGGGGTTCACCTCTAATTCTAAGATGGCTAGATAA GCATCTTTCAGGGTTGTGCTTCTA
TCTAGAAGGTAGAGCTGTGTCGTTCAATAAAAGTCCTCAAGAGGTTGGTAATACGCAT
GTTTAATAGTACAGTATGGTGACTATAGTCAACAATAATTTATTGTACATTTTTAAATAG

*Two hundred and forty bases from a
portion of human chromosome 1.*

The key to translating the code of DNA into a meaningful language is to apply the discovery that converts elements to letters. Based upon their matching values, hydrogen becomes the Hebrew letter *Yod* (Y), nitrogen becomes the letter *Hey* (H), oxygen becomes the letter *Vav* (V), and carbon becomes *Gimel* (G). These substitutions now reveal that the ancient form of God's name, YH, exists as the literal chemistry of our genetic code (underlined letters Figure 6.5). Through this bridge between God's name and the elements of modern science, it now becomes possible to reveal the full mystery and find even greater meaning in the ancient code that lives as each cell of our bodies.

DNA Base	Chemical Element			Hebrew Letter
Thymine(T)	Hydrogen	=	Yod	Y
	Nitrogen	=	Hey	H
	Oxygen	=	Vav	V
	Carbon	=	Gimel	G
Cytosine(C)	Hydrogen	=	Yod	Y
	Nitrogen	=	Hey	H
	Oxygen	=	Vav	V
	Carbon	=	Gimel	G
Adenine(A)	Hydrogen	=	Yod	Y
	Nitrogen	=	Hey	H
	Oxygen	=	Vav	V
	Carbon	=	Gimel	G
Guanine(G)	Hydrogen	=	Yod	Y
	Nitrogen	=	Hey	H
	Oxygen	=	Vav	V
	Carbon	=	Gimel	G

Figure 6.5: The four DNA bases, showing the elements that they are made of, and the equivalent of each element in the Hebrew alphabet. As our genetic code is made of combinations of the DNA bases, sometimes hundreds of letters long, there are a tremendous number of ways that YHVG may be combined in our cells.

In Each Cell of Every Life: The Code Revealed

During an interview, Albert Einstein was once asked to describe his understanding of what God is like. In his reply, he alluded to the fact that, although the Creator is not seen directly, we are shown evidence of His existence in each moment of every day.

"My comprehension of God," Einstein shared, "comes from the deeply felt conviction of a superior intelligence that reveals itself in the knowable world."[37] Through such candid insights, we're given a glimpse into the way one of the greatest minds of the last century perceived the intelligence underlying our world. The discovery linking that intelligence to the elements of life now gives even greater meaning to Einstein's perception.

When we substitute modern elements for all four letters of God's ancient name, we see a result that, at first blush, may be unexpected. Replacing the final *H* in YHVH with its chemical equivalent of nitrogen, God's name becomes the elements hydrogen, nitrogen, oxygen, and nitrogen (HNON)—all colorless, odorless, and invisible gases! In other words, replacing 100 percent of God's personal name with the elements of this world creates a substance that is an intangible, yet very real form of creation!

Indeed, in the earliest descriptions of God, we are told that He is omnipresent and takes on a form in our world that cannot be seen with our eyes. Thus, He can be known only through His manifestations. The *Sepher Yetzirah* describes this nonphysical form of God's presence as the "Breath" of God.

> *"Ten Sefirot of Nothingness: One is the*
> *Breath of the Living God, Life of worlds. . . .*
> *This is the Holy Breath."*[38]

Additionally, the first chapters of Genesis relate that it is in a nonphysical form that the Creator was present during the time of creation (Genesis 1:2). It was "the *spirit* of God" [author's emphasis] that first moved over the face of the earth.

The *Sepher Yetzirah* further describes the first Hebrew letter to emerge from the void of creation as the Mother Letter that made the universe possible: *Alef*. Through a great, mystical "secret," *Alef* then evolved into the first element to appear in our universe, hydrogen, as well as the first letter of God's name: *Yod*. Modern theories of the Big Bang now suggest that hydrogen was the first element to form from the energy released at the instant of creation, and remains as the single most abundant element in the universe. Both accounts appear to be describing the same element!

Exodus reminds us in very specific terms that the name YHVH was revealed as the personal name of God. In equally clear terms, we are shown that humankind is made "in the image" of God.

Perhaps in these statements may be found the most direct clue describing our relationship to the source of all that "is." With a new emphasis, the statement regarding our origins reminds us that we are made only *in the image* of God, rather than being made *as,* or *equal* to, God. Although subtle, this statement suggests that, while we undeniably share in the attributes of our Creator, we're also set apart from YHVH by something that makes us very different.

Substituting modern elements for the ancient letters, it is clear that *although we share in the first three letters representing 75 percent of our Creator's name,* the fourth and final letter of our chemical name sets us apart from God (see Figure 6.6 below). While the presence of God is the invisible and intangible form of the three gases hydrogen, nitrogen, and oxygen, the last letter of our name is the "stuff" that gives us the color, taste, texture, and sounds of our body: carbon. The one letter that sets us apart from God is also the element that makes us "real" in our world.

God's Name As Elements			Humankind's Name As Elements	
Name of God	Chemical Equivalent		Name of Man	Chemical Equivalent
Y	Hydrogen	=	Y	Hydrogen
H	Nitrogen	=	H	Nitrogen
V	Oxygen	=	V	Oxygen
H	Nitrogen	≠	G	Carbon

Figure 6.6: The *H* in the YHVH of God's name is replaced by *G* in the YHVG of Humankind. Through language, this illustrates that, while we share three of the four letters of God's personal name as our genetic code, we are not equal to God—25 percent of our composition is very different. It is this difference that gives us our physicality and accounts for our uniqueness as a species.

This is not to suggest that God is simply a wispy gas made of invisible elements. Rather, it's through the very name that God divulged to Moses over three millennia ago that our world and the

foundation of life itself became possible. God tells us that in the form of hydrogen, the single most abundant element of the universe, He is a part of all that has ever been, is, and will be.

The Name of God in the Body of Man

Legend states that when King Solomon built his holy temple in Jerusalem, an ancient ritual took place, preceding even the laying of the first stone. Preserved through the traditions of the Masons today, that ritual involved the orientation and laying of one stone, the *cornerstone,* to which all other stones of the massive complex would eventually be oriented. It is told that the king placed one sheet of parchment within this cornerstone upon which he himself had inscribed a single name. Symbolically, the name anchoring the cornerstone of Jerusalem's Holy Temple would also become the name upon which King Solomon would base the leadership of his people, the power of his nation, and become the basis for one third of the earth's organized religions. That single name was the tetragrammaton YHVH, the timeless name of God.

An even closer examination of the actual letters that form the name of God and the body of man clarifies precisely what this ancient relationship says to us today. While original versions of the biblical texts fully acknowledge God's name as YHVH, they also refer to the shortened version as YH, as was previously noted. Scholars generally accept the two names YHVH and YH as interchangeable.[39] When translated, the name YH may be read as "the Eternal."[40]

Although the specifics may vary across time and culture, in modern English the meaning of the word *eternal* clearly implies an existence having no beginning or end and functioning beyond the limitations of time.[41] It is precisely this "eternal" aspect that's common to both the name of God, <u>YH</u>VH, and the human body, <u>YH</u>VG, as indicated by the underlined letters. Through both the secret letter codes of antiquity, and the literal translation of DNA as an alphabet, we're shown that something about our existence

remains lasting and eternal. We share that never-ending quality with our Creator through a full 50 percent of the elements that define our genetic code.

YHVH = the name of God
YHVG = the name of Man

YH (God/Eternal) forms one-half of God's name and the name coded into our cells.

The Promise of God in the Body of Man

The second aspect of our chemical name carries our relationship with God to a new level. Further, it describes precisely *how* God exists in our bodies. The next two letters *(VG)* of our name as Hebrew letter equivalents of DNA (YHVG) illustrate the nature of this relationship. In the science of gematria, it's important to note the number codes of ancient alphabets are not sensitive to the order of the letters. Just as 1 + 2 and 2 + 1 both give us the same result of 3, the rules of letter codes permit the same considerations with letter values.

Additionally, within the mysteries of the Kabbalah, the reverse (altered) order of a given set of letters is often associated with alternate realms of creation. While the qualities related to such a mirror may vary, the meaning itself does not change. Thus, with consideration to the *VG* or *GV* of humankind's name, YHVG, we may look to the literal translation for greater understanding.

Within the Hebrew language, the letters *GV* translate to the idea of "within," or more specifically, "the interior of the body."[42] Within the *Sepher Yetzirah's* mysterious 231 mystical gates of creation,[43] *GV* represents *DM,* or the root of the name Adam, meaning "blood." Combining these translations of the message in our cells now offers an unprecedented insight into our relationship to creation through the name of God. By replacing the elements of DNA with their equivalents of Hebrew letters, we

reveal the message that is spelled out within each cell of our bodies (see Figure 6.7b).

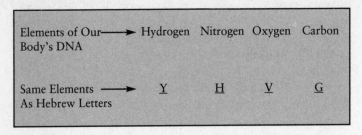

Elements of Our → Body's DNA	Hydrogen	Nitrogen	Oxygen	Carbon
Same Elements → As Hebrew Letters	Y	H	V	G

Figure 6.7a: The elements of our DNA translated into letters of the Hebrew alphabet.

- YH: the abbreviated and accepted form of YHVH/Eternal, the ancient name of God.

- VG/GV: within the body.

A literal translation reveals the message:

"God/Eternal within the body"

Figure 6.7b: The message that is revealed when the chemistry of our cells is translated into the letters of ancient Hebrew.

By substituting these words for our genetic code, we are now able to illustrate how the literal name of God forms the message within each cell of our bodies: God/Eternal within the body. A graphic illustration of this substitution shows that through various combinations of the four DNA bases—adenine, thymine, guanine, and cytosine—it becomes possible to create the substance of life from the name in our bodies (see Figure 6.8). It's equally clear that the bases of the code contain varying degrees of

God's presence "within the body."[44] Previously, we described the letters *T, C, A,* and *G* as abbreviations for the combinations of hydrogen, nitrogen, oxygen, and carbon that make up the DNA bases. As we replace each element with its equivalent Hebrew letter, we are shown precisely how human life is created from variations of God's name in our bodies.

While warranting further study, these correlations open the door to a new, very different way of viewing our relationship to God and creation. Clearly, such a process represents only the beginning of a broader study leading to a much deeper understanding.

Although the links between language and the elements fall short of defining *who* the God of our prayers is, or what such a presence would actually look like, they offer us an unprecedented insight into our relationship with our world and one another. With respect to Figure 6.8, a number of conclusions immediately come to light.

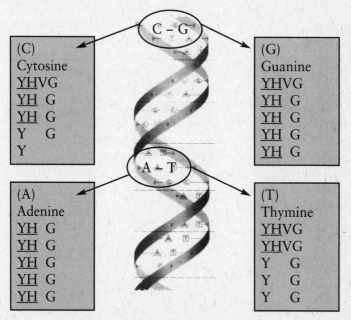

Figure 6.8: A graphic illustration of God's ancient name, YH, within the fabric of our genetic code.

- When correlated with the Hebrew alphabet, the code of all life becomes a translatable message in our cells.

- Different forms of DNA bases produce the message in varying degrees of repetition.

- 50 percent of the message within our cells translates literally to "God/Eternal."

- The remaining 50 percent of our genetic code translates to "within the body," thus describing where we may find God's eternal nature in this world.

In humankind's most cherished traditions, we are reminded of our relationship to a greater power and the lasting nature of that relationship. At the very least, the discovery of God's name within each cell of all life reveals a message, as well as a promise, that transcends any differences that we could ever impose upon one another. In a very real sense, the foundation of our existence is formed of an essence that is limitless, unbounded, and eternal. It is this spark of creation that texts such as the *Sepher Yetzirah* equate to the Creator—a spark clearly shared through at least 50 percent of the name that accounts for our existence—that holds the promise for each of us to become more than the conditions and limitations of our lives.

This is the promise shared by every man, woman, child, and ancestor of our global family, as the living message coded within each cell of our bodies.

CHAPTER 6 SUMMARY

- Due to the infinite nature of God's existence, He is identified by names that describe His manifestations, such as YH (the Eternal), YH YHVH (YH the Lord), El Shaddai, and the Creator.

- The name YHVH was held so sacred in the Hebrew tradition that its approximately 6,800 occurrences in the Torah were replaced with a substitute name to prevent its misuse or dishonoring.

- The structure of all life is made from different combinations of only four DNA bases, with each base made of the four main elements of life—hydrogen, nitrogen, oxygen, and carbon.

- *New discovery:* Replacing the four elements of our DNA with the letters represented by their ancient and hidden number code reveals that the basis of all life is made of various combinations of God's ancient name, YH, meaning "Eternal."

- In addition to the name itself, the letters *VG*, meaning "within the body," are encoded into the remaining building blocks of life.

- The message is a reminder that human life specifically, and all life in general, is united through a common heritage. Though stopping short of describing precisely *how* the code in our cells originated, the fact of its existence and the odds against such a message forming by chance strongly suggest intelligence and an intention underlying our origins.

PART III

The Meaning:
Applying the Message to Our Lives

"God became as we are, that we
may be as he is. God is man
and exists in us and we in him."

— WILLIAM BLAKE

Chapter Seven

MESSAGE FROM THE FIRST DAY:
Reading the Language of God

Reactions to the discovery linking ancient alphabets with modern elements have been varied yet predictable. For some, the revelation of God's name within the code of life holds implications of such magnitude that they feel absolutely overwhelmed. Initial responses have ranged from disbelief to a curiosity bordering on awe and wonder. Always there are questions and a longing to know more. "If the code is real, how could such a thing be possible?" "How could we have overlooked something of such importance for so long?"

For others, the discovery offers welcome relief, scientifically confirming what they already suspect in their hearts and what they live in their lives. Beyond the differences of culture, race, religion, action, or belief, the message reminds us that we're part of something greater than any differences we could ever impose upon one another or ourselves.

In retrospect, the code of life is simple and straightforward. It is only in our world of separation, where we reduce the study of nature to the seemingly unrelated sciences, that the connections have been lost and the message obscured. The discovery of God's name within our bodies shows us the benefit of merging different ways of knowing into a single understanding. By crossing the traditional

boundaries that define chemistry, language, history, and religion, we are shown the power of a larger, integrated worldview. In the simplicity of the code, perhaps the message is just as simple.

Perfection of the Soul

What does the message in our bodies reveal about our role in creation? Previous chapters described how ancient texts linked God's name to the way that His presence was made known at a given point in time: the God of Mercy, the God of Creation, and so on. The Book of Genesis provides some of the most powerful clues to understanding our role in the destiny of our species. In its original language of Hebrew, the text reveals that during the act of creation, God stopped the process *before* it was complete (Genesis 17:1). The English translation of this telling event reads: "I am God the Creator who said enough, now walk before Me and *become* perfect" [author's italics]. The name attributed to this aspect of God is given as *ShaDaY*, a contraction of two Hebrew words, *She-amar Day*, which may be translated as "*He who said enough, stop.*"[1] Within this single phrase, we are shown the potential that God's name allows for us in our bodies, and perhaps why the world and our existence sometimes appears to be less than perfect.

As the name ShaDaY represents only one aspect of God, his personal name remains unchanged; God still identifies himself as YHVH. In the previous applications of gematria, we converted the letters of YHVH to the number code of the Hebrew alphabet. The process revealed that the name of God as a number is 26, which we may further reduce to 8 by adding the digits 2 and 6. Applying the same procedure for the values of our DNA, YHVG, however, yields a number that, while similar, is slightly less.

The hidden number code for the DNA of humankind yields 10 + 5 + 6 + 3, or 24. The sum of 2 + 4 is the coded value of 6. This value states and confirms in number what the texts have already revealed in words. While we *share in the attributes* of God's name, the final letter of our physical body, *Gimel,* reminds us that we are not equal to God (see Figure 7.1).

Name of God	Letter Code	Body (DNA) of Human	Letter Code
Y	10	Y	10
H	5	H	5
V	6	V	6
H	5	G	3
Sum	26	Sum	24
Reduced	8	Reduced	6

Figure 7.1: Comparison of God's name as the elements of our world, and our name as encoded into each of our cells. As tradition reminds us, while we are related to God, our physicality (the carbon or G of Gimel) prevents us from being equal.

The wording of Genesis 17:1 is very precise. It implies that the act of creation was halted only with respect to *what we could become*. In modern terms, this may be read as a statement that is less about our physical perfection and perhaps more about the subtle qualities that we aspire to as humans. Although we were complete as bodies in the moment that God halted the process (that is, in our physical form), we were left to choose the nonphysical and spiritual attributes that would allow us to fulfill our potential and achieve our "perfection." In commanding humankind to "become perfect," God gave us the mandate to change, evolve, and participate in the completion of the world and our essence: the mandate to co-create.

Evolution of Essence

Along with the written history revealed in the most ancient records, the discovery of modern human remains now dated at 160,000 before the present time (see Chapter 2) suggests that our physical form has changed very little from the time of our beginnings. While the fossil record offers physical evidence of an evolving progression, the diversity in our past suggests that there were many twists and turns along the way. In their contribution to the Special Edition of *Scientific American* (vol. 15 no. 2, July 2003), Ian Tattersall and Jay Matternes allude to this phenomenon. "The story of human evolution has not been one of a lone hero's linear struggle. Instead it has been the story of nature's tinkering: of repearted evolutionary experiments. Our biological history has been one of sporadic events rather than gradual accretions." Perhaps the greatest mystery of our evolution lies in the fact that somewhere among these "sporadic events," we have acquired the characteristics that set us apart from all other life.

Tattersall and Matternes address our uniqueness in their article, stating *Homo sapiens* embodies characteristics that are "undeniably unusual," further stating, "Whatever that something is, it is related to how we interact with the external world: it is behavioral. . ." Such observations suggest that while a form of physical evolution has obviously occurred, the qualities of our species that have undergone the greatest change may be in the intangible attributes that make us unique, such as the way we deal with life and one another—our expression of love, compassion, and our powers of discernment that come from thoughts, feelings, and emotions.

Through the very characteristics of feeling and emotion that set us apart from other life,[2] we have clearly "evolved" to become more than our ancestors who precede us by hundreds of thousands of years. This understanding supports the physical evidence regarding our evolution. Our ability to transcend the hurt of life's disappointments or to forgive those who have violated our trust, for example, allows us to redefine what such experiences mean in our lives. As we change our perception, in a very literal sense we redefine our bodies as well. The ability to improve immune functions; shift our hormone levels; and alter heart rate, breath, and metabolism simply by changing the way we feel is well documented in the scientific and medical literature.[3, 4]

The statement from the Torah's version of Genesis: "Now walk before Me and *become* perfect" may be less of an observation regarding our imperfection, however, than an invitation to transcend the challenges that each of us face in our lives. In that way, we fulfill the destiny of a greater perfection, a destiny only one letter removed from the mirror image of God.

Although we outwardly acknowledge the possibility of our relationship to a higher power, is it possible that over time and through the struggle to survive, we have forgotten the meaning that such a relationship implies? If we believe that our human family is the result of a "chance" mingling of molecules that resulted in our complex and intelligent species, then there is a sense that we're alone in the cosmos, and our survival may truly be based upon the strongest and fittest. If, however, we discover that our global family has been "created"—that we are the intentional product of a greater intelligence—then the sense of our role in creation must also change. Perhaps new clues, such as those that we find by reading human DNA as an original language, may help us better understand the nature of our evolution. Ultimately, we may find that the answer to our mystery lies at the heart of our genetic map.

The Mystery of the Human Genome: What Makes Us Different?

In June 2001, a milestone was reached in what future generations may recognize as one of the greatest achievements in the history of science. After 20 years of research, in the largest cooperative effort of its kind, the long-anticipated first draft of the human genome—the chemical recipe for the human body—was completed.

"Mapping the human genome has been compared with putting a man on the moon, but I believe it is more than that," stated Dr. Michael Dexter, the director of the Wellcome Trust, which funded the UK's portion of the project.[5] Elaborating on the significance of creating the first human genetic map, Dexter speculated that in addition to being a key achievement in our lifetime, it may be "the outstanding achievement . . . in the history of mankind." In addition to answering questions of our genetic nature, however, the completion of the first human genetic map revealed a surprise that few were expecting.

To the astonishment of the teams reporting the discoveries, it was announced that the genetic blueprint for a human appears to have far fewer genes than expected. When the project began nearly two decades earlier, it was believed that as many as 100,000 genes were required to define a human body. Among the initial findings reported in the 2001 announcement was the discovery that humans have only about one-third as many genes as had originally been estimated.

According to Craig Venter, president of the firm that led one of the mapping teams, "We have only 300 unique genes in the human [genome] that are not in the mouse."[6] Francis Collins, leader of the U.S. portion of the project, commented on the implication of such findings. "We had a hard time explaining the [genetic] control mechanism when we thought there were 100,000 [genes]. Now we have only a third as many."[7] Taking the findings of his team one step further, Venter said, "This tells me genes can't possibly explain all of what makes us what we are."[8]

In no way detracting from the significance of the Human Genome Project's accomplishments, the findings add to a growing suspicion that something is still missing from our understanding of living organisms. Somewhere along the road of discovery that has led to today's sophisticated explanations of life, a key piece of information appears to have been overlooked, left out, or simply forgotten. Venter reiterated this idea when asked to comment on the significance of the surprise findings. "I believe all of our behaviors, all of our sizes and functions clearly have a genetic component but genes only explain a part of the process."[9]

In the early years of the 21st century, perhaps we are only beginning to understand the implications of such findings, and how prophetic Venter's comment really is. Throughout the seven millennia of recorded history, our spiritual practices, religious traditions, and sacred literature have admonished us to recognize that human life is much more than the bones, flesh, muscle, and hair that is so obvious to the naked eye. Now, through the use of sophisticated instruments and the best minds of our time, a two-decade-long study to map the human genetic code has arrived at precisely the same conclusion. 'We are around as a species,' observed Venter, "because we have an adaptability that goes beyond the genome."[10]

With only 300 genes separating us from a field mouse, what is it that makes us so very different? Ultimately, we may discover that the answer to this question is precisely the key that lies at the heart of our most deeply held beliefs and religious traditions. Almost universally, ancient accounts tell us that with the first of our kind, our species was infused with what has been described as a special "spark," a mysterious thread of spiritual essence that eternally joins us with others of our kind and our Creator. It is this spark that sets us apart from all other forms of life. Perhaps it's the same force that imbues uniqueness into our genetic code as well.

The Force That Is Everywhere, All of the Time, and Responds to Human Emotion

In recent years, some scientists have suggested that our modern world has outgrown the need for spiritually based explanations of life's mysteries. In the German news magazine *Der Spiegel,* renowned theoretical physicist Stephen Hawking illustrated this viewpoint when he stated, "What I have done is to show that it is possible for the way the universe began to be determined by the laws of science. . . .This doesn't prove that there is no God, only that God is not necessary."[11] Recent discoveries in the rapidly evolving field of quantum physics now suggest that Hawking's "laws of science" and the "God" of spiritual traditions may, in fact, be related in surprising and unexpected ways. Ultimately, we may discover that they are references to precisely the same force!

From the studies documenting that many atoms may coexist in exactly the same place, at exactly the same instant in time without bumping into one another,[12] to the Australian National University's announcement of the teleportation of a beam of light (dismantling and then reassembling the beam at another location),[13] and the phenomenon of "twinned photons" (two units of light created from the same parent) mirroring one another's behavior even when separated by distances of many miles,[14] in the last years of the 20th century it was clear that the very foundation of our worldview was changing in a dramatic way.

What could possibly account for such observations? New research began to suggest that the events of creation, from tiny subatomic particles to massive and distant galaxies, are somehow related. Acknowledging the existence of a previously unknown form of energy, scientists suddenly found themselves in the uncharted territory of a world where the line between traditional science and the mystical world of unseen forces became less clear.

Given names such as the "Mind of God," "Nature's Mind," and the "Quantum Hologram," this previously unrecognized field of energy is described as a force that is everywhere all of the time, has been in existence from the time of the Beginning, and exhibits a form of intelligence that responds to our deepest emotions. In modern terms, such descriptions sound strikingly similar to ancient references to the presence of God.

Perhaps the power of the names only begins to hint at the magnitude of the discoveries that this force has yet to reveal. The implications of such a subtle and ever-present force offers clues into the mysteries of bilocating atoms, communication between atoms over great distances, and the health of our bodies.[15] At the same time, the acknowledgment of such a field offers a much-needed bridge between modern science and ancient descriptions of precisely such a force.

In light of the new discoveries in the quantum world, there has been a willingness to revisit the wisdom that is preserved as our earliest accounts of creation. While the languages are obviously from another time, the themes that they describe are remarkably similar to the late 20th-century revelations of science. Much the same way that a single unifying force is now considered key in the study of physics, the principle of a single all-powerful force at the foundation of life also weaves continuity among the oldest and most diverse accounts of life's origins. With such a power in mind, a closer look into the edited and restored texts of ancient Christian, Hebrew, and Gnostic literature offers additional clues into the elusive distinction that sets us apart from other life.

"And Man Became a Living Soul"

One of the first keys to the mystery of our uniqueness is the distinction that these texts make between the human body and the spark of God's essence that animates the body. Through verses found in the restored versions of biblical translations, we are offered clues to this mystery as statements declaring that "YaHWeH . . . formed the human spirit . . ."[16] and the Lord YaHWeH declared, "I shall put my spirit in you . . ."[17] Although such accounts may be accurate, they're lacking in the kind of detail that helps us to make sense of our mysterious existence. From the "lost" Gnostic texts mentioned previously, however, we're given even clearer insight into the subtleties of the human soul and how it came to be.

Among the cache of documents recovered in the Nag Hammadi Library was a rare text of the *Mandaeans,* the only Gnostic sect to survive into modern times. Distinguishing "humankind" as a life that is foreign to this world, the Mandaean texts are focused upon the uniqueness of our experience on Earth. They begin their narration by describing the creation of Adam in a text entitled *Creation of the World and the Alien Man.*

The text makes an unmistakable distinction between Adam's body and the soul that enters his body after it is formed. It is only after Adam is infused with the mysterious force of "Life" that his body awakens and he is animated. Echoing other Gnostic texts, which depict Adam's creation as a collective effort among the angels of the Heavens, the manuscript begins by stating that, under God's direction, "they created Adam and laid him down, but there was no soul in him. When they created Adam, they were unable to cast a soul into him."[18] It is only after "the radiance of Life spoke in him [Adam]" that he "opened his eyes in the bodily trunk."[19]

Another Gnostic text, known as *The Hypostasis of the Archons*, is a mystical interpretation of the first books of Genesis. It is believed to date to the third century C.E.[20] Contained in the narration is an additional description of Adam's creation, this one clearly distinguishing the living essence of Adam's spirit as distinct and separate from his body. "And the Spirit came forth . . . it descended and came to dwell within him, and that Man [Adam] became a living soul. It called his name Adam. . . ."[21]

For even greater clarity into the precise nature of Adam's spirit, we're left to glean clues from the foundations of the Hebrew and Christian traditions, such as the Talmud.

Humankind: The Wisdom of Angels in Bodies of Earth

The Haggadah, for example, in addition to stating that humankind was created specifically as a bridge between the worlds of Heaven and Earth, describes *precisely which qualities* of the angels of Heaven, and creatures of Earth, have merged to create the species of "man." Specifically, we have inherited four qualities from the angels that contribute to our uniqueness.[22] They are:

- our "power of speech,"

- our "discriminating intellect,"

- our "upright walk," and

- the "glance" of our eyes.

Our "power of speech" represents a twofold power that we share with no other life on Earth. Science has demonstrated that vibration affects our physical world in very profound ways. From the magnitude of force that devastates entire cities during an earthquake, to the lesser force that heals our bodies through powerful emotion, the effects result from vibration. Speech allows us to make our vibrations audible. Through our ability to precisely "flutter" the diaphragm in our abdomen and force just the right amount of air between the muscles of our vocal cords, we create the powerful vibrations that heal our bodies and change the world. Additionally, through our words, we preserve the memory of our past, while sharing with others the experiences that move our souls.

It is the power of our "discriminating intellect" that allows us to choose when, how, and even if we share our beliefs with others through our gift of speech. Through our intellect, we may consider the consequences of our actions before we act, rather than living in a state of perpetual reaction, attempting to "fix" the choices that we regret.

Through the gift of our "upright walk," we free the use of our hands and arms, allowing the mobility to perform the actions that we deem worthy of our time. Through our erect posture, we are given the ability to build our world, express our deepest emotions, while caring for one another and ourselves—and in a way afforded to no other creature on Earth. From the perspective of life mirroring consciousness, our upright posture may also be viewed as a metaphor for our ability to "stand tall" and "rise above" the trials and challenges of the earth beneath our feet.

The "glance of our eyes" is perhaps the most telling of our gifts from the angels. It is said that through our eyes we are given "windows to the soul." When we look into one another's eyes, there is much more occurring than simply a process of light and optics. Through the way that we choose to see others and the way that we permit others to see us, we exchange tremendous amounts of information regarding our state of mind, health, feelings, and desires in a way that is unique to us alone. From the angels' gift of the "glance," we each have the power to heal or destroy, love or hate, through the message that we convey.

Balancing the traits that we share with the angels, we also have four characteristics that we've inherited from "the beast of the field"[23]:

1. We "eat and drink."

2. We "secrete the waste matter in our bodies."

3. We "propagate" our kind.

4. We "die."

It's clear that the authors of such texts believed, that as descendants of Adam, we carry the spark that links us with our Creator in a way shared by no other species.

Perhaps some of the greatest detail regarding the nature of the soul itself may be found in the Haggadah as well. With titles such as *The Angels and the Creation of Man* and *The Creation of Adam,* the text offers a narrative of what Adam was like after he received God's essence as his soul. In describing the qualities of God's spark, the text makes a clear and unmistakable reference to the gender of humankind's soul. "For God had fashioned his [Adam's] soul with particular care. *She is the image of God,* and as God fills the world, so the soul fills the human body" [author's italics].[24]

Through this passage, we're given two important clues about God's nature. First, we are told that Adam's body was imbued with a force that was feminine by its very design. While this does not prevent other spiritual aspects of Adam from being masculine, the phrase states clearly that the essence infused into the first of our kind was feminine. Second, contrary to traditional interpretations that identify God as "He," the passage implies that the feminine nature of Adam's soul is, at least in part, identical to that of his Creator.

While such texts may call into question God's gender on Earth, from these examples it is clear that the "spirit" of God is a separate and distinct force that merged with Adam *following* the creation of his body. In the absence of this level of detail in conventional biblical translations, our insight into the nature of body and spirit is generally limited to the familiar passage in the King James version of Genesis: "The Lord God formed man of dust from the ground, and breathed into his nostrils the breath of life; and man became a living being."[25]

Obviously describing the same moment in the creation of human life, this phrase, combined with the older and more specific passages, contributes to our overall understanding of the uniqueness at the core of our existence. Through the mysterious power of our soul, we are offered the opportunity to improve our lives and leave a better world for those who follow in a way afforded to no other creature on Earth.

God's Name in Our Bodies: What Does It Mean?

Perhaps the reason for our uniqueness is that our bodies are designed specifically as containers of God's "spark." Although all life is made from elements that equate to the name of God, ancient sources are clear that it is only within human life that God imbues his personal spirit. The Haggadah supports this distinction, clarifying that man is the only creature under Heaven in whose formation God physically and personally intervened.

"He [man] is the only one who was created by the *hand* of God."[26]

All other creatures, the text continues, were created "from the *word* of God." With this distinction, the body of each human is described as a "microcosm, the whole world in miniature." Conversely, the text identifies the world around us as a mirror of our collective nature, "The world in turn is a reflex of man."[27] It is only in the last years of the 20th century that modern science has confirmed that the world around us does, in fact, mirror our deepest states of emotion.[28] Once again, a powerful concept is offered through a few eloquent words in the language of another time.

If we venture beyond the conventional wisdom suggesting that passages such as those of the Haggadah are simply metaphors for our past, they offer new insight into precisely what it means to carry God's name in each cell of our bodies. The common denominator in the ancient descriptions is that Adam, as the first of our kind, was imbued with a gift that was unmatched throughout the universe.

Through the primal act of creating human life, God shared a part of himself as he "breathed his breath" into our species. In doing so, we assumed the role of "vessels," uniquely endowed with the divine spirit. To this day, our role continues, as the ancient secret to creating such a container is preserved and passed on through the miracle of each new human life. Perhaps the answer to the mystery of what makes us different remains hidden within the tiny molecule that holds life's code itself: our DNA.

From this perspective, our genetic code may be considered as an ancient recipe for the quality of container necessary to hold God's essence. Through phrases that leave little doubt as to their meaning, many spiritual traditions emphasize that our bodies are the specialized structures built to contain Heaven in the realm of Earth. Just as physical temples are built to house the holy space within them, throughout Hebrew, Gnostic, and Christian texts our bodies are referred to as the "temples" that house God's holy essence.

In the New Testament, for example, we see references to our role as temples offered subtly at first. As the mystery of the teachings unfold, the references become more direct. The Gospel of John records that Jesus "spake of the temple of his body."[29] In the third chapter of Corinthians, the reference is more direct, while posed as a leading question to those listening. "Know ye not that ye are the temple of God, and that the spirit of God dwelleth in you?"[30] In the sixth chapter of the same book, the theme becomes a direct statement: *"Your body is the temple of the Holy Ghost which is in you"*[31] [author's italics]. Having clearly made the distinction between the body of man and the Holy Spirit that resides within the body of man, both canonized and Gnostic texts agree that only the human form possesses the ability to house God's spirit.

Elaborating upon the description of our bodies as structures housing God's essence, the Kabbalah invites us even deeper into the mystery, describing how the containers of God's light (the "vessels" described in Chapter 5) shattered and fell into the lower spiritual realms of Earth. Here in the Earthly realms where darkness and light coexist, the vessels reformed and were able to communicate their light to the world of humans.

As an expression of the power of creation, we alone participate in the events of our world, create the quality of our lives, and have the discernment to choose in a way that makes us better people. It is only within our world that each day has a purpose, a beginning, and an end, and may be judged as success or failure. Within each moment of each day, we affirm or deny the gift of our uniqueness through the way we live our lives. As we encounter the greatest challenges of history, the message within each of our cells is a reminder of our power and uniqueness.

A great irony of our time in history is that the same technology that holds the power to destroy all that we have achieved also holds the power to reveal that our lives are an expression of something vast and wonderful. The words within each of our cells have never been subjected to the edits, deletions, and interpretations of conventional texts. The message remains intact, just as it was on the first day of our existence.

When the events of our lives test us beyond reason, the message within our cells stands as a living and immutable symbol, a touchstone reminding us:

- We are not alone.

- We are here "on purpose," as the result of an intentional act of creation.

- We are inextricably linked to one another and all life.

- We share a unique trait—the essence of God—in a way that sets us apart from all other life on Earth.

Life: By Choice or by Chance?

It is in recognizing the odds against life originating by chance that we may fully grasp the meaning of the message within our cells. Chapter 1 offered a definition of living systems from a chemical point of view, and described life as a "behavior pattern that certain chemical systems attain when they reach a certain level of complexity."[32] In a later portion of the same text, the authors further refine their definition, suggesting that life is the result of "complex, organized chemical systems that propagate, grow, metabolize, use their environment and protect themselves from it, and evolve and change in response to long-term changes in the environment."[33] While such sterile-sounding definitions of life may describe *what* life does, they fail to address *how* life has come to exist.

Whether life has arisen by chance or through an intentional series of ordered events has remained a subject of controversy since the birth of the scientific method approximately 400 years ago. The question is this: Did random chemical reactions within the primordial "soup" of creation lead to the first living cells? Or has another, yet unidentified force intervened to play a role in organizing the chemicals of the world to form the life of our bodies?

At the time of this writing, there remains no viable theory describing a chemical origin for life—the creation of life from nonliving matter has never been scientifically documented under laboratory conditions. In fact, scientists acknowledge that the odds of life arising purely by chance are slim at best. Nobel laureate Francis Crick commented upon the many, complex, and varied conditions that would have to be in place for the conditions of the first glimmering of life to appear. "An honest man, armed with all the knowledge available to us now, could only state that that in some sense, the origin of life appears at the moment to be almost a miracle, so many are the conditions which would have had to have been satisfied to get it going."[34] In terms of sheer chance and probability, the odds are staggering.

Noted British astronomer Sir Fred Hoyle and Cardiff University of Wales mathematician/astronomer Chandra Wickramasinghe have given us a context for just how great such odds really are. Assuming that a number of factors supporting the simplest forms of life were in place at some point in our long-forgotten past, they estimate that the odds for a random combination of molecules producing even the simplest life is somewhere in the neighborhood of 1 in $10^{40,000}$ (that is 1 with 40,000 zeros following it!).[35] Even if we reduced this number by a factor of one-half, the odds that elements randomly combined to produce complex life over the estimated 4.5 billion years of Earth's history are exceedingly small.

In his classic text *Molecular Biology of the Gene*,[36] James Watson describes the uniqueness and mystery of living cells. "We must immediately admit that the structure of the cell will never be understood in the same way as that of water or glucose molecules. Not only will the exact structure of most macromolecules within the cell remain unsolved, but their relative locations within cells can only be vaguely known."[37]

There appears to be *something* about the process within the miracle factory of each cell of our bodies that defies explanation through conventional modern wisdom. From such observations, we begin to sense just how unlikely it is that we are the result of a "fluke" of creation. Thus, the message encoded within each of our cells takes on even greater meaning.

Order As a Sign of Intelligence

In nature, *order* is often seen as a sign of intelligence. The existence of predictable and repeatable patterns that can be described by universal formulas is an example of what is meant by the word *order*.

During candid interviews late in his life, Albert Einstein shared his belief of an underlying order in creation, as well as his sense of where such order comes from. During one such conversation, he confided, "I see a pattern but my imagination cannot picture the maker of the pattern . . . we all dance to a mysterious tune, intoned in the distance by an invisible piper."[38] In our search for meaning in life, the very presence of order is often viewed as a sign that something greater is "out there."

It's precisely this kind of order, for example, that was observed among the 60,000 images photographed from the Viking mission to Mars in 1976. The discovery of what appear to be artificial structures on the planet's surface has led to an investigation and controversy that continues today.[39] While the two-, three-, four-, and five-sided pyramidal structures, located among perfectly aligned trenches that stretch for miles, are obvious to the trained eye, the question remains: Are they the product of nature, or the remnants of intentional construction from long ago? While the solution to this mystery may require a manned mission to answer definitively, the presence of key mathematical principles embodied within the structures themselves[40] certainly suggests that they are the product of a willful design.

In a similar fashion, the discovery of order at the very foundation of life may be considered as a sign of intelligence within that life. The revelation that the four elements of life represent key letters of an ancient alphabet, as well as the fact that that alphabet forms a message, carries the degree of order underlying life to an even greater magnitude. Add to these already powerful indications of intent the recognition that each cell of our bodies carries precisely the *same message,* and the significance of this code becomes perhaps greater than the discovery itself.

The presence of God's name encoded as each cell of life preserves not only a special message, but the message carries a special meaning as well.

The Mystery of "God Is One"

Historically, we emerge into our world as the result of the union between a man and a woman, our *mother* and our *father*. Whether by choice or by chance, it is the merging of the DNA contributed by each of their bodies that results in the new life within our mother's womb. One of the mysteries of life and now made even more mysterious by the advent of human cloning is whether or not a sperm and an egg are all that is required to create a human life. Are they enough, or is something more required?

Specifically, what is the unseen force that gives the "command" for cells to grow and divide in precisely the right way at just the right time to produce a healthy baby boy or girl? Precisely who is the "piper" that Einstein referred to as the source of our cosmic "tune"? A closer look at birth, *from the ancient perspective of number,* may offer us a clue.

The following "equation" representing the union of mother and father to produce the human body as Adam is complete only when the numeric value of God is added to it. Chapter 4 revealed that the Hebrew word for the first born of our species "Adam" (written without the vowels) is ADM. Applying the specified number values for each letter, results in the following:

$$\underline{A} \qquad \underline{D} \qquad \underline{M}$$
$$(Alef) = 1 \quad (Dalet) = 4 \quad (Mem) = 40$$

Summing these individual values produces the new combined value of 45, while an additional summing further reduces the value of Adam to 9.

$$1 \quad + \quad 4 \quad + \quad 40 \quad = \quad 45$$
$$4 \quad + \quad 5 \quad = \quad 9$$

In numeric terms, 9 *is* Adam. Through the language of number, we may now explore Adam's relationship to his mother and father. To determine *how* mother and father are related to the 9 of Adam, however, it is first necessary to find their hidden values, as well.

The Hebrew word for *mother* is spelled as the consonants EM.[41]

$$\underline{E} \qquad \underline{M}$$
$$(Alef) = 1 \quad (Mem) = 40$$

Summing these individual values produces the combined value of 41, which may be further reduced to 5. A similar process for "father," spelled as AV,[42] results in:

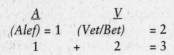
$$\begin{array}{ccc} \underline{A} & & \underline{V} \\ (Alef) = 1 & (Vet/Bet) & = 2 \\ 1 & + \quad 2 & = 3 \end{array}$$

Summing these numbers creates a new value of 3. With the words of *father, mother,* and *Adam* now converted to the common language of number, we may compare "apples to apples" and examine the words on a deeper level.

As Adam (humankind) results from the union of father and mother, we would expect his name to have a value that is equal to the two combined. *This is not the case,* however, when we add the 3 of father to the 5 of mother. The simple operation produces a combined value of 8, which is one less than the 9 of Adam. This apparent mystery is solved through a single passage in the Torah and the insight, once again, of Rabbi Benjamin Blech.

Although many investigators interpret passages in ancient tradition as metaphor, more often than not references in the Torah are specific. Rabbi Blech points out how it is clearly stated in Genesis, for example, that God has a number value. "The Lord is our God, *the Lord is One*"[43] [author's italics]. To some scholars, this is a direct declaration that the numeric value of God is the number 1. Within "1," however, lies an even deeper mystery.

Completing the Equation of Life

In the Hebrew language, the number 1 is associated with the first letter of the alphabet, the *Alef* (א). The deeper reasons and complex issues underlying the creation of *Alef* itself are the subject of entire studies and certainly worthy of further exploration. For the purposes of our mystery as to why "mother" and "father" are one number short of creating "Adam," we'll limit our discussion. By examining the origin of *Alef,* the mystery of the passage "The Lord is One" is solved.

As Rabbi Blech reveals, the ancient letter *Alef* is actually formed from the union of two separate letters, one of them being used two times. In the upper right and lower left corner of *Alef* is found the smallest and first letter of God's name, the *Yod* (י). Between these occurrences of *Yod* the two are divided by a slanted *Vav* (ו). If we separately consider each of the letters that make *Alef*, we solve the mystery.

In the familiar form of analyzing Hebrew letters as numbers, each *Yod* is given the value of 10, while the *Vav* is assigned the value of 6. Summing these individual values (10 + 10 + 6) gives a new combined value of 26—*precisely the same value* held in the ancient name of God: YHVH! In addition to directly representing the number 1 in the Hebrew alphabet, *Alef* is also an indirect, coded reference to God's personal name and presence. "One" is literally equal to "God."

Through the rule of number relationships that we previously explored in Chapter 4, two words that are related in value are also related in nature. From this perspective, "God" is the value that is missing in the equation of mother and father to give Adam wholeness. In addition to the union between the earthly quantities contributed by man and woman, the spirit of God must be present for Adam (humankind) to be complete.

THE EQUATION OF LIFE

Mother	+	Father	+	God	=	Adam
5	+	3	+	1	=	9

More than a message added to life as an afterthought, the fact that the code *is* life tells us that God exists *as* our bodies. What we see as atoms of carbon, oxygen, hydrogen, and nitrogen, the "stuff" of life, *is* God. While the code may not describe precisely *who* God is, it tells us in terms of our own science that we cannot separate ourselves or any life in our world from the presence of a higher power.

With the familiar eloquence that poet William Blake is noted for, he summarizes our relationship to God in a few brief words:

"God is man and exists in us and we in him." Beyond simply describing our relationship to God, Blake continues that God exists as humankind so that humankind may make the choices each day that bring us closer to the perfection of our Creator. "God became as we are, that we may be as he is." By embracing the wisdom of this statement, we are granted the power to transcend the challenges of our lives and any differences that have ever divided us.

CHAPTER 7 SUMMARY

- In the original language of the Torah, we are told that God halted creation before it was complete and commanded humankind to "walk before Me and become perfect" (Genesis 1:17). Scholars suggest that this statement may refer less to our perfection as bodies and more to the spiritual essence within our bodies fulfilling its potential.

- An analysis of the number values representing the DNA in our cells (YHVG) and the values that represent the name of God (YHVH) reveals that, even though we share in the attributes of God's name, we are not equal to God.

- Many scientists, including those responsible for the discovery of the genetic code, suggest that the probability that life has arisen by "chance" borders on the miraculous. There appears to be a force in life for which science has yet to account.

- In nature, the appearance of order that may be described by universal mathematical formulas may be viewed as the sign of an underlying intelligence.

- The facts that the code of life embodies such a high degree of order and that within that order there exists a message, suggests an intelligence of an even greater magnitude.

- In the Hebrew equation of life, the simple union of "mother" and "father" is not enough to produce "Adam," the first of our species. Something is missing. It is only when the numeric presence of God is added to the equation that the numbers balance and the formula is complete.

"People do not fight because they are wicked. . . .
War is waged primarily for the sake of what
is central . . . bread. Help the needy.
Feed the starving. Assuage the pain
of those who are hungry. . . .
It is the means of preventing war
and securing the great blessing of peace."

— RABBI BENJAMIN BLECH

Chapter Eight

WHAT HAVE WE LEARNED?
Surviving Our Future Through the Lessons of Our Past

With the recent turn-of-the-century celebrations still fresh in our minds, many scientists, organizations, and concerned individuals are now asking the single question upon which so many other questions hinge: Will we survive as a species for another 100 years? Specifically, will we survive another century of genetically modifying our foods and enhancing our bodies, and creating industries that deplete the life from our oceans, rivers, and forests? Perhaps most important is whether or not we dare to continue unleashing the awesome power of nature as the most lethal weapon known in the history of humankind.

Until the mid-20th century, it made little sense to ask such questions. Today, that has changed. As a result of scientific innovations developed during World War II, including those of quantum physics, genetics, and miniaturized electronics, our technological choices now carry consequences that will last for hundreds of years and many subsequent generations.

The lingering question for our future is less about developing the technologies themselves than to the wisdom of implementing them in our lives. Just because we have the *ability* to modify the weather patterns over vast regions of the earth and create new forms of life, for instance, *do we have the right* to do such things?

Playing God: What Gives Us the Right?

From the mid 1970s until the early 1990s, I was privileged to work among brilliant scientists and engineers developing some of the most advanced technology in recorded history. For corporations and universities alike, this was a time of tremendous momentum, as our nation was redefining its dependence upon foreign oil, as well as struggling to maintain its superiority during the Cold War and in the space program. Not surprisingly, the period of such intense research was accompanied by equally intense introspection. In a very real sense, scientists were exploring the limits of their new-found capabilities to alter life and our planet at a level historically left to God and nature.

It was the responsibility that comes with such awesome power that often sparked heated debates questioning our moral and ethical right to use such technologies—debates that I enthusiastically joined at every opportunity. Fueling the discussions that erupted in front of vending machines and drinking fountains, and which often continued into restrooms and cafeterias, arguments generally followed one of two schools of thought.

One way of thinking held that our ability to "tweak" the forces of nature was, in and of itself, the license to explore those technologies to their fullest. In other words, because we have the capability to modify weather patterns and create new forms of matter and life, we should do so to see where the technology might lead. This line of reasoning frequently led to yet another level of justification, suggesting that if we were not meant to do such things, we would never have discovered the secrets that made them possible.

A second school of thought was more conservative, suggesting that just because we have the ability to engineer life and nature does not necessarily mean that we have the right to exercise our power. To those supporting this path of reasoning, the forces of nature represent sacred "laws" that should not be tampered with. To customize the gene codes of our children before they're born, and to adjust global weather patterns to suit our needs, is "off limits," they argued, and it violates an ancient and unspoken trust.

Although it's not necessarily spelled out word for word, to cross the line from *user* to *creator* places us in a role where we are competing with the power of God.

The question then becomes one of what gives us the right to do so. This argument was often accompanied by the metaphor of numbers on an automobile's speedometer. Just because the dial may indicate speeds of up to 160 miles per hour, this does not necessarily imply that we should drive our vehicles that fast!

Perhaps it is precisely the metaphor of a speedometer that illustrates yet a third line of reasoning. If a speedometer indicates that a vehicle is capable of traveling at 160 miles per hour, in all likelihood someone will attempt to do so at some point in time. It appears that it is inherent in human nature to test boundaries and carry capabilities to extremes. The key, however, is that when we do test such limits, we also have the power to determine the time, place, and conditions of the test.

We can find a deserted stretch of road with a good surface on a day when the weather is dry and minimize the possibility of injuring ourselves and others—or we can act on an impulse and test the limits of a vehicle on a busy freeway, endangering ourselves and risking the lives of those around us. In either scenario, the boundaries are tested. One is done responsibly, the other carelessly. Perhaps the same principle applies to the way we push the limits to engineer the forces of creation.

During my time in the defense industry, it wasn't uncommon for after-hours conversations to focus on the development of weapon technologies. At the end of the Cold War, when the nuclear arsenals of the superpowers were being reduced, invariably these discussions would lead to the question of what technologies would replace nuclear arms in the future. Ranging from powerful ground-based lasers that can be bounced from orbiting mirrors in space to targets on Earth, to neutron bombs designed to take "only" life, while leaving buildings, automobiles, and homes intact, only one decade earlier the discussion of such now-serious scenarios would have sounded like science fiction.

In addition to these externally based offensive weapons, the discussions would sometimes include internal, defensive technologies as well. In the event, for example, that a rogue power unleashed a biological agent upon unsuspecting populations, could we genetically engineer a change within ourselves to make us immune to the bacteria or virus? Because the technology already exists for each of these scenarios, and others too numerous to do justice to in this book, the debate didn't center on whether or not they were possible—rather, on whether or not we should develop them.

If we reengineer our DNA in response to a near-term biological threat, for instance, how would such a choice affect our bodies' ability to protect us against new threats in the future? What are the long-term consequences of changing the genetic formula for an entire population, one that has taken thousands of years to achieve the successful code that we have today? Is it possible that we could inadvertently threaten the survival of our species through the ignorance of applying what was believed to be a life-saving measure without fully understanding its consequences?

During the days of the Cold War, these are the kind of questions that were asked almost on a daily basis by those whose job it was to bring precisely such possibilities to fruition. More than a decade after the end of the Cold War, they remain among the most urgent questions facing technology-based societies at present, questions that must be answered as we continue our quest into the uncharted territory of engineering nature and life. Today, we find ourselves in a world where we have entrusted science and scientists to lead our journey of exploration, a journey from which there is little likelihood that we will turn back. Our hope is that while we are learning to engineer the forces of creation, we survive our learning process.

10,000 Intelligent Civilizations Possible: Where Are They?

Is it possible that somewhere in the cosmos, or even in Earth's remote past, other civilizations have undergone similar experiences and asked similar questions with regard to their advancement?

Could the technological choices of ancient societies have had consequences so devastating that the civilizations no longer exist? If so, is it possible, as well, that we can learn from their experiences and perhaps avoid the mistakes that led to their absence today?

In 1961, astronomer Frank Drake formulated the now-famous Drake's equation, estimating that there could be as many as 10,000 intelligent civilizations that have formed within the 13- to 14-billion-year history of our universe. With such a number in mind, scientists and researchers are now asking the obvious question: If so many intelligent civilizations are possible, where are they? If even a fraction of those 10,000 intelligent civilizations actually exist, it is reasonable to expect that they have discovered the universal principles of nature that govern time, space, and matter. It is also reasonable to expect that they have incorporated those principles, just as we have, into their way of life. For these reasons, it makes perfect sense to expect that evidence of those technologies would be detected here on Earth in the form of communication signals. To date, no such signals have been acknowledged.

Carl Sagan, astronomer and colleague to Drake, speculated that there might be two reasons for the apparent absence of such signals today. First, he suggested the possibility that we are among the first civilizations to have reached the point in our evolution where we have the ability to engineer the forces of nature—a time that he refers to as "technological adolescence." Due to archaeological evidence that may not have been available to Sagan during his lifetime, this possibility now appears unlikely.[1]

The second possibility is that other intelligent species have, in fact, existed in the past, followed a path similar to ours, and no longer exist. Sagan suggested that the reason we do not detect evidence of these advanced life forms is that they did not survive their learning curve, and destroyed themselves through their misuse of the forces of nature. If this turns out to be the case, then we may be at an exceptionally critical point in the history of our species— in danger of making the same mistakes and suffering the same consequences. This possibility illustrates yet another consideration.

If, in fact, we are living in a period of technological adolescence, then we must mature through that period into the responsibilities

that such power affords us. Not unlike the universal experience of children transitioning into adulthood, through our adolescence we must find a way to navigate the changes in our lives and survive our transition. As parents of young people will attest, when their children burst into puberty, the transition marks a time of confusion and adjustment.

Seemingly overnight, the children's bodies blossom into adulthood, accompanied by all of the pressures and responsibilities that define an adult in our society. In their own way, each young person must make sense of what is happening to them, and they must do it quickly in order to survive.

In much the same way, through our collective time of technological adolescence we must find a way to balance the power of our discoveries with the values of life and nature. In an equally similar fashion, we must do so quickly. Referring once again to our child-to-adult analogy, a pitfall of puberty is that, for many young people, their time of change is accompanied by a feeling that may best be described as that of "invulnerability." Along with their newfound powers, their sense of being indestructible frequently leads to carelessness, as they test the limits of authority and reason. Sadly, it is the feeling of invincibility that is believed to be a key factor in the number-one killer of young people today: automobile accidents attributed to a driver's taking unnecessary risks.[2]

The parallels between the adolescence of children and of our technologically based adolescence are certainly worth considering. Now, more than simply a philosophical discussion, our survival hinges upon our ability to recognize the choices that affirm or deny life in our world.

Reflecting upon the magnitude of the crises that we now face as a global family, futurist Barbara Marx Hubbard clarifies the urgency of our lesson in very simple terms, describing our situation as one in which "If we don't learn [that we are all connected, we are all related, that it's all one living body], we won't breathe!"[3]

Our Greatest Threat

In their 2000 State of the World report, The Worldwatch Institute noted: "The bright promise of a new century is clouded by unprecedented threats to the stability of our natural world."[4] Nearly without fail, the threats cited in the report stem from recent advances in science, and the way that powerful technologies have been unleashed in our lives. From issues of providing enough food and building sustainable economies, to the uncertainties of gene-based technology and the spread of weapons that can render regions of the earth uninhabitable for hundreds of generations, it is clear that humankind is on a destructive course with regard to the survival of our species.

In the late 20th century, many scientists, researchers, and organizations viewed the 1990s as the completion of a cycle and an opportunity to evaluate our mistakes as well as our achievements as a global community. In June of 1995, during a conference in Killarney, Ireland, pioneering psychiatrist Stanislav Grof presented a paper that echoed the concern of many individuals regarding the deteriorating conditions that threaten our world.[5] Among the immediate dangers cited by Grof were those of the "industrial pollution of soil, water, and air; the threat of nuclear waste and accidents; destruction of the ozone layer; the greenhouse effect; possible loss of planetary oxygen through reckless deforestation and poisoning of the ocean plankton; and the dangers of toxic additives in our food and drinks."[6] Mirroring the sentiment of many other scientists, any one of the conditions mentioned by Grof is enough to signal a real and present danger to the life-giving systems of the earth. The fact that all are present at the same time in history presents the potential of a threat that is almost unimaginable.

In his classic paper on the Search for Extraterrestrial Intelligence (SETI),[7] Carl Sagan describes a similar series of scenarios, each contributing to the eventual collapse of global societies, as we know them, if left unchecked. "There are some who look on our global problems here on earth—at our vast national antagonisms, our nuclear arsenals, our growing populations, the disparity

between the poor and the affluent, shortages of food and resources, and our inadvertent alterations of the natural environment of our planet—and conclude that we live in a system which has suddenly become unstable, a system which is destined to soon collapse."[8] He continues his "state-of-the-world" observations with another viewpoint, however, drawn from precisely the same data: "There are others who believe that our problems are soluble, that humanity is still in its childhood, that one day we will grow up."[9]

Interestingly, when we examine the many conditions that have been identified as our greatest threats, we discover a common thread that links them. That thread is humankind. Each of the situations cited by Sagan, the Worldwatch Institute, Grof, and others describes potentially catastrophic scenarios. Additionally, each describes humankind as the only source of the threat.

From such statistics, it is clear that, at the present time, we pose our own greatest danger to the survival of our species! It is equally clear that we alone have the power to ensure the survival of our species and the livability of our world for future generations.

IN WHAT IS PERHAPS one of the most prophetic scenes in the motion picture *Contact,* Dr. Arroway finds herself being questioned by an international panel of experts to determine who will best represent the values of Earth's citizens in the event of extraterrestrial contact. As part of the selection process, she's presented with a hypothetical scenario. Given the opportunity to ask a single question of the presumably advanced civilization that she expects to encounter, what would her question be? Following a brief pause, she thoughtfully responds that she would ask them how they had survived their time of technological adolescence without destroying themselves.

The parallels between this theme in *Contact* and the events unfolding in our world today are unmistakable. Although not necessarily triggered by extraterrestrial contact, as a civilization we are struggling with precisely the same questions and concerns that Dr. Arroway reveals to the panel. How are we to survive the capabilities and awesome power that science and technology have unleashed, especially in the presence of our diversity, and so many different ideas of what our world should look like?

This theme is not a new one in the history of humankind. It is significant to note that in the oldest records of human civilization, rather than tales of miracles and the beauty of life, we are offered a glimpse into the ancient and ever-human struggle with power and its use to back beliefs and ideas. Today, in addition to the environmental problems that have resulted from the evolution of industry, we're faced with a single crisis that may, perhaps, be even more fundamental to our survival.

Along with the hazards that now threaten the natural world, we live in the growing shadow of weapon technologies with the power to destroy civilization and render our planet uninhabitable to all but the simplest forms of life for centuries. The willingness to explore such technologies, the precision with which the resulting weapons have been created, and the ease with which their use is now justified—and even believed to be survivable—creates what is without doubt the single greatest threat to our survival today.

From Ignorance to Intention: Finding Our Way from the Brink of Destruction

The destruction of our planet's life-support systems—the oceans, atmosphere, rivers, lakes, and forests—has resulted largely from our past ignorance of the damage that fossil fuels and chemicals can do to our world. While there have always been "insiders" with access to the dangers of specific technologies, and power and greed have undoubtedly played a role in the way new technologies are implemented, for the most part the general population has been unaware of the consequences that supporting resource-depleting industries may carry.

Balancing two-family careers, PTA meetings, and soccer practice, the average American family has trusted government and industry to maintain safe radiation levels at our nuclear power plants and assure that the water, steam, and residues released from mines and factories are safe. As consumers, few have looked beyond the shelves of their neighborhood malls and supermarkets until recently to see where the products that make life easier for them and their families really come from.

From this perspective, the damage that our planet has experienced may be viewed as largely unintentional, the by-product and consequence of our changing views of progress, economies, and our relationship to our world. Now that the dangers of environment-depleting products have been identified, and the scientific and indigenous predictions validated, we can work together to make changes and "right the wrongs." While this is certainly no excuse for the catastrophic effects (including oil spills, nuclear melt-downs, chemical-plant explosions, and toxic dumping) that have occurred, it serves to clearly distinguish the threat of environmental tragedies from the growing threat of mass-effect weapons, and from the thinking that has led to their creation.

A World Still at War

For many people, the end of the Cold War in the late 1980s signaled the beginning of a relative peace in our world. For the first time in nearly a generation, the constant threat of a nuclear war appeared to lift, and the world breathed a collective sigh of relief as the U.S. and Russia forged new relationships and explored new ways to work together in the post–Cold War era. Although there were no "declared" wars raging on a worldwide scale during this time, the relative peace was precisely that, however: *relative*. In addition to the highly visible struggle for land between Israel and Palestine in the Middle East, at the end of the 1990s, *there were at least 20 other nations actively involved in wars*.[10] Although often referred to only as "conflicts," these hostilities nonetheless have resulted in the same suffering and casualties that are the hallmarks of declared wars.

Receiving little attention from mainstream media, some of the conflicts stem from ancient disagreements and have continued for decades, while others are relatively recent, with death tolls already numbering in the millions. By 1999, for example, the war in the Sudan between northern Muslims and southern Christians had resulted in an estimated 1.9 million fatalities, many of whom included civilians.[11] At the end of the 20th century, nearly one-half of the world's undeclared wars were raging on the continent of Africa, with the remainder in "hotspots" such as Bosnia, Kosovo, Macedonia, Chechnya, Azerbaijan, Tajikistan, Kashmir, India, the Philippines, Indonesia, Tibet, and the Middle East. From civil wars and fights for independence to religious wars and ethnic cleansings, the period perceived by so many as a time of peace in reality has been anything but peaceful.

Following the tragic events of September 11, 2001, the threat of terrorism has focused worldwide attention on countries and cities that many in the West had never heard of before. Suddenly, regions such as Kabul and Tora Bora in Afghanistan became household names, as U.S. troops were deployed in the rugged mountains that serve as a border to neighboring Pakistan. Supporting the principle of preemptive security, within a few short months the search for terrorists primarily harbored in Muslim-based countries changed the landscape of world peace in a way that is unprecedented in recent history.

In the words of Harvard professor Samuel P. Huntington, "The makings of a possible 'clash of civilizations' are present."[12] Perhaps more than at any time in recent history, the world now appears to be divided on how to deal with perceived threats to national interests, the security of continents, and, in the case of countries such as Israel, the very survival of their way of life.

It is within the context of such a world that technology, once again, has become a dominant factor in the peace of our world. The capability of conventional weapons and a sophisticated nuclear arsenal that has given the edge to Western forces for much of the last century is now the same technology that has fallen into the hands of those who consider us their enemies. Although the Cold War may have officially ended in the late 1980s, the weapons that grew from the science of the Cold War era remain.

Why Now?

At end of the last decade, the "nuclear club" (nations that officially admit to having developed and stockpiled nuclear weapons) was acknowledged to have seven members: the U.S., Russia, China, France, England, India, and Pakistan. Additional countries that are actively pursuing a nuclear weapons program now include North Korea, and quite possibly others. During the height of the Cold War, the stockpiles of nuclear weapons that were created between the United States and the former Soviet Union included nearly 70,000 nuclear warheads dispersed throughout North America, Europe, and Asia![13]

These statistics included weapons that were actively deployed, as well as the reserves to replenish supplies during a time of war. Following the treaties that were designed to reduce such staggering numbers of warheads, the nuclear nations began to back down from the overkill of arsenals that would have made it possible to destroy many Earth-size planets. Today, early in the 21st century, the world's still-sizeable nuclear arsenal is approximately half of what it was at the height of the Cold War, at about 36,000 warheads, according to the Natural Resources Defense Council.[14] The Council is quick to report, however, that these numbers do not include the arsenals of undeclared, yet known, nuclear countries such as Israel.

In a time of escalating differences and growing tension between nuclear neighbors, the threat of such stockpiles cannot be underestimated. Although the destruction of a percentage of nuclear stockpiles began following the Cold War, the process appears to have lost momentum. Commenting on the lack of follow-through, Joseph Cirincione, director of the Non-Proliferation Project at the Carnegie Endowment for International Peace, stated, "One of the surprising things is that nuclear disarmament has potentially stopped." With respect to the current state of remaining nuclear weapons in the world today, Jorgen Wouters reported for ABC News that "the major powers still possess more than enough Cold-War weaponry to microwave the planet many times over."[15]

In addition to the nuclear stockpiles among powers that have become enemies, the growing number of chemical and biological weapons add to the already formidable threat of warfare with global consequences.[16] Though declared "illegal" in the Geneva Protocols of 1925 and again in the *Chemical Weapons Convention* (CWC) of 1993,[17] the existence of biological toxins and chemical agents designed for wartime poses a greater threat today than at any time in the last 100 years.

It is clear that the conditions exist for a wartime catastrophe, and the accompanying loss of life, in unimaginable and epic proportions. It is equally clear that it is virtually impossible to prepare for or defend against each one of the multiple threats that is known. In all probability, additional threats exist in the global collection of weaponry that have yet to become public knowledge.

Within the context of such growing arsenals and the escalating tension among the world's powers, I'm often asked the question: "Why now? Why offer this book describing the message in our cells today?" If we are ever to explore the power of a principle that could unify diverse ethnic, religious, and political ideas, this is the generation to do so. In the presence of a global arsenal of weapons with an unprecedented power of destruction, accompanied by the willingness to use them to enforce policies based upon our differences, now is the perfect time to offer the message in our cells.

During a 1949 interview with Alfred Werner that was published in *Liberal Judaism,* Albert Einstein was asked what he thought the weapons of a third world war might look like in the nuclear era. His response was a chilling reminder of the perilous path that we find ourselves on today, as well as the responsibility that we have as a civilization to assure that his speculation never becomes a reality. With the simplicity and candor that he was so well known for, Einstein replied, "I do not know how the Third World War will be fought, but I can tell you what they will use in the Fourth—rocks!"[18]

In the first years of the 21st century, we stand at a perilous crossroads as a global civilization. No longer is it an "American," "Russian," "Chinese," or "European" choice to back down from the brink of global conflict. Through globalization and the spread of technology, conflict anywhere in the world today must be thought of in worldwide terms.

As the nations of Earth align themselves with religious beliefs and political ideals, the civil wars, religious wars, and economic wars—regardless of how "just" they may appear—hold the potential of enmeshing geographic regions and entire continents in ways that were impossible only a quarter century ago.

In the presence of technologies that can incapacitate the most capable armies, wreak havoc on the very basis of life, destroy cities and nations, and vaporize entire populations, the future of our species now rests upon our collective ability to move beyond our differences. In what may turn out to be a great irony of human history, a growing body of evidence suggests that this may not be the first time that humankind has come face-to-face with the prospect of its own destruction through the use of weapons with the power to eliminate entire civilizations from the face of the earth.

Although not acknowledged in conventional history, some of the oldest records of our past detail precisely such a scenario, and the battle that brought an end to two vast empires in a time before our history began. A growing body of archaeological evidence that is considered anomalous in traditional studies hints that at least some of the documents may be the last remaining records of actual historic events. If these events occurred, then we may be witnessing today the modern reenactment of a very ancient lesson, and a new opportunity to choose a new outcome.

Lessons from Our Past

In what has been called the national epic of India, as well as the Hindu Bible, the *Mahabharata* is a literary work unparalleled in terms of the length and breadth of its topic. It may also be the most detailed description of a war using technology so advanced, with consequences so devastating, that to accept the story as a record of historic fact is almost unthinkable. Although the ancient account describes survivors of the last battle in the war, there was no real victory. The price paid by the warring societies in the *Mahabharata* resulted in a destruction of biblical proportions, including the loss of countless numbers of lives, the inability of the land to grow food, and the destruction of an advanced civilization that predates history.

The story was originally recorded in the ancient language of Sanskrit between 2,500 and 3,000 years ago. Containing approximately 100,000 verses, the central theme of the epic describes a struggle between two kings, King Pandu and King Dhritarashtra, ending in a great battle that may have taken place as long ago as 8,000 to 10,000 years ago—well before traditional history suggests that great civilizations and sophisticated technology existed! Interestingly, the last battle described in the *Mahabharata* also marked the end of the last cycle in Hindu cosmology, the *Dvapara yuga*, and the beginning of the last great age of the world. We live in that age today, the time of the *Kali yuga*.

It is the description of the weapons and tactics of warfare in the Indian epic that has captured the interest of historians and generals in times past. The same descriptions are now drawing the attention of scientists and researchers. Unfolding on the plains near what is now Delhi, India, the *Mahabharata's* verses detail the use of a weapon that results in the utter destruction of vast expanses of Earth and all life in those areas. As the mysterious weapon is introduced and discharged in battle, it is described as an "unknown weapon, the iron thunderbolt . . . a single projectile charged with all the power of the universe."[19] The impact resulted in an "incandescent column of smoke and fire, as brilliant as 10,000 suns. . . ."[20]

The verses go on to describe the utter and complete devastation that the weapon leaves in its wake. "The earth shook, scorched by the terrible heat of this weapon. Elephants burst into flames. . . . Over a vast area other animals crumpled to the ground and died. The waters boiled, and the creatures residing therein also died."[21] In the final events of the battle, the text describes the horrible fate of humans caught in the path of such destruction. "The corpses were so burnt that they were no longer recognizable. Hair and nails

fell out."[22] Additional details describe how "pottery broke without cause. Birds, disturbed, circled in the air and were turned white."[23]

If the technology being described and its effects are accurate accounts of what transpired long ago, it is obviously detailing a weapon unlike anything known to exist at any time in history— that is, until atomic weapons were introduced to the world in the mid-20th century. Until recently, the magnitude of destruction described in the verses of the *Mahabharata* was inconceivable from a single weapon. With the 1945 detonation of the first nuclear bomb used in warfare, however, the possibility of such catastrophic proportions became a modern reality.

The relationship between the catastrophic battle in the *Mahabharata* and the power of nuclear devastation has not gone unnoticed in recent times. Following the successful detonation of the world's first atomic bomb at the Trinity test site in 1945, physicist Robert Oppenheimer quoted directly from the Bhagavad-Gita, a portion of the *Mahabharata*. Referring to the role of both creator and destroyer assumed by the Hindu god Shiva, Oppenheimer recited Shiva's declaration from the epic as he witnessed the fury of the blast: "Now I am become death, the destroyer of worlds."[24]

Interestingly, in addition to the epic poems of India, a number of other ancient cultures, including the native North Americans and the Tibetan Dzyan, also describe a time of great destruction in our past. Each attributes the devastation that followed to the ancient struggle between good and evil and humankind's quest for power. Is it possible that, at some point in our distant past, nuclear technologies, including those built for warfare, could have existed on Earth? Could an advanced civilization have climbed the ladder of technological evolution thousands of years before convention history began, only to crumble in the ruins of its own destruction?

A growing body of evidence, and an increasing number of scientists, are beginning to give serious consideration to precisely such questions. As early as 1909, when scientists were first beginning to understand the power that could be unleashed from the atom,

physicist Frederick Soddy commented, "I believe that there have been civilizations in the past that were familiar with atomic energy, and that by misusing it they were totally destroyed."[25]

If, in fact, an ancient civilization possessed the science and technology to harness the power of the atom, and actually used that power for warfare, we should still see evidence of the resulting destruction today. While anomalous discoveries of charred mountain tops, the sand of ancient deserts fused into vast sheets of glass, and ancient radioactive skeletons have been reported throughout the world,[26] perhaps the most telling finds are being unearthed near the legendary battle site described in the *Mahabharata* itself.

Early in the 20th century, archaeologists began excavating the remains of an unknown civilization in the Indus River Valley of northern India and Pakistan. While nomadic peoples had been known to inhabit the area for thousands of years, historical timelines had previously linked organized development in the region to the Aryan invasions around 1,500 B.C.E. With the discovery of two major cities—Harappa and Mohenjo Daro—that date was pushed back to approximately 3,000 B.C.E.

British archaeologist Sir John Marshall first excavated the ancient city of Mohenjo Daro in the 1920s, and his work was followed by the further excavations of Sir Mortimer Wheeler in 1946.[27, 28] Their digs revealed a surprisingly well-planned urban center, with a sophistication that is absent in many of the towns and villages of the area today. The architects of Mojenjo Daro built their city in a square grid pattern defined by main streets that were 30 feet wide. Many of the structures within the grid had running water and closed sewage systems, as well as a number of large enclosures believed to be public or ritual baths. Accompanying the advanced design in the cities themselves, the inhabitants of the Indus Culture used a forgotten form of writing—now known as Indus Valley Script—that has never been translated or deciphered. Without being able to read what inhabitants left behind, we have only the physical artifacts themselves to tell the story of Harappa and

Mohenjo Daro.

Perhaps the greatest mystery that the ancient cities leave for us today is why they were forgotten. What was the cause of their abandonment? Wheeler's discoveries may offer a clue. When the dig reached the level of the ancient streets, the workers found a number of human skeletons oddly scattered in disarray. Many of the skeletons were contorted in awkward positions, and a few were still holding hands, as if some disaster had unexpectedly overtaken them. Accounts from other excavations in the area describe similar findings: "Groups of skeletons in postures of flight have been found on the stairways at some sites."[29] What happened to these people, and why did their skeletons remain so intact? What circumstances prevented the bodies from being scattered by wild animals, natural decay, or looters after their deaths?

Perhaps the answer to these questions lies in less-publicized discoveries of similar skeletons found near the present-day Indian city of Delhi. While excavating in preparation for the construction of a housing project, workers reportedly uncovered something that should not exist. In an area that had already been recognized as producing an alarmingly high number of cancers and birth defects, they discovered a thick layer of radioactive ash beneath the earth's surface.[30]

Further investigation revealed that the ash covered an area of approximately three square miles (for comparison, the greatest area of devastation in the Japanese city of Hiroshima covered approximately four square miles). In his book *Riddles of Ancient History*, Russian archaeologist A. Gorbovsky reported the discovery of at least one human skeleton in this area with a level of radioactivity approximately 50 times greater than it should have had due to natural radiation![31] What could possibly explain these "anomalous" findings from a civilization that reached its peak, then perished, nearly 2,000 years before the time of Jesus of Nazareth?

Clearly, much more work remains to be done at this and similar sites. Through additional research, we'll be able to validate the finds and unlock the secrets that such remains hold for us today. Even in the absence of a focused study, however, these findings contribute to a growing body of evidence indicating that something happened long ago that had such thoroughly devastating effects that an entire civilization disappeared as a result.

Do the discoveries of Wheeler, Marshall, and others reveal the evidence and aftermath of an advanced civilization and their failure to survive their "technological adolescence"? The effects of nuclear blasts are well documented today. With the similarity of those effects to the findings in such ancient sites, the parallels are clear, and the comparisons unavoidable. When we combine the tangible evidence of today with the written records from our past, a single question comes to mind: If we have been down the path of self-destruction before and obliterated an entire civilization through the misuse of power, are we in danger of making the same mistake again?

Is it possible as nations align themselves against one another in age-old struggles for land, ancient blood lines, and religious and political beliefs, that such differences could draw the world into yet another global conflict in our time? Will we allow the differences between capitalism and socialism; the diversity within Christian, Hebrew, and Muslim values; and conflicting perspectives on what the word *progress* means to divide the world in a way that appears irreconcilable? In considering the destructive power of the world's nuclear, chemical, and biological arsenals, can we afford to risk finding the answer to such a question?

History has shown, in the heat of conflict, "might" often becomes the justification to use whatever means are deemed necessary to back deeply held values and beliefs. The *Mahabharata* is the story of a powerfully lethal weapon, used as a last resort, by an army that believed if they weren't victorious in battle they would lose their civilization and way of life. If a comparable scenario were to manifest today, future generations could well be reading of our time as an epic of the great war of the 21st century, justified by similar beliefs. If the Indian literature is, in fact, an accurate record of historic events, then humankind has experienced the consequences of such thinking in the past, and barely survived. The next time we may not be so fortunate.

In what appear to be the many and complex issues that stand at the root of the world's problems today, the simplicity of their origins sometimes goes unnoticed. The source of the greatest threat to our survival is the way we perceive our diversity. Most present-day conflicts are based upon differences between people, races, religions, and beliefs. Real or perceived, in the 21st century the recognition of a single principle that transcends our differences, unifying people of all beliefs and walks of life, now becomes a strategic asset in addition to a spiritual understanding. The universal nature of God's name in the cells of our body may become the foundation of such a principle.

Beyond Our Differences: Survival Through Unity

The history and experiences of those who have come before us can sometimes be our best teachers regarding how to proceed into the uncharted territory of new ideas. Although times have changed and we are now dealing with factors of science and technology that our ancestors 100 years ago couldn't even imagine, in many respects the principles of coping with change are the same.

Whether we're speaking of native North American communities trying to preserve their way of life during the 17th century, or our global family attempting to survive the threats of the 21st century, at the most basic levels the experience is the same: We are talking about honoring life. *One of the great lessons that history has taught us is that unity and cooperation offer a greater chance of survival than can ever be realized from competition and conflict.*

DURING THE EUROPEAN COLONIZATION of North America, indigenous communities that had been indifferent and at times even hostile to their own neighbors foresaw only too well the necessity to overcome their differences. When the first explorers and settlers arrived on the shores of what is now the American northeast, tribes and families that had lived in the areas for many generations generally welcomed them. Diaries from the settlers at Jamestown, Virginia, which was the first permanent European settlement in North

America, attribute their survival of the devastating winter of 1607 to 1608—a winter for which they were poorly prepared—to the advice and support of the native peoples who helped them.

Quickly, however, it became clear that the two ways of life were incompatible; the native way of life could never survive the mind-set of the European worldview. To the indigenous communities that had successfully balanced the needs of daily life with the cycles of nature for hundreds of years, the very idea that land could be claimed was as inconceivable as the idea of ownership of air around them and the rain from the skies. Because the concept that nature could be "owned" made so little sense, many natives didn't take the threat posed by the European colonists seriously. They simply did not understand what was happening to them and their culture.

Among a handful of leaders from the same tribes, however, there was a growing realization about the impending threat. Although these visionaries may not have fully understood the intentions of the settlers in their lands, they did recognize that the various tribes had to cooperate and speak with a single voice in order to preserve their way of life or it would become lost forever. They knew that their survival would depend upon their ability to do so! Sadly, the leaders also witnessed the consequences of their communities' failure to unify, organize, and act until it was too late.

Perhaps one of the most poignant illustrations of their lesson in unifying for a greater good may be seen in the accounts of the Narragansett tribe and their leader, Chief Miantonomo. The chief recognized that the threat posed by the colonization of North America extended beyond the members of his immediate tribe, to surrounding tribes, some of which his people had experienced tension and disputes with in the past. Reaching out to the Mohawk peoples, he proposed a unified alliance to create what historian Ian K. Steele has called a "general Amerindian resistance movement."[32] In 1642, the chief reportedly said:

> *We [must] be one as they [the English] are,* otherwise we shall all be gone shortly, for you know our fathers had plenty of deer and skins, our plains were full of deer, as also

our woods, and of [turkeys], and our coves full of fish and fowl. But these English having gotten our land, they with scythes cut down the grass, and with axes fell the trees; their cows and horses eat the grass, and their hogs spoil our clam bakes, and we shall all be starved" [author's italics].[33]

Unfortunately, another one of history's lessons shows how well-intentioned efforts in one area of life do not always resolve problems in other arenas. During a war between tribes that was occurring at the same time that the native peoples were losing their way of life to the Europeans, Chief Miantonomo was captured by members of the Mohegans, who placed him in the custody of the English as a "rebel." Because he was not within the jurisdiction of the British Colonies, however, the English reasoned that they had no legal right to try his case. As a solution, they turned the chief over to the Uncas tribe, who carried out his execution with English witnesses to confirm the punishment.

This account clearly illustrates the value of putting individual differences aside and unifying in the face of a common threat. While there is no guarantee that the genocide of the estimated 20 million native peoples in North America would have resulted any differently, there is the possibility that a combined effort by the natives during the early years of colonization may have made a difference in terms of *how* the colonization occurred. With little doubt, the colonization of North America would have taken place, regardless of any efforts on behalf of the indigenous inhabitants. The wave of discontent that was felt so strongly throughout Europe in the 17th century and the technology that allowed for the colonization of a "New World" generated a momentum that could not be stopped.

The way that the development occurred, however, might have been reshaped in the presence of the estimated 50,000 native inhabitants of Virginia in 1607. Backed by the strength of their sheer numbers, their knowledge of how to survive in the "new" land, and through the power of a single voice, it is possible that the native peoples could have persuaded the settlers to work with them, rather than against them, regarding the way the colonization took place.

Through infighting within the tribes and differences in opinion, values, and goals, that unified voice was not formed soon enough. By the time the tribes of North America could see what was happening to their land and their way of life, they were so weakened by the diseases (such as smallpox) that the Europeans introduced, and so overpowered by the advanced weapons of rifles and artillery (as well as the use of horses, wagons, and forts) that they could do little more than resist.

The key here is that in their failure to overcome localized differences and unify in the name of a common good, the original inhabitants of North America lost all that they loved and held dear: their culture, the land that they had been stewards of for hundreds of generations, and, ultimately, much of their way of life. Though late in coming, the reality of this tragedy is recognized today. Remnants of this vast and ancient way of life are now being restored and preserved in some of the most pristine, rugged, and beautiful lands remaining in North America. Additionally, growing numbers of people not content with conventional forms of medicine, worship, and lifestyle are turning to the ancient ways held sacred by America's first inhabitants.

The story of Chief Miantonomo and the early colonization of our country is only one of many such accounts that could be told. The reason for offering this particular example is that it graphically illustrates a powerful lesson in survival that we can learn from today. The lesson is simply this: For the survival of their group, it is in the interest of families, communities, and nations to look beyond the differences that challenge their way of life and work cooperatively to overcome the issues that threaten their existence.

The same principle may be applied on a grander scale to our entire planet. Although this observation may intuitively appear obvious, history is laced with examples of the failure to recognize this fundamental principle of survival. In addition to seeming like good common sense, we see direct evidence of the power of unity and cooperation as examples in other species.

Nature:
The Blueprint for Unity and Cooperation

Although the theory of evolution itself has come under sharp criticism, the observations that Darwin made while developing his theory have become classic examples in studies of social behavior. While the species are different, the principles are similar in insects, animals, and humans. Contrary to the conclusion that Darwin seemed to have drawn regarding strength and survival in *The Origin of Species*, his later works described survival strategies based on unity and cooperation rather than "survival of the fittest." In his next book, *The Descent of Man*, Darwin summarized these observations, stating, "Those communities which included the greatest number of the most sympathetic members would flourish best and rear the greatest number of offspring."[34]

Early in the 20th century, Russian naturalist Peter Kropotkin reinforced Darwin's later work with his own observations, illustrating how he'd found cooperation and unity the keys to the success and survival of a species. In his 1902 classic *Mutual Aid: A Factor of Evolution*, Kropotkin eloquently describes the benefits experienced in the insect kingdom through the instinctual ability of ants to live as cooperative, rather than competitive, societies.

> Their wonderful nests, their buildings, superior in relative size to those of man; their paved roads and over-ground vaulted galleries; their spacious halls and granaries; their cornfields, harvesting and "malting" of grain; their rational methods of nursing their eggs and larvae and of building special nests for rearing the aphids whom Linnaeus so picturesquely described as "the cows of the ants"; and, finally, their courage, pluck, and superior intelligence—all of these are the natural outcome of the mutual aid which they practice at every stage of their busy and laborious lives.[35]

Dr. John Swomley, professor emeritus of social ethics at the St. Paul School of Theology in Kansas City, leaves little doubt that it is to our advantage to find peaceful and cooperative ways to build the global societies of our future. Citing the evidence presented by Kropotkin and others, Swomley states that the case for cooperation rather than competition is more than just a benefit of a successful society. In a simple and straightforward fashion, he cites that co-operation is "the key factor in evolution and survival."[36] In a paper published in February of 2000, Swomley quotes Kropotkin, stating that competition within or between species "is always injurious to the species. Better conditions are created by the elimination of competition by means of mutual aid and mutual support."[37]

In the opening address at the 1993 Symposium on the Humanistic Aspects of Regional Development, held in Birobidzhan, Russia, symposium co-chair Ronald Logan laid the foundation for the participants to view nature as a model for successful societies. In a direct reference to Kropotkin, he stated, "If we . . . ask Nature: 'who are the fittest: those who are continually at war with each other, or those who support one another?' we at once see that those animals which acquire habits of mutual aid are undoubtedly the fittest. They have more chances to survive, and they attain, in their respective classes, the highest development of intelligence and bodily organization."[38]

At a later point in the same address, Logan cited the work of author Alfie Kohn (*No Contest: The Case Against Competition*), describing in no uncertain terms what his research had revealed regarding a beneficial amount of competition in groups. After reviewing more than 400 studies documenting cooperation and competition, Kohn concluded, "The ideal amount of competition . . . in any environment, the classroom, the workplace, the family, the playing field, is none. . . . [Competition] is always destructive" (*Noetic Sciences Review,* spring 1990).[39]

Nature is widely recognized as a proving ground for experiments in unity, cooperation, and survival among insects and animals. From nature's lessons, we are shown, without question, that unity and cooperation are advantageous to living beings.

Such time-tested strategies from the world around us may ultimately lead to a blueprint for our own survival. To apply such a strategy, however, an additional factor must be accounted for in our world that does not appear in the animal kingdom. As individuals, and as a species, we generally must know "where we are going" and what we can expect when we get there, before we change the way we live. We need to know that the result is worthwhile and something to look forward to!

A Future to Believe In

Some of the most brilliant scientists, futurists, and visionaries of our time have speculated about what we would achieve as a species if we were to continue at the present rate of technological advancement, uninterrupted for decades and even centuries.

Although each vision is different, all foresee a time when the conditions that have brought the greatest suffering to humankind become memories of our past. They see an emerging world where disease is eliminated, where life spans are measured in hundreds of years, and where even immortality is a possibility. They envision us evolving into an interplanetary and galactic species, where space travel, time travel, and *Star Trek* kinds of technology are commonplace. Almost universally, these futurists see the darkest conditions of the world as temporary obstacles—stepping-stones that must be crossed—leading us to the time of their visions.

In his book *Visions,* Michio Kaku describes his perspective of what our future as a planet may hold. Drawing upon interviews that he conducted with more than 150 scientists from a number of different disciplines over a ten-year period, Kaku describes an era of possibilities that sounds so fantastic that it's almost too good to be true. At the same time, he cautions that a future of unlimited supplies of energy, immortality, global cooperation, and wormhole travel is only possible if we survive the present crisis of fossil-fuel-based economies and the tendency to use technology to destroy ourselves.

To form a framework for how such a future might unfold, Kaku refers to the attempt by Russian astronomer Nikolai Kardashev to classify the development of civilizations by their ability to harness the elements of nature as sources of energy. He places the degree of such achievements into a broad scheme based upon three levels that he calls *Type I, Type II,* and *Type III* civilizations.[40] The key characteristics that separate each type of civilization are the amount of energy that they consume and the source of their energy. The difference in energy consumption between each type is roughly ten billion times the previous level and can be "bridged" in relatively short periods of time.

In this simple and straightforward scheme, Kardashev envisioned civilizations from a global perspective surviving their periods of technological adolescence, wars, and inevitable differences in a way that prevents them from destroying themselves over long periods of time. It is such expanses of time that allow the longevity of civilizations to be measured in periods of thousands of years, rather than hundreds in duration.

Kardashev describes the first level of progress as *Type I* civilizations. Their defining characteristic is that they will have harnessed the powers of nature and draw their energy from the planet itself. Using ocean, wind, and deep-earth technologies, they will have transcended the limitations of fossil fuels, as well as the risks and dangers of nuclear-powered economies. The vast supplies of energy available to a Type I civilization eliminate the need for competition and war over limited fuel sources. At the same time, their technology makes the energy for the basic necessities of life widely available to a presumably growing population.

Type II civilizations are characterized by their ability to reach beyond their immediate planet and draw their energy from the nearest sun. Having achieved lengthy life spans, the energy requirements of Type II civilizations will eventually force them to look beyond their planet for new and limitless supplies of energy. Harnessing the energy of their sun will involve technologies more sophisticated than passively collecting the sun's rays in way we do today. Some theorists suggest that as a Type II civilization, we'll actively travel

to the sun with collectors that deflect massive amounts of solar radiation to sites on Earth, designed to convert such quantities into usable energy.

Of the benefits enjoyed by a Type II civilization, Kaku describes a world that is no longer vulnerable to the forces of nature. Through the technology of climate regulation and planetary adjustments, the longevity of such a civilization will allow for preparations involving planetary cycles that are lost over centuries in today's world.

The most sophisticated advances described in Kardashev's classification scheme are those of the *Type III* civilizations. Having advanced beyond the kind of energy harnessed by their local sun, a Type III civilization will expand its search for energy to other stars, and perhaps even tap the fabric of the galaxy itself as it expands into a galactic civilization. In Kaku's vision, the science of a Type III civilization may even master the elusive *Planck's energy,* allowing the opening of space/time to create shortcuts between stars and galaxies as wormholes. Both life and civilization would be immortal, having outgrown the limitations of "natural" deterioration and the possibility that "chance" phenomena could destroy them. As fantastic as such scenarios sound today, many scientists, researchers, futurists, and visionaries believe that such technologies and futures are not only possible, they are our destiny.

The key to reaching such levels of advancement
is that we must live through the present.
We must survive our learning curve and find a
way to become greater than the differences
that have separated us in the past.

Within this classification scheme, humankind has yet to achieve even the first level of a Type I civilization! Based upon the conditions of our world and the development of science and technology, at the dawn of the 21st century, we're classified as a *Type 0* civilization. We still rely upon limited supplies of fossil fuels, whose use also threatens our environment. At the same time, the ownership of these fuels has defined our world's populations as "haves"

and "have-nots," and has justified conflict throughout much of the industrialized world age.

A signature of Type 0 civilizations is their inability to pool their collective knowledge into a wisdom that benefits the species as a whole. In Kaku's words, "On earth we are still a Type 0 civilization: we are still hopelessly fractured into bickering, jealous nations and deeply split along racial, religious and national lines."[41] As a ray of hope, he identifies an additional trend that is building at the same time. In the presence of civil, ethnic, and religious wars, we're becoming increasingly more dependent upon one another through the globalization of world economies. He cites the formation of trade organizations, such as the European Union, as evidence of this trend.

Where will these trends lead us? In a very real sense, the answer to that question is being created now, as we search for new ways to settle our differences and marry our beliefs about precisely what the world should look like.

If the achievements of the past 200 years are any indication of what is possible for our species, then the future, indeed, holds a promise that many today can only imagine in their dreams. The key to overcoming the suffering and tragedy that appear to be so prevalent is that we must live long enough to build the world that so many have envisioned. We must survive what is, perhaps, the greatest time of change ever experienced by our species. We must cooperate and bridge our differences. Within each cell of every life is preserved the message giving us the reason to believe in our future, and the key to bridging the differences that make such future civilizations possible.

Perhaps author and visionary Jean Houston best describes the magnitude of our time in history. With regard to the degree of change that we face today, what we may expect in the future, and with the eloquence that has become the hallmark of her work, Houston states, "The only expected is the unexpected. Everything that was, isn't anymore and everything that isn't is coming to be. Ours is an era of quantum change, probably, the most radical de-construction and re-construction the world has ever seen. And we are the ones to carry on."[42]

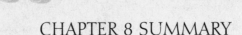

CHAPTER 8 SUMMARY

- With the millennium still fresh in our minds, scientists ask the question of whether or not we will survive another 100 years of unleashing the forces of nature as weapons and technology, without fully understanding the consequences of doing so.

- Drake's equation estimates that there could be as many as 10,000 intelligent civilizations that have developed in the 13- to 14-billion-year history of our universe. The question that so many are asking is: Where are they? Carl Sagan speculated that they might not have survived their technological adolescence.

- Do the archaeological discoveries of a massive city dating back between 8,000 and 12,000 years indicate a previously advanced civilization on Earth, at a time before our history began? Do the remnants of radioactive human skeletons, melted pottery, and sand fused into glass support the theory that they destroyed themselves with atomic weapons, as suggested by the great battle described in the ancient Hindu epic the *Mahabharata*? If so, are we making the same mistakes?

- With at least 20 active civil, religious, and political wars raging today, the "peace" following the Cold War has been a relative peace only. Global tension and growing stockpiles of mass-effect weapons make a planetary conflict with catastrophic results more likely now than at any point in the last 100 years.

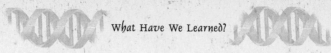

- Examples from Native American traditions and observations in nature clearly show that unity and cooperation offer a better chance of survival for a species than do competition and aggression. Unity and cooperation are now considered strategic assets, as well as spiritual truths. The message in our cells offers a reason to believe that such unity is possible.

- Futurists envision a time in our not-too-distant future where the disease and suffering of today are memories of the past. The key to reaching such a time is that we, as a civilization, must survive long enough to attain the necessary scientific and spiritual understandings.

"As Five-fingered Humans, we are given
the gift of thought and life into our hands.
As Five-fingered Humans, we are all the same."

— LINDA DEE (DINE' NATION)

Chapter Nine

THE GOD CODE:
A Reason to Believe

I have always been fascinated by masses of people. There is a feeling, often described as "electricity," that only occurs when hundreds or thousands of people converge in the same place at the same moment in time. In the organized chaos of so many individuals, each one immersed in the business of their lives, it's easy to suspect that such experiences play a less obvious role in a much greater plan. Focused on their errands, meetings, or the person walking beside them, shoppers and commuters are generally unaware of the history of those that surround them, sometimes only inches away. Yet, within any crowd, from concerts and restaurants to boardrooms and playgrounds, every person is the product of all of the hurt and personal tragedy, as well as the success and joy, that has led them to the place where they share their brief moment in time.

Strolling through exotic markets in Peru, the bazaars of Cairo, massive airports that have become self-contained communities, or seated at a sidewalk café in almost any city, it is at such times that a single question often comes to mind: "What would it take to bring so many people together in a shared moment of unity?" Similar to the way a national anthem carries people beyond their differences of culture, religion, and status, what truth could be revealed that would have a similar effect? What sentence could be stated with the power to transcend the beliefs that may have separated so many people in the past, and offer a unity that continues long after the moment has gone by?

Experiences That Unite

Through informal discussions during seminars and conferences, I often ask audiences precisely this question. The most common response is one based upon personal experience and historic perspective. In recent memory, when we think of people uniting, it's generally in response to the *need* to unite, such as a shared tragedy or common goal.

During the last half of the 20th century, there is a sense that our global family has experienced an inordinate number of catastrophic events, both man-made and natural. This suspicion is borne out statistically, as the last 100 years have produced the greatest extremes in droughts, storms, floods, and wildfires—as well as industrial and environmental disasters—ever recorded.[1] From the devastation of Hurricane Andrew and the floods of Eastern Europe, to the Oklahoma City bombing and the meltdown of Russia's Chernobyl reactor, the tragedies that have left their indelible mark in our memories have also provided some of the best opportunities for cooperation.

Clearly, during the same span of time, we've also experienced a sense of unity stemming from happy events as well. Among people who are complete strangers, the joyous spectacles of royal weddings, Super Bowl playoffs, and Olympic competitions have provided moments of exhilaration and a reason to revel in a shared experience. These moments, however, have often been short-lived bursts of emotion rather than life-changing events that genuinely shaped the course of history. More often than not, it's the tragedies that my audiences cite as the greatest opportunity for unity.

The images of September 11, 2001, will remain fresh in the minds of *this* generation, and, in all probability, many generations to come. Who can forget the sight of people from every walk of life and nationality imaginable suddenly being drawn together on one day, staggering away dazed from burning buildings with their bodies covered in a layer of eerie gray ash? Who can forget the conflicting emotions of horror and pride as we witnessed police officers and firefighters running into the same buildings to save others, only to disappear and ultimately vanish in the ensuing inferno?

Suddenly bankers, commodity traders, deli chefs, and street vendors were working side by side with rescue teams and bystanders to pull as many people as possible from the rubble that had once been the pride of New York City's skyline. On that day, in stark contrast to the horrors resulting from the worst expression of our species, we also witnessed the very best of our kind. In countless instances of selfless heroism, caring individuals risked their lives without a moment's hesitation so that others could live.

In addition to what such events have shown us about ourselves as a society, they have also taught us something about ourselves as human beings. Although the events are the *catalysts* that bring us together in examples of "unity through tragedy," the power that they awaken within us comes from something more than the remains of smoldering buildings. During interviews with those surviving such moments, they confide that the outward surge of strength that others perceive as heroism stems from the surreal and sometimes "mystical" feeling of a greater force moving within them.

When asked in post-tragedy press conferences what was going through their minds in the instant they acted, it's not uncommon for those honored for their superhuman efforts to reply that they had "no choice." The direct experience of another human in need spoke to them on a gut level. Bypassing the logic that would typically lead them *away* from danger, the experience evoked something much deeper within them, and they acted.

Those who have worked side by side in a frantic effort to save lives often convey that their strength is more than simply the spirit of cooperation with other rescuers. It's as though a "fusion" of souls results from knowing that, together, they are capable of accomplishing something greater than any individual could do alone. In these and similar instances, it is the *meaning of the experience,* rather than the events themselves, that forever changes people's lives.

From this perspective, when I ask myself the question "What would it take?" I'm really asking, "What experience could be shared by so many people that would awaken all of us to a greater sense of unity and purpose? What would it take to go beyond simply getting our attention in the moment, to lead our hearts and minds to a new reality of life-honoring cooperation and peace?" Surely, there must be an answer to such questions. And that answer must be linked to the *feeling experienced* in the moment of the event.

Whatever the catalyst, we would each need to share in a feeling that was so deep, so personal, and so real that it would be impossible to ignore. It would require a gut-level "Aha" that transcended our everyday routines. It would need to penetrate to the very core of our essence, raising the tiny hairs on the back of our necks and bringing tears to our eyes, just because we know it's true! If an experience of such magnitude could occur for those within the airport, bazaar, or café where I asked the question, then it would be possible for others beyond our immediate vicinity as well.

Through the personal effect of allowing such a shared moment, we would grant ourselves a rare opportunity: the chance to see our world and, perhaps more important, one another in the light of a greater possibility. It is the undeniable feeling of such a direct and deeply personal experience that lingers well beyond the moment. Through the feeling, we find a reason to believe that we're part of something greater, and the strength to make a difference in our world.

The Power of the Moment

In the instant of such a life-affirming experience resulting from the message in our cells, every man and woman—each laborer, office professional, parent, and educator, every farmer and tribe member, warrior, and priest, regardless of heritage, race, or religion—could stand firm in the knowledge of their relationship to a greater power. Embracing that knowledge without doubt or hesitation, they could look into the eyes of those around them with a new sense of confidence, self-esteem, and honor. In the presence of others whom they may never have understood, tolerated, or even liked in the past, the experience would allow them to see something that they may have never seen before: concrete evidence of their combined role in a greater plan.

Precisely where such a moment can lead may be less significant than our willingness to allow the moment to occur. The message within our cells has the power to carry us, as a family, beyond the looming crises of runaway technology, global war, and disease to the certainty that we are worth more than the value we have placed on wealth, heritage, technology, and borders.

We are a family—quite possibly one-of-a-kind within the vast expanse of creation. As in any family, the experience of one member signals a possibility that all may experience at another time. Each member represents a potential for the whole. As remote as the possibility may appear, the tragic extremes of famine, disease, war, and poverty that befall one people, society, or nation at a given point stand as testimony that others may experience similar tragedies at another time.

Likewise, the success of one part of our family becomes the model for the success and survival of others as well. Each time one of us discovers a way to overcome disease, intolerance, life-denying technology, and hate, the door is opened for others to follow.

Although there are many issues upon which world leaders disagree, there is one trend about which there appears to be little argument: The leading indicators of planetary change show that the family of man is confronting the greatest challenges to survival in recorded history. Some of the best minds of our time agree, stating that unless we change the thinking that has led to such conditions, we're on a collision course with disaster. In addition to the threat of a midcentury collapse in our ecosystems, the spread of rogue viruses that are immune to any known drug therapy, and

shifts in weather patterns that are already altering our ability to grow life-sustaining crops, we now face the very real threat of global war.

In the presence of such large-scale problems—each of which threatens the future of our species—killing one another over differences in ancestors, the color of our skin, and the way we worship God makes very little sense. Clearly we have "bigger fish to fry"!

The Power of a Message

Before his death in 1996, Carl Sagan speculated about the impact that the discovery of intelligence beyond Earth could have upon our attitudes and societies. In his classic SETI paper,[2] he identified the search for other life as part of a curiosity that is as old as humankind itself. In the first sentence, he stated, "Through all of our history we have pondered the stars and mused whether mankind is unique or if . . . there are other beings who contemplate and wonder as we do—fellow thinkers in the cosmos."[3] Sagan further remarked that even if we chose not to reply to the source of an extraterrestrial transmission, the detection of the signal itself could have benefits that directly affect the direction of scientific research and the views of society in general. Beyond simply answering the question of whether or not we are alone, Sagan suggested that such a discovery would offer a clue as to the survivability of our technological path.

In all likelihood, a transmission from deep space would originate from a civilization that is much older and presumably more advanced than we are today. Communications of radio-like transmissions move at the speed of light and take tremendous amounts of time to travel the vast distances between stars and planets. Assuming that other civilizations still exist, scientists estimate that the average distance between them is about 300 light years. If we were to detect a signal from a neighboring star, this means we'd be receiving it 300 years after it was originally sent.

If we then chose to respond to the signal, another 300 years would pass before our transmission was received, making the total time for a single communication 600 years! Due to the sheer number of stars in our galaxy, the odds are that our first message would come from somewhere *beyond* our nearest neighbor. This means that before reaching our world, the signal would have traveled a distance so great that any meaningful conversation would be nearly impossible!

From Sagan's perspective, however, simply receiving such a signal would tell us that the civilization of its origin had survived their technological evolution. In doing so, they would have mastered the consequences of acquiring technology, without destroying themselves in the process. "A single message from space," he stated, "will show that it is possible to live through technological adolescence."[4] Additionally, Sagan suggested that while it is not likely, it is quite possible that "the future of human civilization depends upon the receipt and decoding of interstellar messages."[5]

If simply receiving a signal could have such a cohesive impact upon our global family, imagine what it would mean if the signal were meaningful—a message that could be read!

Contact!

With Sagan's speculation in mind, what would happen if we were to apply the benefits of receiving an extraterrestrial signal to a message of a different kind? What if we applied all that we know about the significance of discovering other-worldly intelligence to the message within each cell of our bodies? In a very real sense, the name of God in our cells *is* from beyond our world, as well as being firmly grounded *as* our world. Rather than receiving the symbolic message of an electronic signal from deep space, would the tangible message of God's name from within our bodies produce a similar experience, with a similar effect?

As studies imply, it is the magnitude of a shared experience that ignites the greatest sense of unity among people of different

backgrounds. Evidence of God's presence, resulting from a multi-nation, multidecade search such as the Human Genome Project, could hold the potential to produce precisely such an effect.

If we define "contact" as our receipt of a viable message in a recognizable form, and from a source that originates beyond our world, then the discovery of God's ancient name within the human genetic code may very well be viewed as contact!

The Perfect Time

"Stay tuned! We'll be right back after the news at the top of the hour!" the host of the program announced as we approached the second half of our interview. I heard the familiar burst of radio static and the "beep" indicating that we were off the air for a few moments during the break. Suddenly, the moderator's voice shouted into the telephone: "Great interview, Gregg—powerful stuff! We're off to a good start!" For the previous 30 minutes, the topic of our discussion had been the scientific proof of the unified field of consciousness that envelops our world and the power of that field to serve as a conduit for prayers of peace. I had just shared the studies confirming that when a certain number of people achieve what is called "coherent emotion"—such as the kind created through unified feelings of peace—the effect is documented to extend *beyond* the group that is praying into the families and communities where the studies are conducted.

While the host's reaction to such studies was not uncommon, it is what he said next that sent chills throughout my body. He began by sharing his belief that we (humankind) are the product of a vast and ancient intelligence. "If this is true," he reasoned aloud, "then somewhere in our past that intelligence must have left evidence of its existence. Somewhere in this world there must be a sign that is unmistakable—our Creator's 'calling card'—to remind us that we're part of something bigger than ourselves." Barely taking a breath between thoughts, he continued, "Someday, I believe that we'll find that evidence, and it will become a reason for us to stop fighting ourselves. I just hope that we find it soon! What do you think, Gregg? Do you believe that it's out there somewhere?"

His words caught me completely off guard! The man on the other end of the phone had no way of knowing that for 11 years I had searched for precisely such evidence! My mind reeled as I considered how to answer his question honestly without betraying my agreements not to discuss my findings until the work had reached a completion point and could be shared responsibly. Within a fraction of a second after asking the question, however, my dilemma disappeared, as I heard the host's voice again. "Ten seconds and we're back on the air," he said, and the next segment of the program began. I never had the opportunity to answer the question, and it was never asked again. The fact that such a question was asked at all, however, is the key to this story.

If we are, in fact, all connected through a shared consciousness, there are probably very few secrets in our world and certainly fewer "accidents." From this perspective, while the interviewer asked the question as one person, it was as if, collectively, our shared awareness had asked the question for everyone—that is, we were asking ourselves for help!

What the interviewer had no way of knowing was that I had recently come to a particularly frustrating point in my research. While never questioning the existence of the code itself, I had begun to question my approach to finding it. Hearing the words "I just hope that we find it soon!" was precisely what I needed as encouragement at that point in my life. To me, the tone and urgency of his voice sounded almost like a plea, and his comments inspired me to continue to the breakthrough only months later that led to this book.

I believe that, on an unconscious and unspoken level, we all work together in this way. By simply being honest in our conversations, we often speak precisely the right words, in precisely the right moment, and that we are heard by others in ways that we may never imagine. On that evening, I heard "us" asking ourselves to find the kind of evidence that the host had described, giving us a reason to believe that peace in our world is possible. The fact that the question was asked also suggests that now is the perfect time to share the message in our cells.

The statistics on lost life that I shared in Chapter 1 stand as a dark testament to historian Eric Hobsbawm's statement that the 20th century was the "most murderous century" in recorded human history. Especially astonishing is that the statistics illustrate what many people have already suspected—as a species, we alone are responsible for the loss of more of our kind, due to intentional acts of violence and a disregard for the well-being of others, than the effects of natural disasters and disease. Facing these dismal reminders of our past, I am often asked to share my sense of how likely it is that a single piece of information can bring about life-affirming change and contribute to reverse the trend of cruelty that has dominated our world for at least the last four centuries. Is it possible for such change to occur on a meaningful scale? My answer is an emphatic *yes!* In addition to being possible, I believe that this magnitude of change is achievable and necessary. The message of God/Eternal within our cells may be precisely the catalyst to "jump-start" such a change!

It may be precisely because we have yet to see such a level of change on a large scale that now is the perfect window of opportunity. If we lived in a time when radical shake-the-foundation-of-our-core-beliefs information was revealed on a routine basis, like the proverbial cry of "wolf," the impact of the message could be lost. The convergence of so many conditions today, each of which stands alone as a threat to our future, makes this the perfect moment to discover that our "sameness" is greater than our differences.

A notable by-product of the September 11 events was the ongoing intensity with which the mass media reported the aftermath of the tragedy. Within hours of the first reports, we were inundated by a new format of journalism: television reporting enhanced with powerful graphics and carefully composed theme music that augmented the already-riveting drama that was playing out before our eyes. In the days and months that followed, while we were searching for a new kind of "normal" in our everyday lives, we continued to receive our news with the same intensity, as if each new day held a new crisis. Since then, the vigor of such relentless, high-tech coverage has produced another by-product that was, perhaps, unexpected.

To varying degrees, the general public has become desensitized to powerful reports of war and terror. In much the same way that Americans became calloused to the statistics of war casualties during the Vietnam era, news events that would have commanded our undivided attention before the tragedy of September 11 have become routine in our lives as well.

The nature and style of presentation that is now required to hold our attention for more than a few moments had gone well beyond what we were accustomed to in the past. Even the effectiveness of sex and taboo innuendo now requires additional shock value, of an even greater degree, to stand out from the routine programming of every day. It is within this context that the opportunity for meaningful change presents itself, through the power of a message that touches every member of our global family.

Since more than 95 percent of our global family believes in the existence of a higher power, to know so clearly that we carry a message from that power may rival even the most powerful media broadcast available to us today! Knowing of the message within our cells, however, does not guarantee that a fundamental change in the way we view ourselves will occur. It simply sets the stage, providing a poignant reason and the opportunity. It is a place to begin.

A Species of Change

Change appears to be a fundamental part of human nature. The brief history of our species is punctuated by changes in varying degrees. While some have required little more than adapting a new attitude, others have required quick and innovative thinking just to survive. Approximately 10,000 to 12,000 years ago, for example, our ancestors experienced a degree of change that is almost unthinkable in the modern world. Geologic evidence suggests that toward the end of the Pleistocene epoch, a rare magnetic reversal occurred! Within a matter of hours and days, those living at the time witnessed a 180-degree shift, as Earth's magnetic North Pole become the South, and the South Pole become the North.

We can only imagine what this phenomenon meant in the absence of science and communications to explain it. Accompanying the reversal, tree-ring data and fossil evidence indicate that a tremendous shift in weather patterns also occurred. Judging from the remains of prehistoric mammoths, frozen in mid-stride with their last meals still in their mouths, the shift in climate and the accompanying deep-freeze occurred very quickly. Suddenly, portions of the earth that had formerly been mild and fertile experienced drought, while historically arid and desert locations became cold and wet. Our ancestors had to adapt quickly in order to survive, and apparently did so successfully.

In addition to the catastrophic effects of natural events, during the last 500 years or so we have experienced the exploration, conquering, and enslavement of entire continents and populations—traumas of unimaginable proportions. Accompanying the history of expansion and domination, we've also witnessed the merging of cultures, religions, and races, examples of our ability to respond to change. We are a species of survivors, capable of adapting to unexpected conditions. From such a history, it's clear that change is an important part of who we are. Hopefully, we are now also willing to do whatever it takes to assure our collective future.

The question remains, however, as to what evidence exists that a powerful experience of unity, and the change that it implies, could be accepted on a mass scale. In response, I rely upon what I believe is the key to making meaningful and life-affirming choices in a world that, at times, appears to be poised on the brink of self-destruction. That key is human nature itself.

A Species of "Goodness"

At first, the tug was barely noticeable. I'd grown accustomed to the bumps, nudges, and close encounters that accompany touring with others in close quarters. In the spring of 1998, I had the honor of facilitating a 23-day pilgrimage into the mountains of central Tibet, a journey that would take us to elevations as high as 17,000 feet above sea level. To accustom our bodies to such extremes, we had scheduled a 48-hour layover in the country of Nepal, situated at about 4,000 feet in elevation. While the numbers for the temperature and humidity rivaled one another as they raced high into the 90s, this brief visit would allow us a gradual ascent onto the Tibetan plateau, as well as time to immerse ourselves in the Nepalese culture. Standing with our group in the open plaza of Katmandu's historic Bharkor Square, we found ourselves straining to hear the thick Pakistani accent of our guide over the sounds of street vendors calling us to their booths.

I could have ignored the gentle tug at the pleat in my pants if it were not so deliberate. Instinctively I glanced downward to the source of the distraction. I wasn't prepared for what I saw. My eyes were met by the intense gaze of an ancient-looking man whose sparsely bearded face barely rose above the height of my knees. The clear whites of his eyes peered from behind long, silver strands of hair kept in motion by the hot wind whipping over the stone slabs in the square. Nearly naked, while the white ash that traditionally covers holy men clung to the dampness of his skin, there were patches between that revealed the darkness of his body underneath, made only darker from years of exposure to the high-altitude sun.

It took a moment for me to make sense of what my eyes were seeing. As I searched below his waist to the place where the man's legs should have been, there were only the limp folds of a soiled loincloth cascading onto the ground. In place of his limbs, there was a short piece of board with rollers attached to the underside, which was stained and darkened through years of use. This "roller board" appeared to be his only means of moving from one point to another.

Instinctively, I backed away, a little startled by the experience. Without speaking a word, the man slowly placed both of his palms on the ground and rolled himself forward in my direction. I glanced up to see if anyone else had noticed what I was seeing. Those around me appeared to be absolutely oblivious to what was happening on the ground below their eyes. It was as if the events were playing out for the man and me alone. Having grown accustomed to the tremendous poverty that we had seen through the course of the past days, my immediate assumption was that this man was a beggar hoping for a handout. I reached into my backpack and handed him whatever Nepalese money I could find. What happened next was a powerful lesson for me in judgment, expectations, and assumptions.

With one palm still on the ground for balance, the man on the board refused my offer. Shaking his head to the left and right in the universal gesture of "no," he pushed the money back toward me with his open hand. Using the same hand, with a single motion he gestured to a building behind us. Looking up, I saw a very beautiful and very old temple that towered above the place where we stood. For some reason, our group had not noticed it when we entered the plaza. We had walked right past the green moss that covered the intricately crafted façade framing the building's windows and doors. Squinting my eyes to adjust for the distance, I began to make out the tremendous detail of what must have been thousands upon thousands of tiny humanlike figures carved into the ancient wood, many of them Hindu gods.

As I glanced back down to thank the man for directing my attention to such a beautiful place, he was gone. I searched the ground, my eyes darting around the bodies of pilgrims and tourists as they strolled through the square. Suddenly I saw the man's back as he moved away, slowly and deliberately pushing himself across the stones on his board to the edge of the square. Although I considered following him to say thank you, I did not. I felt that he had accomplished what he had come to do or else he would have stayed. I have learned that such brief experiences often hold powerful lessons, and I had no doubt that this was one of those moments.

At first I had judged the man, placing him into the category of the beggars regularly asking for handouts that have become so commonplace throughout the world. Not only did he not *want* a handout, the man had *refused* the money that I offered to him. In that moment was the lesson: Here was a man who, in all probability, had no home and no family to care for him, and who obviously had no legs and probably owned little more than the loincloth around his waist and the board beneath his body. In his state of having nothing, he had approached me not to ask for something. Rather he came to *give!* While my mind had made an assumption and was racing through all of the awkwardness of whether or not I should offer something useful to the beggar (our guide and translators had asked us not to), the man on the board simply wanted to share a part of his world with me—and that was *all* he wanted.

In that moment, I glimpsed an example of what I believe is the truest essence of human nature. In our most basic state, free from the encumbrances that lead us to believe that we are needy, taken advantage of, or engaged in competition for survival, we are fundamentally a kind and giving species—*a species of goodness.* I thought about the man later in the day and I realized that I missed him. I missed his beard, the smell of ash on his body, and the look in his eyes. I began to consider how different my world would be if we had never met, and I felt good knowing that such a man existed "out there" somewhere. Through the aftermath of such powerful feelings, I realized that he had given me much more on that day than simply pointing out a building.

On the most fundamental level, my sense is that we are a kind, compassionate, and caring species, as demonstrated by the man on the board. At the same time, *out of necessity,* we are also a species of warriors and survivors. When driven to extremes, we have the power, capacity, and will to override our fundamental nature and become violent, to protect and survive. Our violence can be triggered by circumstances, *either real or perceived,* that we believe threaten us as individuals, families, communities, or nations. At other times, we strike out in acts of sheer desperation at circumstances that seem beyond our control. Regardless of the rea-

son that we betray what has been called our fundamental "goodness," it is in such moments that we witness the very worst and most frightening aspects of our nature.

As with any sweeping generalizations concerning people, there are always exceptions. In every society, there are statistics that seem to refute our goodness, as individuals polarize toward the darkest traits that we shun and abhor. Living the worst nightmares as the reality of their lives, nearly every generation has experienced the terror that may be best described as "evil incarnate," such as serial killers Jack the Ripper or Ted Bundy, wreaking havoc within otherwise life-honoring communities and neighborhoods.

On rare occasions, such individuals have risen to places of tremendous power. Using charisma to seduce entire armies into carrying out their schemes, they commit atrocities against other races, other nations, and even their own people. Today, that terror has taken on a new dimension, evolving from individuals and small, poorly funded groups to well-funded international organizations. Such moments of darkness for our species, however, may illustrate more of what we *do* under extreme circumstances, rather that what we *are* by nature. Fortunately, "Adolph Hitlers," "Slobadan Milosevics," and organizations of terror are the exception rather than the rule, and are few and far between.

In the absence of conditions that drive us to be animal-like in our actions, a growing body of ancient, scholarly, and scientific evidence suggests that when given the opportunity, we prefer to live peaceful and considerate lives that honor the benevolent aspects of our species.

Our Truest Nature

The sense of our benevolence was eloquently expressed by the 13th-century scholar St. Thomas Aquinas: "The goodness of the species transcends the goodness of the individual, as form transcends matter."[6] Four hundred years later, philosopher, statesman, and naturalist Francis Bacon echoed a similar sentiment when he wrote: "The inclination to goodness is imprinted deeply in the nature of man. . ."[7] *It is our uniqueness as a species, coupled with our fundamental character of goodness, that opens the door for the message in our cells to seed real and lasting change in our lives.*

In my experience of traveling to every continent of the world with the exception of Antarctica, there is a common theme I have found among the people with whom I have had the privilege of sharing time, meals, nature, and daily life. From the remote villages and monasteries in the mountains of Egypt, Tibet, and South America; to the street vendors in the bazaars of Luxor; as well as throughout Europe and the rural towns and cafés of Australia and North America, people appear to be basically "good" by nature. As individuals and families, we find ways to be happy in whatever circumstances we find ourselves. From homeless beggars and salt-of-the-earth people who work the land, to brilliant minds in positions of technical and political power, in general, all appear to be searching for the same things in their lives: peace, food, shelter, health, the opportunity to make a good life for their families, and a better understanding of their place in creation.

Abraham Maslow, one of the great psychologists of the 20th century, first distinguished himself through his work with the social behavior of primates. In his later years, however, he dedicated himself exclusively to the study of human nature, noting "wonderful possibilities and inscrutable depths" of our existence. Even in the presence of colleagues such as Sigmund Freud, who proposed lust, selfishness, and aggression as our basic nature, Maslow's studies led him to believe that "people are all decent underneath."[8] His unwavering faith in our goodness remained through the last days of his life, when he wrote that humankind "has a higher nature" as part of our essence, and our species can be "wonderful out of their own human and biological nature."[9]

Beyond wishful thinking, our fundamental "goodness" is borne out by innumerable examples that demonstrate the power of this quality in our lives. More than simply a modern phenomenon, from battlefield heroics of the Christian Crusades to recent tragedies of floods, hurricanes, and terrorism, it's not uncommon to see one human lay down their life for the benefit of another. Faced with circumstances that threaten one of our kind, more often than not a basic instinct to preserve life becomes stronger than the fears and concerns that we have for ourselves, and we act. This instinct appears to be so deeply ingrained into the fabric of our nature that we even extend it beyond our species to the animal kingdom as well.

In August of 2002, portions of Europe experienced the heaviest rainfall and floods in nearly a century. I was leading a tour in Southern Peru as record amounts of rain devastated historic sites in Austria, Germany, and the Czech Republic. Throughout the week, I caught brief glimpses of the chaos and devastation carried by satellite to the one-station televisions in our rural mountain hotels. Of all the images that I witnessed during that time, among the most powerful for me personally were those of authorities attempting to save a captive elephant from drowning in her enclosure at a zoo in the city of Prague.

Risking their own lives as mountains of water and debris rushed toward them, officials worked feverishly to free this 35-year-old Indian elephant, named Kadir, while she panicked and thrashed in the rising water. In the end, the efforts failed, and in a moment of desperation, the officials chose to take Kadir's life quickly rather than subject her to the slow death of drowning.[10]

It would have been much easier and certainly acceptable, in the presence of so much chaos, for the workers to devote their energy to saving themselves, their homes, and families. Faced with the choice, however, something within them transcended logic, and they acted on Kadir's behalf. In recent years, similar stories have aired across the networks, regarding horses in flooded canyons of the American West; as well as dogs, cats, and even hamsters being saved from burning homes, all at the risk of their rescuers' lives.

In the wake of September 11, a little-publicized project focused on going door-to-door in Lower Manhattan's crumbling apartment buildings, collapsed hotels, and burned-out homes in search of peoples' pets that had been abandoned in the chaos. The reward of those who risked their lives in unstable buildings and toxic smoke brought tears to the eyes of the reporters covering the story. One by one, family pets were retrieved—hungry, dehydrated, *and alive*—wagging their tails or softly whimpering in response to human touch. Once again, in the hours and days following September 11, to concede the loss of animal life as a consequence of such a catastrophe would have been acceptable, and certainly justified by the magnitude of the tragedy. The point is that, as a species, we did not. Something about our fundamental nature found it acceptable to risk human life in an effort to save animal life.

Building Blocks of Change

Nature shows us that to move from one level of order to another requires a period of chaos in between. It is from the collapse of an existing pattern and the ensuing chaos that a new pattern and greater order may be found. To borrow from the popular metaphor of the "calm before the storm," this time of chaos may be viewed as the "storm before the calm." Whether we are talking about the chaos of divorce that precedes the happiness of a new marriage, or the layoff from one job that leads to a whole new career, each benefit is preceded by a time of unsettled change. This principle is clearly illustrated in what appear to be some of the most mystical, yet effective, forms of change among native peoples today: the healing of body and mind through the use of sound.

The idea is that "life" has an inherent blueprint of wellness, one that is always present, even when it appears that chaos has replaced order in the form of disease. Through the very precise use of chanting, drums, rattles, chimes, gongs, tones, and songs, the subtle life patterns of the individual being "healed" are disrupted and thrown into chaos. When the sound stops, because wellness is the blueprint of life, the healthy patterns find one another and reestablish themselves. As the disease has no blueprint, it cannot "find itself" and reassemble. It simply disappears and the result is that the person is "healed."

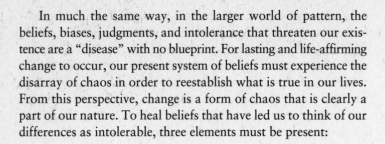

In much the same way, in the larger world of pattern, the beliefs, biases, judgments, and intolerance that threaten our existence are a "disease" with no blueprint. For lasting and life-affirming change to occur, our present system of beliefs must experience the disarray of chaos in order to reestablish what is true in our lives. From this perspective, change is a form of chaos that is clearly a part of our nature. To heal beliefs that have led us to think of our differences as intolerable, three elements must be present:

1. We must be willing to change.

2. We must believe that the change is worth making.

3. We must believe that the change is possible.

Within such a framework, two of the factors required for a single piece of information to make a meaningful difference in our world are already in place:

1. History shows that our willingness to change is our nature.

2. The escalating threats to our existence make the prospect of change worthwhile.

The remaining element necessary is also the most obvious. Before we make a change in our lives, whether as individuals or societies, we need *a reason to believe* that the change we are about to make can be accomplished. We need a sign that it is doable!

God's Signature: A Reason to Believe

In recent months, scientific and lay magazines alike have described what is now called the epidemic "obesity" of America. Statistics show that as much as half of the U.S. population is clinically overweight.[11] Lifestyle factors such as diet, exercise, alcohol, and smoking are cited among the principal factors contributing to this plague that is sweeping our nation, even though all are habits that can be changed relatively easily. For most Americans, the results of such studies, and this kind of news, come as no surprise—we already know about our weight and where it comes from!

Even armed with the clearest knowledge, many individuals are reluctant to make changes that could contribute to their longevity, quality of life, and healthier relationships. Sadly, it is only after experiencing personal health crises—often directly related to lifestyle—that they find the reason to believe that change is necessary. Through the challenge of their personal experience, they discover a reason to believe.

The example of national obesity illustrates one way in which we appear to learn. More often than not, we must experience what we *do not* want in our lives before we know that we don't want it! Rather than choosing the way we prefer to live (for example, healthy choices of nutrition and lifestyle) we react to what life shows us, making our decisions after the fact.

As a global society, it appears that we may learn in the same way. We had to experience the horrors of genocide and global oppression before we began to condemn the policies that support them. As a nation, we had to experience segregation by race and status before we recognized that we were more than our beliefs and the color of our skin. Historically, it is new ideas, solidly based in truth, that have opened the door to entirely new worlds of change and possibility. Until Copernicus presented his evidence that the earth moves around the sun, rather than the sun around the earth, there was no reason to believe otherwise. It was only after Antoni van Leeuwenhoek witnessed bacteria through his handmade magnifying lenses, that the world of microbes invisible to the naked eye was taken seriously. Until they were seen, there was no reason to believe that they existed.

As a species, we have arrived at a precarious moment on our evolutionary path, where we're learning how our access to nature's forces fits into our lives: the time that Carl Sagan identified as

technical adolescence. The key to our survival is that we must recognize the fundamental principles of our relationship to life, one
another, and the cosmos before we can apply what we've learned!

Certainly, on a very different scale than the discoveries of
Copernicus and van Leeuwenhoek, yet in a very similar vein, the
time appears to be right to infuse a new wisdom into our era of
change. While the vast majority of the world professes to believe
in a supreme power of some description, for many, the realities of
suffering and cruelty have created doubt about just how intimately we are connected to the Creator and one another. The
recognition of God's name within each cell of every person, past,
present, and future, offers an unprecedented reason to believe
that a change is worthwhile. It is precisely this magnitude of catalyst that is necessary to turn the strength of our doubt into the
power of trust. In the uncertainty of a changing world, such evidence serves to renew our faith that there is something "out there"
to believe in, while offering us a reason to believe in ourselves.

Beyond Our Differences

While our religions, beliefs, and lifestyles are a part of how we
identify ourselves outwardly, we may be on the threshold of the
era where we outgrow the need to separate ourselves through differences. At the very least, the discovery of God's name within our
bodies carries a message that may elevate us to a greater sense of
respect and tolerance for our uniqueness as individuals. Nature
teaches that it is our diversity—the very differences that have been
used to justify seemingly senseless acts of fear and hate—that
holds our greatest chances for survival as a species. Once again,
let's look to nature for clarity.

In a study of moths conducted in the 1950s, for example, it was
discovered that the coloring of the wings within the same species
changed with the environment, allowing individuals to blend with
their background. The wings of moths living on the tree trunks in
the area where they were released for the study assumed a

"barklike" appearance that made it difficult for birds to detect them while searching for food. Similarly, the moths that were concentrated in a rocky landscape assumed coloring that allowed them to blend in with the rocks of their surroundings. Moths that did not change their wing color, however, had shortened lives, as they became easy prey for birds and other insects. It was the diversity produced by the moths' ability to adapt, and the ease with which they were able to change, that led to their survival.[12]

In much the same way, it's our ability to think differently and adapt to the conditions of our changing world that assure our survival as a species. In a now-famous statement, Einstein encapsulated this concept: "The significant problems we face today cannot be solved at the same level of thinking we were at when we created them." If we all perceived the world in precisely the same way and had precisely the same solutions for our problems, the first time our collective answer was wrong could well be the last time we had the opportunity to change.

Perhaps it is no accident, then, that God's name translates into the same letters and implies the same meaning—even in languages that appear to support the most diverse religions and beliefs of our world today. Although scholars acknowledge, for example, that both the Jewish and Islamic traditions share a common ancestry through the patriarch Abraham, it is their interpretations of Abraham's teachings that have become widely varied over centuries. *Even in the presence of such differences, the hidden number code for the Hebrew and Arabic alphabets reveals precisely the same value and produces precisely the same secret of God's name in our bodies.* In doing so, the code carries the same message of possibility and hope to the three religions that account for over one-half of the world's population: Judaism, Islam, and Christianity.

Figure 9.1 illustrates how this powerful link bridges even these diverse religious traditions. The first block to the left shows the code of life as the elements of DNA—hydrogen, nitrogen, oxygen, and carbon. In the middle block, the same code is shown as the equivalent letters in the Hebrew alphabet: *Yod, Hey, Vav,* and *Gimel* (YHVG). The block to the right illustrates the code once again, this time in Arabic.[13] In the middle and right-hand blocks, the value for each letter is noted immediately to the right, under the column "Value." The result is obvious, the implications enormous.

DNA As Elements	DNA As Hebrew Letters		DNA As Arabic Letters	
Chemistry	Hebrew	Value	Arabic	Value
Hydrogen	Yod	10	YA	10
Nitrogen	Hey	5	HA	5
Oxygen	Vav	6	WAW	6
Carbon	Gimel	3	JYM	3
Combined Value		6		6

Figure 9.1: Comparison of the elements of life, and their equivalents in the Hebrew and Arabic alphabets. Though the outward languages are different, the underlying number codes are the same, and produce the same message in both languages.

The message within our DNA reads precisely the same in both the Arabic and Hebrew languages.

These relationships graphically show us what we already sense on an intuitive level. The letters of God's name within our bodies are universal, regardless of our differences. Within each cell of every body, we find the same code, yielding the same message; and transcending the language, faith, and race of the individual without bias, prejudice, or exception.

Although many have suspected that such a message must exist *somewhere,* through the code within our cells, this suspicion becomes a reality. As the code is based in consistent, repeatable, and verifiable values, the fact of its existence is clear. Beyond metaphor or wishful thinking, and regardless of the way that we interpret the message, the presence of the code, in and of itself, cannot be denied.

Although the literal text of the message "God/Eternal within the body" will undoubtedly be subject to various interpretations, the fact that the message exists at all speaks volumes. Regardless of "who" or "what" we believe is the source of our genetic code, the tremendous degree of order implied by the message says that something else is "out there." This reminds us that we're part of a bigger picture, and perhaps a greater plan. For these reasons, the message in our bodies is unprecedented in its role of providing a platform of common ground in the resolution of our differences.

A Place to Begin

In recent years, the study of conflict resolution has become recognized as a specialized and evolving science. Perhaps the fastest growing branch of this field is Alternative Dispute Resolution (ADR), which is designed to create new and innovative solutions for parties in volatile solutions. Ultimately, the goal of ADR is perhaps best stated in a paper regarding water conflicts among contemporary indigenous peoples. Published in the journal, *International Negotiation,* Aaron T. Wolf, an assistant professor at Oregon State University, defines ADR as a number of approaches "with which parties in conflict voluntarily seek to reach a mutually acceptable settlement."[14] While the term may be recent, he suggests that many modern techniques actually have ancient roots in indigenous societies, and "apparently, have been used by indigenous people for centuries if not millennia."[15]

Not unlike the situation that we find ourselves in today as a global society, to survive the challenges of their existence, ancient communities discovered that it was in their collective best interest to work together in solving the issues that threatened their future.

One of the clearest examples of these traditional methods at work may be seen in a practice known as *shared-vision* exercises. Wolf describes these techniques in his research on the water disputes between the Berber peoples in the M'goun Valley region of Morocco.[16] Through their shared vision, each individual offers a view of what the conflict could look like if it were to be resolved successfully, as well as a view of what may happen if the negotiations fail. The purpose of the vision is to provide a forum that contributes to the foundation of what they would like to accomplish together. In this way, both sides have ownership in the outcome and feel included in the process. Additionally, when tempers flare and resolution seems unlikely, the shared vision becomes a point of reference to fall back upon, reaffirming the common thread that brought them together in the beginning.

Through sharing their hopes and dreams of what a positive solution can look like, conflicting parties create a bridge between the conflict of the moment and the possibilities of a greater future. Additionally, their vision may be used to defuse the anger that often erupts when the parties meet face-to-face, as well as a reason to believe in the process. Using the visions, the *hak'm* (a regional judge who uses a combination of customs and traditions that honor both parties) "puts the dispute in the larger context of their shared histories and values."[17] Through the successful use of shared visions applied to a variety of issues, only rarely are the tribal disputes of the M'goun Valley elevated to a higher authority.

Deceptively simple, the theme of the shared vision represents the possibility of a shared experience as well. While a collective future of world peace is the hope of many today, at the same time we witness examples of hate that are so strong, with mistrust and hurt so deep, that to envision a common good is likened to asking the impossible.

Similar to the way people may lose trust in their bodies when the power of illness appears to be greater than the possibility of healing, people who have been at war require a starting place from which to overcome their mistrust and begin healing. From Kosovo's Muslims and Serbs to Israel's Palestinians and Jews, the memory of recent atrocities and violence have created a sense of mistrust between opposing sides that leaves little room for peace. In instances such as these, it has been difficult just to envision the end of a day without violence, let alone a shared and peaceful future. To ask these people to create the vision of a common future pushes the limits of their sensibilities.

It's under precisely such circumstances that the message in our cells may serve an even greater good. While envisioning a shared future may be difficult in the midst of seemingly unending conflict, the acknowledgment of a common identity—knowing that each individual is imbued with the indelible signature of the same God—offers a fact that cannot be denied. In this single, immutable piece of evidence lives the truth of a family, a common past, and a place to begin. With the knowledge of a greater presence within the very fabric of our bodies, the vision of a shared future begins to make sense.

In the first years of this new century, many of the most violent conflicts, which have taken the greatest numbers of lives, have been justified through extreme interpretations of religious texts. Based in the way specific phrases of Christian, Jewish, or Muslim scripture is read, families have been destroyed, children orphaned, and nations left in ruin. It is within this type of conflict that the message within our cells may have an even greater power, and assume an even deeper meaning. The presence of God's name in our bodies stands as an indelible reminder that a single presence—a force greater than our changing ideas of "right" and "wrong"—exists as life itself.

For individuals and nations battling one another for reasons justified by their religions—whose principles are based upon the God that lives within the bodies of their "enemies" as well as themselves—the battles begin to make very little sense. In this way, the message in our cells holds even a greater possibility of unity for those whose conflicts are in the name of God.

Interestingly, in both the Berber and Bedouin communities that Wolf describes in his paper, the resolution of the conflict is often followed by ceremony called a *sulha,* which is a public ritual of forgiveness followed by a celebration. The moment of the sulha marks a turning point in the relationship between the parties that have been in conflict only days or weeks before. Ideally, the ritual occurs *only when both parties* feel that the situation of conflict has been resolved. Through the ritual of forgiveness and celebration, the slate is "wiped clean" and the agreement becomes legally binding. In this way, there is closure to the entire experience, and life begins anew.

As nations find themselves backing away from the conflicts that threaten the well-being of their citizens and our global community, the power of an outward sign of forgiveness is something that appears to be missing. The effectiveness of such an honoring gesture of strength toward a lasting completion cannot be underestimated.

Our One Immutable Truth

Seated next to the window, I glanced up from the papers in my lap to see what all the commotion was about. As I listened to the bits and pieces of the conversation, it became apparent that the woman who had been seated next to me when I boarded the plane had a friend that she wanted to sit with in another section. She had convinced the man already sitting next to her friend to exchange seats with her, and now they were stepping over one another in an attempt to maneuver into their new seats before the plane left the gate. When all was said and done, I found myself next to an Air Force officer returning to his wife and children at a military base in New Mexico.

Before the plane had even left the ground, we were engaged in the usual "airplane conversation," exchanging the courtesies of describing where we had been, where we were going, and what we would do when we got there. As soon as the use of electronics was permitted, the man opened up his laptop computer and became very focused on the information blazing across his LCD screen. Clearly feeling at ease from our earlier conversation, he began describing his job to me and how it had changed following the World Trade Center and Pentagon attacks of September 11. As he elaborated on the new strategies of national security and how terrorism had redefined his role in the military, I found that my fascination was less about the topic itself and more about this man's passion for what he believed in and the pride with which he approached his responsibilities. I began to think about the irony of the moment.

The officer's job was to tap in to the resources of the most powerful military, weapons, and technology systems in recorded history, and to use that force to combat those who threaten our homes and way of life. On the other hand, following my time in the aerospace industry during the Cold War, my focus had been to bridge the wisdom of our past with what we know today to help us avoid the need for precisely such war. I wondered to myself what the odds were that the shuffling and reseating that had led to our conversation had occurred purely by "chance."

After the officer finished describing his new responsibilities, our conversation shifted. It was obvious that this man was very good at his job. What he contributed to the military arose from a personal place of professionalism, determination, and the pride that comes with knowing that those efforts contribute to a greater effort. I expressed my appreciation to him for the way he approached his job. "I'm glad that you do what you do and do it so very well," I began. "Because I could never do your job."

"Really?" he replied. "That's interesting. And what is it that you do?" he asked. Following a brief description of my search for the wisdom to avoid war, he laughed for just a moment. Then he returned my compliment and said, "I'm glad that you do what you do, because I could never do *your* job. It's such a different way of thinking!"

We shared a laugh at the irony of our lives and continued to solve the problems of the world through the remainder of our flight. By the time we landed in Albuquerque that evening, it had become very clear to both of us that we wanted the same things for our families and the world, and were contributing to that common goal in very different ways. As we made our way to the baggage-claim area, we wished each other good luck and said our good-byes. As I went down the escalator, I began to realize that, within the small conversation between us, the officer and I had experienced a mirror of the way that consciousness appears to work on a much larger scale.

Assuming that a unified field of consciousness links us, there can be no "them" and "us" as the events of our world unfold.

There is simply a "we." Together, *we* are resolving our differences and solving our problems in the only ways that we know how. Part of us relies upon the tried and proven methods of our past—battles, war, and old ideas implemented through modern technology—to resolve the issues that arise between people and nations. At the same time, however, another part of us strives to change the thinking that has led to the need for the weapons and armies that make war possible. We are living through a time in history when both views must coexist, while together we choose the path that we will follow into our future.

The irony of our time in history is that both ways of thinking are supported by good people working toward a better world in the only ways they understand. Recognition of this may well be the key to surviving this transition. While the old ways buy us precious time, the question is whether or not we have the wisdom to use that time wisely to change the thinking that believes war is the solution to our differences.

My conversation with the officer only strengthened my belief that we are working together as a global family, perhaps in ways that we have yet to recognize or fully understand. While we continue to discover just how deep the roots of our "family tree" really extend, however, of one thing we may be absolutely certain: As "blood" unites the most distant relatives through the knowledge of their heritage, the message in our cells unites us in the knowledge that we each carry the same history and the same signature of the same Creator. With that message, we are assured that, in addition to sharing our planet, our past, and our future, we're intimately enmeshed within the choices of those around us, the only family that we know.

Once we know the truth of our human family, we cannot "un-know" it. Once we see the evidence in black and white, it is impossible to "un-see" it. From that moment forward, we can no longer plead ignorance as a reason to justify the hate, suffering, and atrocities that have marked the last century.

Beyond any reasonable doubt, we each share the ancient name of God in our bodies in the most intimate way imaginable. Each fiber of muscle, each crystal of bone, the tears that we shed, and the by-products of life that we call "waste"—all are God.

Within this simple yet powerful realization lives the thread of our unity and the key to our survival. While we may not know precisely what challenges we will face in our collective future, of one thing we may be certain: Whatever our tests entail, we will face them as a global family. Whatever fate befalls one community, people, or nation is possible for all others as well. It will require every ounce of our collective wisdom, our passion to preserve life, and the strength that can only come from our diversity for us to become more than our tests.

For hundreds of generations, we have each carried the key to our survival as a message to ourselves in a form that, once recognized, could not be mistaken. Perhaps in anticipation of the day when the search for our origins would lead us to the essence of life, it is only through our discovery and acceptance that we are one with the world that the message could ever be revealed.

Beyond Christian, Jew, Muslim, Hindu, Buddhist, Shinto, Native, Aboriginal, white, black, red, or yellow; man, woman, or child, the message reminds us that we are human. As humans, we share the same ancestors and exist as the children of the same Creator. In the moments that we doubt this one immutable truth, we need look no further than the cells of our body to be reminded.

This is the power of the message within our cells.

CHAPTER 9 SUMMARY

- Experience has shown that humankind has an extraordinary ability to unify during moments of common need. Historically, tragedies have provided the greatest opportunity for large and diverse populations to rally around a common cause.

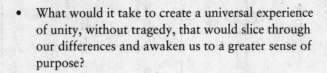

- What would it take to create a universal experience of unity, without tragedy, that would slice through our differences and awaken us to a greater sense of purpose?

- In his landmark paper on the Search for Extraterrestrial Intelligence (SETI), the late Carl Sagan suggested that our detection of a message from beyond our world would serve as a powerful unifying factor in human consciousness.

- In many respects, the discovery of a universal message within our cells may achieve the same kind of unity among people of diverse cultures and beliefs.

- Many of the issues that led to the 20th century's distinction as the "bloodiest 100 years" in history have continued into the new millennium. At the same time, many feel as though our differences in religion, heritage, and beliefs have never been greater. The time is ripe for the acceptance of a powerful, unifying message of hope—something to believe in.

- Faced with evidence of humankind's "inhumanity to man," history and science suggest that we are basically a species of "goodness," although capable of violent acts in extreme circumstances.

- Nature offers a blueprint of how unity and cooperation offer a greater chance of species' survival than violent competition. Human history, such as the clash between cultures during the exploration of North America, supports this idea.

- The "signature" of God's ancient name in the cells of our species offers an unprecedented common denominator from which to resolve our differences. Such tangible evidence also gives us a reason to believe that peace is achievable and worthwhile.

- Indigenous traditions of conflict resolution offer a viable model for transcending the differences that threaten our survival as a species.

- As citizens of our world, we are more than any religion, heritage, belief, lifestyle, border, or technology that divides us. In the moments when we doubt this one, immutable truth, we need look no further that the message in our bodies to be reminded. This is the power of the message within our cells.

Appendix A

THE SECRET ORDER OF
THE ARABIC ALPHABET
Shown with Number Codes

[Used with permission and courtesy of David Allen Hulse[1]]

Letter	Letter Name	Number Value	Letter	Letter Name	Number Value
A	ALF	1	O	OYN	70
B	BA	2	F	FA	80
J	JYM	3	S	SAD	90
D	DAL	4	Q	QAF	100
H	HA	5	R	RA	200
W	WAW	6	Sh	ShYN	300
Z	ZA	7	T	TA	400
H	HA	8	Th	ThA	500
T	TA	9	Kh	KhA	600
Y	YA	10	Dh	DhAL	700
K	KAF	20	D	DAD	800
L	LAM	30	Tz	TzA	900
M	MYM	40	Gh	GhYN	1000
N	NWM	50	A	HMZ	NO VALUE
S	SYN	60			

(Underlined letters of the Arabic alphabet above correspond to the same values of God's name in the Hebrew alphabet.)

 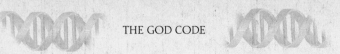

Arabic Letters of God's Name   Hebrew Letters of God's Name
Y (*YA*) = 10   ⟶   Y (*Yod*) = 10
H (*HA*) = 5   ⟶   H (*Hey*) = 5
W(V) (*WAW*) = 6 ⟶   V (*Vav*) = 6

Appendix B

THE PERIODIC TABLE
of Elements

IA															
H 1.0															

Legend

H 1.008 ← Element Name
← Atomic Mass

IIA												IIIA	IVA
Li 6.9	Be 9.0											B 10.8	C 12.0
Na 22.9	Mg 24.3						VIIIB					Al 26.9	Si 28.0

		IIIB	IVB	VB	VIB	VIIB				IB	IIB		
K 39.0	Ca 40.0	Sc 44.9	Ti 47.8	V 50.9	Cr 51.9	Mn 54.9	Fe 55.8	Co 58.9	Ni 58.6	Cu 63.5	Zn 65.3	Ga 69.7	Ge 72.6
Rb 85.4	Sr 87.6	Y 88.9	Zr 91.2	Nb 92.9	Mo 95.9	Tc 98	Ru 101.0	Rh 102.9	Pd 106.4	Ag 107.8	Cd 112.4	In 114.8	Sn 118.7
Cs 132.9	Ba 137.3	*	Hf 178.4	Ta 180.9	W 183.4	Re 186.2	Os 190.2	Ir 192.2	Pt 195.0	Au 196.9	Hg 200.5	Tl 204.3	Pb 207.2
Fr 223	Ra 226	**	Rf 261	Db 262	Sg 263	Bh 262	Hs 265	Mt 266	Uun 269	Uuu 272	Uub 277		

0
He 4.0

Note: The four elements of DNA, carbon, oxygen, hydrogen, and nitrogen are highlighted with darker shading.

VA	VIA	VIIA	
N 14.0	O 15.9	F 18.9	Ne 20.1
P 30.9	S 32.0	Cl 35.4	Ar 39.9
As 74.9	Se 78.9	Br 79.9	Kr 83.9
Sb 121.7	Te 127.6	I 126.9	Xe 131.2
Bi 208.9	Po 209	At 210	Rn 222

*	La 138.9	Ce 140.1	Pr 140.9	Nd 144.2	Pm 145	Sm 150.3	Eu 151.9	Gd 157.2	Tb 158.9	Dy 162.5	Ho 164.9	Er 167.2	Tm 168.9	Yb 173.0	Lu 174.9
**	Ac 227	Th 232.0	Pa 231.0	U 238.0	Np 237	Pu 244	Am 243	Cm 247	Bk 247	Cf 251	Es 252	Fm 257	Md 258	No 259	Lr 262

Appendix C

THE NUMBER OF HYDROGEN, Nitrogen, Oxygen, and Carbon Atoms in Each of the Four DNA Bases

In the DNA base *thymine,* there are six hydrogen atoms, two nitrogen atoms, two oxygen atoms, and five carbon atoms present.* Cytosine is composed of different amounts of exactly the same elements, with five hydrogens, three nitrogens, one oxygen, and four carbons. The remaining bases vary accordingly and are noted below. In this way, a tremendous number of variations become possible, simply by using different arrangements of the same four elements.

The following chart illustrates the four DNA bases and the number of atoms for each element that makes each base unique.

DNA Base	Chemical Element	Number of Atoms	DNA Base	Chemical Element	Number of Atoms
Thymine(T)	Hydrogen	6	Adenine(A)	Hydrogen	5
	Nitrogen	2		Nitrogen	5
	Oxygen	2		Oxygen	0
	Carbon	5		Carbon	5
Cytosine(C)	Hydrogen	5	Guanine(G)	Hydrogen	5
	Nitrogen	3		Nitrogen	5
	Oxygen	1		Oxygen	1
	Carbon	4		Carbon	5

*Number of atoms calculated from *Lehringer's Biochemistry Textbook* (a medical standard). Dr. Todd Ovokaitys confirmed my interpretation of the data.

Appendix D

EXPANDED ILLUSTRATION
of the Hydrogen, Nitrogen, Oxygen, and Carbon Atoms in Each DNA Base, Showing Their Equivalents As Hebrew Letters

In the thymine, cytosine, adenine, and guanine that follow on the chart, we see that the letters/elements responsible for the uniqueness vary in each base. Additionally, we note that the presence of God's name within the code, as YH does not always guarantee that the "within the body" (VG) is held within that portion of DNA.

For example, in cytosine, while YH is repeated in the base three times, only once, in the first instance, is the code complemented by the VG indicating "within the body." For 66 percent of the cytosine base, the "Eternal" name of God as YH simply exists, without the specification as to where the eternal nature of the code is directed, or resides. The extreme of this example may be seen in adenine, where there are four instances of God's name, while there are no instances within this base of the Eternal being directed within the body.

DNA Base	Atom/ Element	Hebrew Letters	Number of Atoms	Literal Illustration
Thymine(T)	Hydrogen	Y	6	<u>YYYYYY</u>
	Nitrogen	H	2	<u>HH</u>
	Oxygen	V	2	**VV**
	Carbon	G	5	**GGGGG**
Cytosine(C)	Hydrogen	Y	6	<u>YYYYYY</u>
	Nitrogen	H	3	<u>HHH</u>
	Oxygen	V	1	**V**
	Carbon	G	4	**GGGG**
Adenine(A)	Hydrogen	Y	5	<u>YYYYY</u>
	Nitrogen	H	5	<u>HHHHH</u>
	Oxygen	V	0	*********
	Carbon	G	5	**GGGGG**
Guanine(G)	Hydrogen	Y	5	<u>YYYYY</u>
	Nitrogen	H	5	<u>HHHHH</u>
	Oxygen	V	1	**V**
	Carbon	G	5	**GGGGG**

Applying the number values of the Hebrew alphabet to the elements of our DNA reveals that the basis of all life stems directly from the ancient name of God.

Key: <u>YH</u> (underline) indicates the "Eternal" aspect of God's ancient name.
VG (bold) indicates how the "Eternalness" resides "within the body."

ENDNOTES

Epigraph

1. Text taken from Almaliah Gad's artistic interpretation of Hebrew scripture. Gad has designed coins and medals for the Israeli government, as well as the emblem for the Six-Day War. His work is displayed at the Ahava Galleries in Boca Raton, Florida.

Part I
Introduction

1. *Penzias and Wilson's Discovery Is One of the Century's Key Advances,* online article including the biography of the researchers and the significance of their discovery. Website: **www.bell-labs.com.**

2. Michio Kaku, *Visions: How Science Will Revolutionize the 21st Century* (New York: Anchor Books, 1998), p. 5.

3. Between 1998 and 2000, at least 50 nations or occupied regions were engaged in armed conflict. Jeffrey Boutwell and Michael T. Klare, "A Scourge of Small Arms," *Scientific American* (June 2000): p. 51.

4. Randall Ingermanson, Ph.D., *Who Wrote the Bible Code? A Physicist Probes the Current Controversy* (Colorado Springs: WaterBrook Press, 1999), p. 19.

5. Michio Kaku, *Hyperspace: A Scientific Odyssey Through Parallel Universes, Time Warps, and the Tenth Dimension* (New York: Anchor Books, 1995), p. 289.

6. Barbara Marx Hubbard, onstage quote from *The Prophet's Conference* (December 2001), in Palm Springs, California.

Chapter 1

1. Richard Leakey, quoted from article in *National Geographic,* February 1998. Website: **www.kirjasto.sci.fi/leakey.**

2. Eric Hobsbawm, "War and Peace in the 20th Century," *London Review of Books* (February 2002). Hobsbawm's statistics show that by the end of the

century, over 187 million people—*a number that represents more than 10 percent of the world's population in 1913*—had lost their lives to war.

3. Zbigniew Brzezinski, *Out of Control: Global Turmoil on the Eve of the 21st Century* (New York: Simon and Schuster, 1995), p. 12.

4. Matthew White, *Twentieth Century Atlas*. See "Historical Body Count, Selected Death Tolls for Wars, Massacres, and Atrocities Before the 20th Century." Website: **http://users.erols.com/mwhite28/warstat0/htm.**

5. Ibid.

6. Ibid.

7. Brzezinski, *Out of Control*, p. 4.

8. Terese Pencak Schwartz, "Five Million Forgotten: Non Jewish Victims of the Shoah." White paper (1997) on the five million non-Jewish victims of the Holocaust, quoting the following sources: Richard C. Lukas, *The Forgotten Holocaust* (Lexington: Univ. Press of Kentucky, 1997) and Stefan Korbonski, *The Jews and the Poles in World War II* (New York: Hippocrene Books, 1998). Website: **www.remember.org/forgotten/**

9. The figure of 1.2 million Tibetans is the estimated death toll for the two decades immediately following the uprising in 1959. It represents approximately one-fifth of the region's population, and may not account for those who died in prison or during the destruction of over 6,000 monasteries, temples, and cultural buildings. Website: **www.tibet.com.**

10. R. J. Rummel, *Statistics of Democide: Genocide and Mass Murder Since 1900* (Charlottesville: Transaction Publishers and Rutgers Univ., 1997). Virginia Center for National Security Law, School of Law, University of Virginia.

11. R. J. Rummel, "War Isn't This Century's Biggest Killer," *The Wall Street Journal* (July 7, 1986).

12. Rummel, *Statistics of Democide*.

13. Brzezinski, *Out of Control*, p. 12.

14. Report on the AIDS epidemic, with global statistics from UNAIDS: The Joint UN Programme on HIV/AIDS. Website: **www.unaids.org.**

15. Matthew White, *Twentieth Century Atlas*. See "Worldwide Statistics of Casualties, Massacres, Disasters, and Atrocities." These statistics were taken from a December 20, 1999, press release by the Munich Reinsurance Company. Website: **http://users.erols.com/mwhite28/warstat0/htm.**

16. Jonathan Steele, "The Century that Murdered Peace," *Guardian Unlimited* (December 12, 1999). Website: **www.guardian.co.uk.**

17. Summary of active United Nations peacekeeping missions in 2002 by country and year deployed. As of March 2002, there were a total of 46,445 personnel and civilian police involved representing 87 countries. Website: **www.un.org.**

18. Neil Armstrong, quoted in the article, "Contact, Are We Alone?" *Florida Today* (1999). Website: **www.flatoday.com.**

19. Ibid.

20. Ibid.

21. Carl Sagan, "The Quest For Extraterrestrial Intelligence." *Smithsonian,* vol. 1, no. 2 (May 1978). His classic paper regarding the search for extraterrestrial life—its costs and its benefits—may be read online. Website: **www.bigear.org/vol1no2/sagan.htm.**

Chapter 2

1. G. Y. Craig and E. J. Jones, *A Geological Miscellany* (New Jersey: Princeton Univ. Press, 1982).

2. Additionally, Hutton suggested that the forces changing the earth's crust, including volcanoes and the uplifting and sinking of continents, were forces that had remained constant since the beginning of time. It was from the sense that earth processes are *uniform* over long periods of time that Hutton derived his theory's name: the principle of *uniformitarianism.*

3. In 1830, Hutton's ideas were popularized through the work of another Scottish scientist, Charles Lyell, in his now-classic work *The Principles of Geology.*

4. Charles Darwin, 1859. Cited by the Galapagos Conservation Trust, a resource dedicated to preserving and disseminating Darwin's discoveries from the Galapagos Islands. Website: **www.gct.org.**

5. References to *high altitude* are usually considered to be elevations between 5,904 and 19,680 feet above sea level, with higher elevations considered *extreme altitudes.* Although villages of full-time inhabitants are known to exist as high as 19,000 feet above sea level, populations at such extreme elevations are rare.

6. Stephen Molnar, *Human Variation: Races, Types, and Ethnic Groups* (New Jersey: Prentice Hall, 1992), p. 218.

7. Unless noted, these dates are from the Special Edition of *Scientific American* (vol. 12, no. 2) released in July of 2003, New Look at Human Evolution.

8. The fossilized remains of the genus *Australopithecus* cover a broad expanse of time. As of this writing, the oldest known representation of this lineage, *Australopithecus anamensis,* dates to approximately 4.1 million years old, while the youngest representation, *Australopithecus boisei,* dates to approximately 1.4 million years old. The most widely publicized example of *Australopithecus* was that of a young female discovered in 1974 near Hadar, Ethiopia. Nicknamed "Lucy," this is most complete representation of *Australopithecus* discovered to date.

9. S. J. Gould and N. Eldridge, "Punctuated Equilibria: The Tempo and Mode of Evolution Reconsidered," *Paleobiology,* vol. 3: pp. 115–151. For the first time in over a century, Darwin's theory of evolution is now challenged by a viable alternative, known as *Punctuated Equilibrium.* Proposed by Niles Eldridge and Stephen Jay Gould, the theory suggests, "Instead of a slow, continuous movement, evolution tends to be characterized by long periods of virtual standstill ('equilibrium'), 'punctuated' by episodes of very fast development of new forms."

10. Igor V. Ovchinnikov, et al, "Molecular Analysis of Neanderthal DNA from the Northern Caucasus," *Nature,* vol. 404 (March 30, 2000): p. 490.

11. Press release from the University of Glasgow, "Rare Tests on Neanderthal Infant Sheds Light on Early Human Development," March 28, 2000. Website: **www.gla.ac.uk.**

12. *Genes in Chimpanzee chromosome 12 or 13 (correspond to human chromosome 2).* Portion of gene sequence retrieved from the *GenBank International Nucleotide Sequence Database.* Web source: **http://sayer.lab.nig.ac.jp/ ~silver/chimp/chromosome-12/top-1213.html.**

13. R. Avarello, et al, "Evidence for an Ancestral Alphoid Domain on the Long Arm of Human Chromosome 2," *Human Genetics,* vol. 89, no. 2 (May 1992): pp. 247–9.
    The following is an excerpt from the paper's abstract. "Since it is supposed that human chromosome 2 originated by the telomeric *fusion of two ancestral primate chromosomes,* these findings indicate that not only the telomeric sequences, but also the ancestral centromere (or at least its alphoid sequences), have been conserved" [author's italics].

14. "Origin of Human Chromosome 2: An Ancestral telomere-telomere Fusion," Proceedings of the National Academy of Sciences of the United States of America, vol. 88, no. 20 (October 15, 1991): pp. 9051–5.
    The following is an excerpt from the paper's abstract. "We conclude that the locus cloned in cosmids c8.1 and c29B is the relic of *an ancient telomere-telomere fusion and marks the point at which two ancestral ape chromosomes fused to give rise to human chromosome 2*" [author's italics].

15. Don Lindsay, "An Inversion Between Man and Chimpanzee Chromosomes." This is a brief, nontechnical description and diagram of the phenomenon of identical genes in different locations in the DNA of humans and chimpanzees. This simple online reference is available at: **www.cs.colorado.edu/~lindsay/creation/inversion.html.**

16. L.S.B. Leakey, Arthur T. Hopwood and Hans Reck, "Age of the Oldoway Bone Beds, Tanganyika Territory," *Nature,* vol. 128, no. 3234 (October 24, 1931): p. 724.

17. Ibid., pp. 239–244.

18. Richard E. Dickerson and Irving Geis, *Chemistry, Matter, and the Universe: An Integrated Approach to General Chemistry* (Menlo Park, CA.: W. A. Benjamin, 1976), p. 629.

19. Frank Crane, *The Lost Books of the Bible and the Forgotten Books of Eden* (New York: New American Library, 1963).

20. Dickerson and Geis, *Chemistry, Matter, and the Universe,* p. 529.

21. Darwin, *The Origin of Species,* p. 168.

22. Francis Crick, *Life Itself* (New York: Simon and Schuster, 1981), p. 88.

Chapter 3

1.There are a number of very good references for the life, history, and teachings of Baal Shem Tov and his transition from Israel ben Eliezer. The following reference specifically pertains to his relationship to the *Book of Adam.* Baal Shem Tov Foundation Website: **www.baalshemtov.com.**

2. Crane, *The Lost Books of the Bible and the Forgotten Books of Eden,* p. 13.

3. Ibid., p. 14.

4. Ibid., p. 11.

5. Hershel Shanks, *The Mystery and Meaning of the Dead Sea Scrolls* (New York: Random House, 1998), dust flap.

6. *The Dead Sea Scrolls,* translated and with commentary by Michael Wise, Martin Abegg, Jr., and Edward Cook (California: HarperSanFrancisco, 1996), p. 8.

7. James M. Robinson, ed., *The Nag Hammadi Library,* translated and introduced by members of the Coptic Gnostic Library Project of the Institute for Antiquity and Christianity, Claremont, California (HarperSanFrancisco, 1990).

Dating to the 4th-century C.E., the Nag Hammadi Library begins at the approximate time that the Dead Sea Scrolls leave off. The Gnostic traditions originated during the time that early Christian doctrine was being reshaped and defined. Identifying with the teachings as they were preserved by earlier generations, the Gnostics chose to separate and honor the original traditions, rather than follow the trend that was being led by the Church. Their texts and way of life were largely discounted, and eventually eliminated from Christian teachings. Through finds such as the Nag Hammadi Library, rare books including the *Gospel of Mary,* the *Apocalypse of Adam,* and the *Book of Enoch* survive today as a testament to the depth of Gnostic wisdom and their dedication to preserving a timeless teaching for future generations.

8. *The Book of Enoch the Prophet,* translated by Richard Laurence from an Ethiopian manuscript in the Bodleian Library (San Diego: Wizards Bookshelf, 1983), p. iv.

9. Ibid., pp. iv–v.

10. Ibid., p. vii.

11. Ibid., chapter I, verse 1, p. 1.

12. Ibid., chapter LXIII, verse 1, p. 77.

13. Ibid., chapter IX, verse 5, p. 9.

14. Ibid., chapter LXVIII, verse 7, p. 85.

15. Ibid., chapter XLI, verse 2, p. 46.

16. Ibid., chapter XLII, verses 1–2, p. 47.

17. *The Other Bible*: *Ancient Alternative Scriptures,* Willis Barnstone, ed. (California: HarperSanFrancisco, 1984), p. 25.

18. Ibid.

19. Ibid., p. 26.

20. *Sepher Yetzirah: The Book of Creation,* Aryeh Kaplan, ed. (York Beach, ME: Samuel Weiser, 1997), p. xvi.

21. Ibid., verse 1:1, p. 5.

22. Ibid., verse 2:2, p. 100.

23. Ibid., 1:1, p. 22.

24. Karen Armstrong, *A History of God: The 4,000-Year Quest of Judaism, Christianity and Islam* (New York: Alfred A. Knopf, 1993), p. 216.

25. *Sepher Yetzirah*, p. xxv.

26. Ibid.

Part II
Chapter 4

1. *The Other Bible*, "The Creation of Adam," p. 26.

2. *The Holy Qur'an*, translation and commentary by Maulana Muhammad Ali, chapter 22, section 1, verse 5 (Columbus, OH: Ahmadiyyah Anjuman Isha'at Islam Lahore, 1995), p. 648.

3. Ibid., chapter 25, section 5, verse 54, p. 705.

4. Ibid., chapter 22, section 1, verse 5, p. 648.

5. *The Torah*, A Modern Commentary, ed. W. Gunther Plaut, ed. (New York: Union of American Hebrew Congregations, 1981), Genesis 2:7, p. 29.

6. Manly P. Hall, *The Secret Teachings of All Ages: An Encyclopedic Outline of Masonic, Hermetic, Qabbalistic and Rosicrucian Symbolical Philosophy,* (Los Angeles: The Philosophical Research Society, 1988), CLIII.

7. Roger Bacon (1214–1294 C.E.) is considered to be the first "true" alchemist in Medieval Europe. He was a Franciscan whose work led him to conclude, "Experimental science. . . reveals truths which reasoning from general principles would have never discovered."

8. The present whereabouts of the original *Emerald Tablets of Thoth* and the later *Emerald Tables of Hermes* are uncertain. Scholars suspect that they may have been among the 532,000 documents lost when the Great Library of Alexandria was destroyed by fire in 48 B.C.E. Before that fire, the Roman historian Kallimachos noted that the entire knowledge of the Greek civilization, including astronomy, medicine, science, and philosophy had been recorded and stored in the library. We can only assume that Thoth's revelations were among those documents.

9. Z'ev ben Shimon Halevi, *Kabbalah: Tradition of Hidden Knowledge* (New York: Thames and Hudson, 1979), p. 7.
   The Sefirot enclosed with a dotted line immediately below the Crown on the Tree of Life, is known as the "non-Sefirot" of *Knowledge*. It represents a unique

place among the names of God on the Tree, for although it is given a place on the Tree, it remains unmanifest in our experience of creation.

10. *Sepher Yetzirah,* appendix 1, chapter 2, verse 2, p. 286.

11. Halevi, *Kabbalah,* p. 6.

12. *Sepher Yetzirah,* chapter 1, verse 9, p. 68.

13. Ibid., appendix 1, chapter 4, verse 2, p. 288.

14. Ibid., verse 6, p. 289.

15. Ibid., verse 7, p. 289.

16. Ibid., chapter 3, verse 4, p. 145.

17. Ibid., verse 7, p. 152.

18. Ibid., verse 8, p. 154.

19. Ibid., verse 9, p. 155.

20. Ibid., appendix 1, chapter 2, verse 2, p. 286.

21. "Prayer Helps Patients Heal, " United Press International (1999). Online report of the studies comparing the recovery and outcome for patients who received prayer with those that did not. Website: **www.applesforhealth.com/prayerhelps1.html.**

22. Ibid., p. 1.

23. Kaku, *Visions, p.* 4.

24. In January 1958, the United States launched its first unmanned satellite, *Explorer I,* to gather information regarding our atmosphere and the earth, as part of the IGY. Through Explorer's onboard instruments, scientists were given new insight into the composition of Earth's atmosphere, oceans, and continents.

25. The precise amounts of our atmosphere's composition may vary due to factors of temperature and elevation. In general, Earth's atmosphere is made of 78 percent nitrogen and 21 percent oxygen. Under a section entitled "Composition of the Atmosphere," a reference is available on the NASA Website: **http://liftoff.msfc.nasa.gov/academy/space/atmosphere.html.**

26. While the precise amounts of oxygen dissolved in water may vary due to temperature and salinity (fresh water/salt water), the ratios are similar. Though a

number of references are available, I chose this particular one because it shows how the percentages are derived. The results: water is approximately 88.89 percent oxygen and 11.11 percent hydrogen. Website: **www.citycollegiate.com/chapter3a.htm.**

27. Together, hydrogen (71percent) and helium (27.1percent) account for over 98 percent of our Sun's composition. In trace amounts, the elements oxygen, carbon, nitrogen, silicon, magnesium, neon, iron, and sulfur account for the remaining percentage. NASA Website: **http://imagine.gsfc.nasa.gov/docs/ask_astro/answers/961112a.html.**

Chapter 5

1. Although researchers have been successful in tracing many ancient alphabets to the point where they branched from an earlier linguistic tree, the precise roots of the tree itself remain murky. While archaeologists have recovered examples of ancient forms of writing, and they are in agreement as to *who* created the tablets, scrolls, and rock drawings of times past, the mystery of precisely *where and how* written language originated remains.

For the moment, evidence appears to suggest that the many and diverse languages of the world today originated from a common "mother" language over 5,000 years ago. Direct links have been established from the earliest cuneiform tablets, for example, to the Greek, Hebrew and Phoenician foundations of modern language.

2. In the science of physics, for example, the letter E is an example of a logogram. Here, E is one symbol representing the force of "energy" and all of the implications that mathematics and physics associate with energy. It is a logogram using this symbol that has become what is perhaps the most recognized mathematical equation in history: $E = mc^2$.

Syllabograms are symbols that represent the syllable of a word as it is spoken. The late J. T. Hooker, University of London Emeritus Reader in Greek and Latin language, describes the significance of using symbols to represent syllables as the "most important advance in the history of writing." J. T. Hooker, *Reading the Past* (London: British Museum, 1990). Ancient languages, such as Chinese, where every word is one syllable, made tremendous advances in their ability to preserve details of history through the use of syllable signs. In English, once again, it is the language of science that offers an example of a syllabogram as the mathematical constant "pi" (Π). Here the symbol is also the entire word "pi," and is used to represent a relationship between the circumference of a circle and its and diameter.

3. *Sepher Yetzirah,* appendix 1, chapter 4, verse 4, p. 288.

4. David Allen Hulse, *The Key of It All: An Encyclopedic Guide to the Sacred Languages & Magickal Systems of the World, Book Two: The Western Mysteries* (St. Paul, MN: Llewellyn Publications, 1993), pp. 461–538.

 THE GOD CODE

5. *The American Heritage College Dictionary,* Third Edition, definition 2 (New York: Houghton Mifflin Company, 1997), p. 1221.

6. The study of gematria may, in fact, be one of the oldest sciences in existence. Almost universally, ancient traditions have associated the letters of the major alphabets, including English, Greek, Latin Coptic, Sanskrit, Hebrew, Arabic, Chinese, Cuneiform, and Tibetan with number values. For more information on this topic, please see Hulse's two-volume treatise, *The Key of It All* (see note 4 above).

7. The use of gematria to study the deeper "hidden" relationships between words and phrases has been recognized, honored, and practiced by scientists and philosophers alike, for hundreds, if not thousands, of years. Perhaps the most visible example of the acceptance and study of gematria relates to the mystical science of the Hebrew Kabbalah.

   The principles of gematria may be explored on many levels of meaning beyond simply adding the values of letter-numbers together, and includes the use of reduced, integral reduced, absolute, and ordinal values. While there are a number of very good texts on this subject, one of the best Web references that I am aware of is hosted by *Gal Einai Institute of Israel,* with information taken from the teachings of Rabbi Yitzchak Ginsburgh. Website: **www.inner.org/gematria/gematria.htm.**

8. Rabbi Benjamin Blech, *The Secrets of Hebrew Words* (New Jersey: Jason Aronson, 1991), p. 129.

9. *The Other Bible,* Haggadah, p. 25.

10. Robert Lawlor, *Sacred Geometry: Philosophy and Practice* (New York: Thames and Hudson, 1982), p. 9.

11. Ibid., p. 10.

12. Michael Drosnin, *The Bible Code* (New York: Simon and Schuster, 1997), p. 25.

13. "Atomic mass" is calculated as the mass of an atom relative to one-twelfth the mass of carbon-12, the most abundant form of carbon.

   In the Periodic Table of Elements (Appendix B), each element is assigned the value of atomic mass. (Although the terms *atomic mass* and *atomic weight* are often used interchangeably and the values associated with them are very similar, they are actually measures of two different properties. Atomic weight may be defined a measure of the force with which a planet pulls on mass.)

14. "Matter" is defined as anything that occupies space and had has mass. "Mass" describes the inertia of a moving object, and how easily that object can

be influenced or stopped. For example, a bird flying at ten miles per hour may be easily influenced by a gentle breeze; the bird is said to have little mass. To a heavily armored military tank traveling at the same speed, however, the breeze does not have much effect. In this instance, the *mass* of the tank is said to be greater than that of the bird. In terms of chemistry, when we ask "how much" of something is present, we are really asking, "What is the mass" of that something?

15. Following are key characteristics that make the elements of the Periodic Table of Elements unique. Of the 17 possibilities, only one characteristic links the most abundant elements of the universe with the hidden number values of ancient alchemy. That key is the characteristic of *atomic mass*.

KEY CHARACTERISTICS THAT MAKE EACH ELEMENT UNIQUE

Atomic Number	Atomic Shells	Melting Point
Electro-negativity	Atomic Radius	Ionization Potential
Density	Atomic Weight	**Atomic Mass**
Boiling Point	Covalent Radius	Specific Heat
Oxidation States	Heat of Fusion	Thermal
Conductivity	Heat of Vaporization	Filling Orbital

16. *Sepher Yetzirah*, chapter 1, verse 13, p. 80. In the Saadia version of the *Sepher Yetzirah*, we find the three Mother Letters mentioned almost immediately in the first chapter. Here, a distinction is made between the Basics (Mothers), the Doubles, and the Elementals.

> *"Twenty-two letters, a foundation of three Basics, seven Doubles and twelve elementals." "The three Basics are A,M,Sh. . . ."*
> *"The seven Doubles are B,G,D,K,P,R,T. . . ."* "The twelve Elementals are H,V,Z,Ch,T,Y,L,N,S,O,Tz,Q."
> [Author has added commas between letters for readability.]

17. Ibid., p. 140.

18. Ibid.

19. Using the principles of gematria, the Hebrew letter Yod is found to resolve to the value of 1.
(ʼ) *Yod* = 10

$$1 \quad + \quad 0 \quad = \quad 1$$

In the Periodic Table, there is precisely one element with the whole number value that matches the "1" of Yod: the element hydrogen.

Hydrogen
A.M.   =   1.008
Whole Number (Integer Value)   =   1

Through a similar process, we discover a match between the letter *Hey* and the element nitrogen (value 5), and the letter *Vav* and oxygen (value of 6).

20. *Sepher Yetzirah,* chapter 1, verse 12, p. 77.

21. A principle used in the logic of deciding among scientific explanations when one or more possibilities are involved. The name is attributed to William Occam, a medieval philosopher, and is often called the *principle of parsimony*. In general, the principle states that "one should always choose the simplest explanation of a phenomenon, the one that requires the fewest leaps of logic."
  Website: **http://pespmc1.vub.ac.be/asc/PRINCI_SIMPL.html.**

22. Dickerson and Geis, *Chemistry, Matter, and the Universe,* graph from inside front cover of hardback edition.
  Interestingly, when compared to the abundance of the four elements in the universe, the human body is shown to share the elements in concentrations that are many times greater than the world around us. (From Dickerson and Geis, *Chemistry, Matter, and the Universe,* 165.)

ABUNDANCE OF ELEMENTS IN THE UNIVERSE AND OUR BODIES
(Values shown as atoms per 100,000)

Element	Entire Universe	Human Body
Hydrogen	92,760	60,560
Nitrogen	15	2,440
Oxygen	49	25,670
Carbon	8	10,680

Part III
Chapter 6

1. *Golden Treasury of Bible Stories,* Arthur Whitfield Spaulding, ed. (Nashville: Southern Publishing, 1954).

2. Halevi, *Kabbalah,* p. 5.

3. *Tanakh: The Holy Scriptures* (Philadelphia: The Jewish Publication Society, 1985), Torah, Exodus 3:14, p. 88.

4. Halevi, *Kabbalah,* p. 9.

5. *Zohar: The Book of Splendor,* Gershom Scholem, ed. (New York: Schocken Books, 1949), p. 3.

6. *Sepher Yetzirah,* p. 5.

7. *Tanakh,* Torah, Exodus 3:13, p. 88.

8. *The Torah,* commentary, "The Divine Name Ehyeh," p. 405.

9. Ibid., Exodus 3:15, p. 400.

10. Ibid., footnote 4, p. 405.

11. Ibid., commentary, "My Name YHVH," pp. 424–425.

12. Ibid., commentary, "Hidden," p. 408.

13. Ibid.

14. *The New Jerusalem Bible: The Complete Text of the Ancient Canon of the Scriptures, Standard Edition* (New York: Doubleday, 1999), Exodus 20:7, p. 70.

15. YHVH is also known as the *Tetragrammaton,* a description derived from the Greek language literally meaning "four-lettered word."

16. *The Torah,* commentary, "Linguistic Excursus on the Name YHVH," p. 426.

17. This photo is a section of the best-preserved scroll from Cave I, the First Isaiah Scroll (1Qisa). The document is 23.5 feet in length and in this slide is opened to the columns that contain the text of Isaiah 38:8 through 40:28. [Photographer: John Trevor]

18. *The Torah,* footnote 6: 3, p. 426.

19. *Sepher Yetzirah,* p. 17.

20. Dana M. Pike and Andrew C. Skinner, *Qumran Cave 4, XXIII: Unidentified Fragments,* Discoveries in the Judean Desert XXXIII (England: Oxford Univ. Press, 2001), Plates, Plate XIX, fragment number 66.
    Scroll fragment with the name YHVH. Although this is not the only occurrence of God's ancient name on a scroll fragment, this is one of the best examples that I could find, as well as one of the oldest. This image was released in 2001 as part of the series of volumes documenting the contents of the Dead Sea finds. This image is reprinted courtesy of Oxford University.

21. Hershel Shanks, "Publishing Every Last Fragment," *Biblical Archaeology Review* (March/April 2002): p. 6.

22. David Allen Hulse, *The Key of It All, Book Two: The Western Mysteries* (St. Paul, MN: Llewellyn Publications, 1994), Introduction, p. cvii.

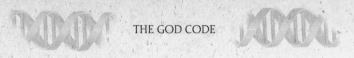

23. *Sepher Yetzirah,* appendix 1, chapter 1, verse 1, p. 285.

24. *The Torah,* commentary, "Linguistic Excursus on the Name YHVH," p. 426.

25. Ibid.

26. *Sepher Yetzirah,* p. 15.

27. *The Torah,* Exodus 15:2, p. 488.

28. *The Other Bible,* Haggadah, p. 32.

29. *Sepher Yetzirah,* pp. 19–22.

30. Ibid., chapter 2, verse 2, p. 100.

31. NASA press release, "Hubble Reads Age of Universe." *Spaceflight Now* (2002).

32. J. D. Watson and F. H. C. Crick, "A Structure for Deoxyribose Nucleic Acid." *Nature,* vol. 171 (April 1953): p. 737.

33. Robert Wright, *Time 100: Scientists & Thinkers—James Watson & Francis Crick.* The Time Archive, 1. Website: **www.time.com/time/time100/scientist/ watsoncrick.html.**

34. President Clinton, "Announcing the Completion of the First Survey of the Entire Human Genome," from a White House press conference on June 26, 2000.

35. Beyond the scope required for the focus of this text, the key to understanding the arrangement of the bases on the double helix is that the sequence of bases running in one direction, forming one side of the ladder, are the complements of the sequence on the other side of the ladder, running in the opposite direction. As only specific bases can pair with other bases, the chance for errors in the code are tremendously reduced by this structure.

36. The four bases of DNA are actually a kind of shorthand notation, an abbreviation for the elements represented by the letters. While the same elements of hydrogen, nitrogen, oxygen, and carbon are present in each DNA base, *it is the amount of each element* that varies. Rather than going through the tedious process of writing out how may times the actual element occurs each time the base is noted, they are simply implied by the letter *A, T, C,* or *G.* (Also see Appendix C.)

37. *The Expanded Quotable Einstein,* Alice Calaprice, ed. (Princeton, N.J.: Princeton Univ. Press, 2000), p. 203.

38. *Sepher Yetzirah,* chapter 1, verse 9, p. 68.

39. *The Torah,* commentary, "Linguistic Excursus on the Name YHVH," p. 426.

40. *Sepher Yetzirah,* p. 15.

41. *The American Heritage College Dictionary,* Third Edition, definition 1, p. 471.

42. The following references are from my personal conversations and written correspondence with scholar and author David Allen Hulse. Regarding the order of Hebrew letters as numbers, he states, "In the numeric sense, the order of the [Hebrew] letters makes no difference." As each letter is associated with a number value, just as 2 plus 1 produces the same value as 1 plus 2, we may consider the VG in our DNA as GV.

In Hebrew, GV has a number of possible translations, all supporting the same general theme—GV translates to the "back," "spine," or "interior of the body." Hulse offers examples of this in a biblical context with GV the back (spine) (Ezekiel 23:35) and interior (Job 30:5). The gematria of this word and the Hebrew word for "Adam" reveal an interesting, and telling, relationship. The sum of the values for GV = 9 (G (3) + V (6) = 9). This is the same value for the name representing the first of our species, Adam (A = 1 + D = 4 + M = 40, with 45 further reducing to 9). From the perspective of this deeper relationship revealed by number, the body of our species, and the VG/GV within our cells are describing the same thing. Thus, the last two letters of the message in our cells may reasonably be viewed as a reference to "within" or "interior" to the body.

David Allen Hulse is widely recognized as a leading expert in deciphering the mystical relationship between ancient languages and their significance to number. The author of a number of texts, including *The Key of It All, Book One: The Eastern Mysteries, The Key of It All, Book Two: The Western Mysteries* and *New Dimensions for the Cube of Space* (York Beach: Samuel Weiser, 2000), he also contributed to Israel Regardie's final book, *The Complete Golden Dawn System of Magic* (Malaysia: Falcon Press, 1984).

43. From my research regarding the significance of the letters VG and GV, it is clear that in the traditions of the *Kabbalah,* the reverse order of the letters may be associated with alternate, or "reverse" realms of creation. The *Sepher Yetzirah,* for example, makes reference to these realms by describing the process of combining each of the 22 Hebrew letters with the remaining letters of the alphabet, in a nonrepeating sequence, to create the 231 possibilities (Gates) of creation (*Sepher Yetzirah,* chapter 2, verse 5, 124). Hulse describes the significance of GV/VG as the 44th Gate of Creation. Here the value of the coded gate is DM, meaning "blood" in Hebrew, and the root of the word for the first created member of our species, *ADM,* (Adam).

44. Each DNA base contains a different degree of "within the body." For example, in the base of thymine (T) there are six hydrogen atoms, two nitrogen atoms, two oxygen atoms, and five carbon atoms. Considering each element from the perspective of the Hebrew letters, only twice in thymine is the "God/Eternal" aspect completed as VG, meaning "within the body." The remainder of the base exists simply as the Y and the G of the code. (See Appendix D for an illustration of this principle.)

Chapter 7

1. Blech, *The Secrets of Hebrew Words,* p. 22.

2. Gregg Braden, *The Isaiah Effect: Decoding the Lost Science of Prayer and Prophecy* (New York: Harmony books, 2000), pp. 187–192.

3. Rollin McCraty, Mike Atkinson, William Tiller, Glen Rein, and Alan D. Watkins, "The Effects of Emotions on Short-Term Power Spectrum Analysis of Heart Rate Variability," *The American Journal of Cardiology,* vol. 76, no. 14 (November 15, 1995): pp. 1089–1093.

4. Rollin McCraty, M.A., Bob Barrios-Choplin, Ph.D., Deborah Rozman, Ph.D., Mike Atkinson, and Alan D. Watkins, "The Impact of a New Emotional Self-Management Program on Stress, Emotions, Heart Rate Variability, DHEA and Cortisol," *Integrative Physiological and Behavioral Science,* vol. 33, no. 2 (1998): pp. 151–170.

5. "Rough Map of Human Genome Completed," *CNN.com Health,* June 26, 2000, 1–2. Website: **www.cnn.com.**

6. Tom Abate, "Genome Discovery Shocks Scientists," *San Francisco Chronicle* (February 11, 2001): p. A-1. Website: **www.sfgate.com.**

7. Ibid.

8. Ibid.

9. Ibid.

10. Ibid.

11. Stephen Hawking, quoted in *Der Spiegel* magazine in 1989. The original text is in German. As I was unsuccessful in obtaining a copy in English, this is taken from an online source of his thoughts, quotes and philosophy. Website: **www.nobeliefs.com/great-quotes.htm.**

 Endnotes

12. Bose-Einstein Condensate Homepage: a new form of matter at the coldest temperatures in the universe. Website: **www.colorado.edu/physics/2000/bec.**

13. "Scientists Conquer Laser Beam Teleportation," *Australian Broadcasting Corporation Online,* Sci-Tech, June 18, 2002. Website: **www.abc.net.au.**

14. Press release, "Geneva University Development in Photon Entanglement for Enhanced Encryption Security and Quantum Computers," Department of Physics, Geneva University, 2001. Website: **www.geneva.ch/entanglement.htm.**

15. Braden, *The Isaiah Effect,* pp. 89–93.

16. *The New Jerusalem Bible,* Standard Edition, Zechariah 12:1, p. 1100.

17. Ibid., Ezekiel 36:27, p. 1006.

18. *The Other Bible,* Mandaean Gnosticism, "Creation of the World and the Alien Man," p. 134.

19. Ibid., p. 136.

20. Ibid., commentary, "The Hypostasis of the Archons," p. 75.

21. Ibid., p. 77.

22. Ibid., Haggadah, p. 25.

23. Ibid.

24. Ibid., p. 28.

25. *Holy Bible: Authorized King James Version*, Genesis 2:7 (Grand Rapids, MI: World Publishing, 1989), p. 2.

26. *The Other Bible,* Haggadah, p. 25.

27. Ibid., p. 26.

28. Braden, *The Isaiah Effect,* pp. 207–211 and 233–238.

29. *Holy Bible,* John 2:21, p. 67.

30. Ibid., I Corinthians 3:16, p. 119.

31. Ibid., chapter 6, verse 19, p. 121.

32. Dickerson and Geis, *Chemistry, Matter, and the Universe,* p. 529.

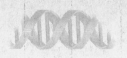

33. Ibid., p. 529.

34. Crick, *Life Itself*, p. 88.

35. Sir Fred Hoyle and Chandra Wickramasinghe, *Evolution from Space* (New York: Simon and Schuster, 1981), pp. 23–27.

36. James D. Watson, *The Molecular Biology of the Gene* (Menlo Park: W. A. Benjamin, 1977).

37. Ibid., p. 69.

38. *The Expanded Quotable Einstein*, p. 208.

39. Graham Hancock, *The Mars Mystery: The Secret Connection Between Earth and the Red Planet* (New York: Crown Publishers, 1998), pp. 73–78.

40. Richard Hoagland, *Hoagland's Mars: Volume II, The UN Briefing, The Terrestrial Connection* (video) (New York: B.C. Video, 1992).

41. Blech, *The Secrets of Hebrew Words*, p. 143.

42. Ibid.

43. Ibid., 23.

Chapter 8

1. Cremo and Thompson, *The Hidden History of the Human Race*, Summary of Anomalous Evidence Related to Human Antiquity, pp. 267–278.

2. "More teens have been killed in automobile accidents during the last ten years than soldiers lost in the Vietnam War." Approximately 58,000 soldiers lost their lives in the Vietnam War, compared to the 60,000 young people that have been killed over the last ten years in automobile accidents. Source: Am I Safe? (Teen Driver Safety Program). Website: **www.AmISafe.net.**

3. Barbara Marx Hubbard, onstage quote from *The Prophet's Conference* (December 2001), Palm Springs, California.

4. Press release, "New Century to Be Marked by Growing Threats, Opportunities," *Worldwatch Institute* (January 16, 1999). Website: **www.worldwatch.org.**

5. Stanislav Grof, M.D., "Consciousness Evolution and Planetary Survival: The Psychological Roots of Human Violence and Greed." Abstract of paper presented

at the 13th International Transpersonal Conference on the Theme of Spirituality, Ecology, and Native Wisdom, Killarney, Ireland, June 1995.

6. Ibid., p. 3.

7. Carl Sagan, "The Quest For Extraterrestrial Intelligence." *Smithsonian,* vol. 1, no. 2 (May 1978).

8. Ibid., p. 12.

9. Ibid., p. 13.

10. "When to Jump In: The World's Other Wars," *Time* (April 19, 1999): p. 30.

11. Monty G. Marshall, Director, Center For Systemic Peace, "Major Episodes of Political Violence 1946–1999." The tables describe 291 episodes of armed conflict in the world between 1946 and 1999. Website: **www.members.aol.com/ CSPmgm/warlist.htm.**

12. Samuel P. Huntington, "The Age of Muslim Wars," *Newsweek,* vol. 138, no. 25 (December 17, 2001) pp. 4–9.

13. Jorgen Wouters, "The World's War Machine." ABCNEWS.com, April 22, 1998.

14. Ibid.

15. Ibid.

16. Some of these agents, such as the *Anthrax* bacteria, have become household words from the extensive media coverage following their appearance in the U.S. Postal Service in 2001. Others have names that are seldom reported and even more difficult to pronounce. The U.S. Centers for Disease Control and Prevention (CDC) lists no fewer than 16 substances that pose a threat in the event of a domestic biological attack. These include nerve agents such as *Sarin* and *VX,* blister agents such as mustard gas, and psychoactive agents such as *Agent 15,* in addition to the familiar bacterial and viral toxins of *Botulinum* (botulism), *Aflotoxins* (cancer-causing poisons), *Clostridium perfringens* (gangrene bacteria), and *Anthrax.* The agency has an equally detailed list for chemical agents.

For a complete list and description of these agents, please search "Chemical Warfare Agents" on the National Library of Medicine's Website: **www.sis.nlm.nih.gov/Tox/ChemWar.html.**

17. The Chemical Weapons Convention, formally know as the *Convention on the Prohibition, Production, Stockpiling and Use of Chemical Weapons, and Their Destruction,* was completed in 1993 and signed by 159 states in 1995. In

addition to chemical and biological agents, this international treaty addresses nuclear technologies and missile development that may be used as delivery systems as well. The following is an online reference to the document itself. Harvard Sussex Program on CBW Armament and Arms Limitation Website: **www.fas.harvard.edu/~hsp/chemical.html.**

18. *The Expanded Quotable Einstein,* p. 181.

19. There are a number of translations for the *Mahabharata* available. Due to its immense size (over 100,000 verses), the translations are usually published in sections, with the classic the *Bhagavad-Gita* the most recognized. The quotes that I have used come from author and researcher David Hatcher Childress, referring to the translation of Charles Berlitz and his book *Mysteries of Forgotten Worlds* (New York: Doubleday, 1972).

Childress, a lifelong researcher and explorer, has amassed an impressive body of evidence suggesting that advanced forms of technology have existed in past, including his book *Technology of the Gods: The Incredible Sciences of the Ancients* (Adventures Unlimited Press, 2000).

For those interested in reading sections of the text itself, one of the better translations that I have found is through the work of Pratap Chandr Roy. A portion of his translations may be viewed electronically for academic and research purposes (noncommercial), specifically pages 446–447 and 489–481, at: **www.abob.libs.uga.edu/bobk/maha/mahbfr.html.**

20. Ibid.

21. Ibid.

22. Ibid.

23. Ibid.

24. "The American Experience: Race for the Superbomb," written, produced and directed by Thomas Ott. This program first aired on the Public Broadcasting System in January 1999. Transcripts are available online. Website: **www.PBS.org.**

25. Frederick Soddy, Nobel Prize in Chemistry, 1921, *The Interpretation of Radium* (1909).

26. Numerous discoveries of large areas of desert sand fused into sheets of high-quality glass are found throughout the literature, which includes: Giles Wright, "The Riddle of the Sands," *New Scientist* (July 10, 1999); Margarethe Casson, *Rocks and Minerals,* no. 396 (1972); Childress, *Technology of the Gods.*

A representative excerpt of these studies may be viewed online at: **www.world-mysteries.com/pex_6.htm.**

27. Sir John Marshal, *Mohenjo-Daro and the Indus Civilization* (3 Vol. 1931).

28. Sir Mortimer Wheeler, *The Indus Civilization* (3d ed. 1968).

29. Peter N. Stearns, Michael Adas, Stuart B. Schwartz, *World Civilizations: The Origins of Civilizations.*

30. A. Gorbovsky, *Riddles of Ancient History* (Moscow: Soviet Publishers, 1966), p. 28.
Although I could not find an original source for this statement, I felt that it was important to include it in the text, as it is referenced frequently in the open literature. It is consistent with the views of other well-respected historians, such as Kisari Mohan Ganguli, who feel that ancient writings from India describe a battle using weapons based in advanced science.

31. Ibid.

32. Ian K. Steele, *Warpaths: Invasions of North America* (Oxford: Oxford Univ. Press, 1994), p. 94

33. Ibid., p. 94.

34. Darwin, *Descent of Man,* p. 110.

35. Peter Kropotkin, *Mutual Aid: A Factor of Evolution* (Boston, MA.: Porter Sargent Publishers, 1902), p. 14.

36. Dr. John Swomley, "Violence: Competition or Cooperation," *Christian Ethics Today* 26, vol. 6, no. 1 (February 2000): p. 20.

37. Ibid.

38. Opening Address of the Symposium on the Humanistic Aspects of Regional Development, *Prout Journal,* vol. 6, no. 3 (September 1993).

39. Ibid.

40. Kaku, *Visions,* pp. 322–330.

41. Ibid., p. 329.

42. Jean Houston, onstage quote from *The Prophet's Conference* (December 2001), Palm Springs, California.

Chapter 9

1. National Atmospheric and Atmospheric Administration (NOAA) database for climate and fire records. National Climatic Data Center. Website: www.ncdc.noaa.gov/oa/reports/weather-events.html#HISTORICAL.

2. Sagan, "The Quest For Extraterrestrial Intelligence."

3. Ibid.

4. Ibid.

5. Ibid.

6. St. Thomas Aquinas, *Summa Contra Gentiles,* Volume 11, p. 45. Quoted by Arthur O. Lovejoy, *The Great Chain of Being: A Study of the History of an Idea* (Cambridge, MA: Harvard Univ. Press, 1936), p. 76.

7. This quote is cited from Francis Bacon's classic text on human nature, *Of Goodness and Goodness of Nature.* This particular chapter, "Essays, Civil and Moral" (Chapter XIII) is available online as part of the Harvard Classics series (1909–1914). Website: www.bartleby.com/3/1/13.html.

8. Abraham H. Maslow, adapted from the editor's introduction to the third edition of *Toward a Psychology of Being* (New York: Wiley, 1999).

9. Ibid.

10. "Prague Faces 'Worst Moment,'" *CNN.com/World,* August 14, 2002. Website: www.cnn.com.

11. "Obesity Trends: Prevalence of Obesity Among U.S. Adults, by Characteristics," reported by the Centers for Disease Control, National Center for Chronic Disease Prevention and Health Promotion. Statistics from A.H. Modkad, M. Serdula. and W. Dietz, "The Continuing Epidemics of Obesity and Diabetes in The United States." *Journal of the American Medical Association,* vol. 286 (September 12, 2001): pp. 1195–1200.

12. Jonathan Wells, "Second Thoughts About Peppered Moths, This Classical Story of Evolution by Natural Selection Needs Revising," *The Scientist,* vol. 13, no. 11 (May 24, 1999): p. 13.

13. Hulse, *The Key of It All: Book One,* pp. 188–189.

14. Aaron T. Wolf, "Indigenous Approaches to Water Conflict Resolution and Implications for International Waters," *International Negotiation*, vol. 5, no. 2 (December 2000): pp. 357–373. The report cited for this text was reviewed before its publication in the journal.

15. Ibid.

16. Ibid.

17. Ibid.

Appendix A

David Allen Hulse, *The Key of It All, An Encyclopedic Guide to the Sacred Languages & Magickal Systems of the World, Book One: The Eastern Mysteries*, pp. 188–89.

INDEX

Page numbers in *italics* refer to sidebars. An "n" after a page number refers to a footnote.

 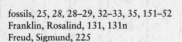

ACKNOWLEDGMENTS

Rarely in life do we have the opportunity to acknowledge the people whose contributions make our achievements possible. While it was necessary to cross the traditional boundaries of science, religion, and history to create this book, it is through the dedication of experts in these very fields that I am able to share my work with certainty and confidence. This section is my opportunity to thank those individuals, as well as to offer my gratitude to everyone who contributed to the completion of *The God Code*, sometimes in ways that they did not even know!

I am especially grateful to:

The spark of divinity within all life that makes itself known through our creations. Thank you for being with me always.

Ned Leavitt, my literary agent. Ned, to you I send my heartfelt appreciation for helping mold this discovery into a meaningful book, and for shepherding it through the publishing world. From the first day that we considered the implications of a message in the code of life, your guidance has been invaluable, your integrity impeccable, and your trust in me a constant.

Stephanie Gunning, my editor and now my friend, through our conversations to flesh out the essence of this book, you always asked just the right questions in precisely the right way to lead us to the clearest choices! Many thanks for your professionalism, the dedication and skill that you embody in all that you do, and your patience with my words and schedules. Most of all, thank you for helping me take the complexities of science and transform them into the joy of empowering wisdom!

Dr. Todd Ovakaytis and Mary Kennedy, I am deeply grateful to you both for your willingness to work with me during our lengthy period of nondisclosure, without even knowing where our work was leading! For two years following that first meeting in our Paris hotel, your expertise in molecular biology, medicine, and statistics has helped pave the way to the next level of exploration. You embody a rare combination of brilliant minds, kind hearts, and a willingness to share, for which I feel both blessed and thankful.

David Allen Hulse, my dear friend, thank you for following your passion to unravel the Great Mystery, your willingness to share your findings with others, and your intuition to respond to that very first e-mail that led to our friendship. Without knowing precisely to what your expertise in the ancient languages was contributing, your willingness to work with me has exemplified an inspiring degree of trust for which I remain eternally grateful. It has been an honor to collaborate toward a greater wisdom, and I sense that our work together is far from complete!

Hank Wesselman, your offer to review this book came to me in precisely the right way, at precisely the right time. Please accept my heartfelt thanks for sharing the up-to-the-minute discoveries of evolution and our past that make this book as accurate as possible. Your willingness to follow the call that beckons from beyond our accepted worldview paves the way for us to become better people and create a better world.

To all of the great people at Hay House, I offer my sincere appreciation and deepest gratitude. To Reid Tracy, president and CEO, thank you for your vision and unwavering faith in my work. Following five years of interesting twists and unexpected turns, we are working together on a project at last!

To Jill Kramer, my in-house editor, many, many thanks for your guidance, honest opinions, and the years of experience that you have brought to bear upon each of our conversations. You are truly a master of your craft. Your words of encouragement during our edits meant more than you could have known, and I now keep your comment sheet in my office for support and inspiration!

A very special thanks to Katie Williams, Jacqui Clark, Jeannie Liberati, Margarete Nielsen, and John Thompson. I could not ask for a nicer group of people, or a more dedicated team to

support this book. Your excitement and professionalism are unsurpassed. Through your trust in me, I have felt welcome in the Hay House family.

To Melissa, I offer my deepest gratitude for your patience through the demands that undertaking a project of this magnitude creates. Thank you for taking the time to listen, support, suggest—and especially for your artist's eye. Throughout the time that you've seen me at my best, and very worst, your friendship has remained a constant, your belief in me unfailing.

To the beautiful spirit of our furry four-legged pooch, Brillo (pronounced *Bree-oh*), thank you for the happiness that you bring into our lives, for reminding us of what it means to "be here now," and for your company into the wee hours of countless mornings as you slept on the yoga mat by my desk while I was writing.

T.K., Charlene, and all of our friends at the Bent Street Café; and Angela, Tony, and all the great staff at the Apple Tree Restaurant . . . over the years, your kindness has been there for me at just the right time in ways that you could not possibly know. My deepest appreciation and many thanks for always taking such good care of me, and for preparing the beautiful meals that have kept me strong and focused through my travels and during the writing process.

To my mother, Sylvia Braden, and my brother, Eric, thank you for your unfailing love and for believing in me. My gratitude for all that you bring to each day of my life extends beyond any words that I could possibly inscribe upon this page. Through the freedom that comes from such support, we have seen one another more, and become closer as a family today than at any time in the past. Although our family by blood is small, together we have found that our extended family of love is greater than we have ever imagined.

I am proud to be part of the virtual team that has become the dedicated family helping me share my work throughout the world. To Lauri Willmot, my favorite (and only) office manager, I send my admiration and innumerable thanks for being there always, and especially when it counts! As our work reaches into the minds and

hearts of an increasing number of people, I find myself appreciating you more with each passing year.

To Tom Park of Park Productions, and Jerry and Robin Miner of Source Books/Sacred Spaces Productions, I send my thanks for your love, support, and willingness to "stick with it" as we honor the principles that originally brought us together. Together, we have learned new and creative ways of merging business and family while weathering the uncertainties of our changing world!

To M. A. Bjarkman and Rae Baskin, the founders of The Conference Works!; and Carol Simmons, Sharon Kreig, Darrin Owens, Kathalin Walker, and the entire team behind the scenes, thank you for your vision and dedication, and for sharing my passion and being open to the possibilities.

To Robin and Cody Johnson, founders of the Prophets Conferences, I send an enormous bundle of gratitude for your skill in bringing together many diverse minds working toward a better world, and for including me in that vision. A special thanks for reminding us that everyone is a prophet. To all, my sincere appreciation and great respect for your willingness to explore new ways of working together in our world of change!

I am honored by the trust of all who have shared in our live presentations. Through your response, I have learned to become a better listener, and heard the words that allow me to share an empowering message of hope and possibility. To you, I remain grateful always.

ABOUT THE AUTHOR

New York Times bestselling author **Gregg Braden** has been a featured guest at international conferences and media specials, exploring the role of spirituality in technology. A former senior computer systems designer (Martin Marietta Aerospace), computer geologist (Phillips Petroleum), and technical operations supervisor (Cisco Systems), Braden is now considered a leading authority on bridging the wisdom of our past with the science, technology, and peace of our future.

His journeys into the remote mountain villages, monasteries, and temples of times past, coupled with his background in the hard sciences, uniquely qualify him to bring the benefit of long-lost traditions to the forefront of our lives today.

From his groundbreaking book, *Awakening to Zero Point*, to his pioneering work in *Walking Between the Worlds* and the controversy of *The Isaiah Effect*, Gregg Braden ventures beyond the traditional boundaries of science and spirituality, offering meaningful solutions to the challenges of our time.

Website: **www.greggbraden.net**

For further information, please contact Gregg's office at:

Wisdom Traditions
P.O. Box 5182
Santa Fe, NM 87502
505-424-6892
ssawbraden@aol.com

NOTES

NOTES

NOTES

NOTES

NOTES

We hope you enjoyed this Hay House book.
If you would like to receive a free catalog featuring
additional Hay House books and products,
or if you would like information about the
Hay Foundation, please contact:

Hay House, Inc.
P.O. Box 5100
Carlsbad, CA 92018-5100

(760) 431-7695 or (800) 654-5126
(760) 431-6948 (fax) or (800) 650-5115 (fax)
www.hayhouse.com

Published and distributed in Australia by:
Hay House Australia, Ltd. • 18/36 Ralph St.
Alexandria NSW 2015 • *Phone:* 612-9669-4299
Fax: 612-9669-4144 • www.hayhouse.com.au

Published and distributed in the United Kingdom by:
Hay House UK, Ltd. • Unit 202, Canalot Studios
222 Kensal Rd., London W10 5BN • *Phone:* 44-20-8962-1230
*Fax:*44-020-8962-1239 • www.hayhouse.co.uk

Published and distributed in the Republic of South Africa by:
Hay House SA (Pty), Ltd., P.O. Box 990, Witkoppen 2068
Phone/Fax: 2711-7012233 • orders@psdprom.co.za

Distributed in Canada by: Raincoast
9050 Shaughnessy St., Vancouver, B.C. V6P 6E5
Phone: (604) 323-7100 • *Fax:* (604) 323-2600

Sign up via the Hay House USA Website
to receive the Hay House online newsletter and stay
informed about what's going on with your favorite authors.
You'll receive bimonthly announcements about: Discounts and Offers,
Special Events, Product Highlights, Free Excerpts, Giveaways, and more!